Dr Annie George's work, *Children's Perceptions of the Role of Biblical Narratives in Their Spiritual Formation,* provides a perspective of storytelling in religious and secular traditions and its crucial role in the transformation of the hearers' worldview and the formation of their faith, character and spirituality. The study makes a valuable contribution to understanding and evaluating children's spirituality in a church context where storytelling is predominantly the teaching method for children. It is a must-read for Christian educators in Indian Christian churches concerned with the spirituality of their children.

Orbelina Eguizabal, PhD
Professor of Christian Higher Education,
Talbot School of Theology, Biola University, California, USA

Children's Perceptions of the Role of Biblical Narratives in Their Spiritual Formation

Annie George

© 2017 by Annie George

Published 2017 by Langham Academic (Previously Langham Monographs)
An imprint of Langham Publishing
www.langhampublishing.org

Langham Publishing and its imprints are a ministry of Langham Partnership

Langham Partnership
PO Box 296, Carlisle, Cumbria, CA3 9WZ, UK
www.langham.org

ISBNs:
978-1-78368-236-2 Print
978-1-78368-237-9 ePub
978-1-78368-239-3 PDF

Annie George has asserted her right under the Copyright, Designs and Patents Act, 1988 to be identified as the Author of this work.

All rights reserved. No part of this publication may be reproduced, stored in a retrieval system or transmitted, in any form or by any means, electronic, mechanical, photocopying, recording or otherwise, without the prior written permission of the publisher or the Copyright Licensing Agency.

All Scripture quotations, unless otherwise indicated, are taken from the Holy Bible, New International Version®, NIV®. Copyright ©1973, 1978, 1984, 2011 by Biblica, Inc.™ Used by permission of Zondervan.

British Library Cataloguing in Publication Data
A catalogue record for this book is available from the British Library

ISBN: 978-1-78368-236-2

Cover & Book Design: projectluz.com

Langham Partnership actively supports theological dialogue and a scholar's right to publish but does not necessarily endorse the views and opinions set forth, and works referenced within this publication or guarantee its technical and grammatical correctness. Langham Partnership does not accept any responsibility or liability to persons or property as a consequence of the reading, use or interpretation of its published content.

Contents

Abstract xv
Acknowledgements xvii
Chapter 1 1
Introduction
    Description of the Problem 2
    Background and Significance of the Study 4
        Children's Spirituality – A Brief Overview 5
        Retrospection 8
    Children in India 10
        Children in Pre-Independent India 10
        Children in Independent India 11
        The Locale of the Proposed Research 13
    Explanation of Key Terms 13
        Children 13
        Narratives/Stories 14
        Spiritual Formation 14
        Christian 15
        Pentecostal/Charismatic Churches 15
        Perception 15
    Statement of the Research Questions 16
    Population and Sample 16
    Assumptions of the Study 18
    Delimitations of the Study 20
    Summary 21

Chapter 2 23
Review of Relevant Literature
    Rationale for the Domain of the Research 23
    Children's Spirituality Domain 24
        Summary 41
    Storytelling in Religious and Secular Traditions 42
        Formation and Transformation of Worldview 42
        Religious Education 44
        Character Formation 50
        Faith Formation 53

  Spirituality 59
  Children's Perceptions of Stories 71
 Chapter Summary 78

Chapter 3 81
Christian Worldview: Integration and Synthesis
 The Bible – the Story that Needs to be Told 81
  The Bible – the Story 82
  The Bible – the Story to be Told 84
 The Old Testament and New Testament Use of Stories 87
  The Use of Stories in the Old Testament 88
  The Use of Stories in the New Testament 93
 Spirituality of Children 99
  The Old Testament 99
  The New Testament 106
 That the Next Generation Might Know:
 Psalm 78:1–8 111
  An Introduction to the Psalm 112
  Exegesis 113
  Summary 118
 Chapter Summary 119

Chapter 4 121
Research Methodology
 Statement of the Research Questions 121
 Research Design 122
  Description of the Schedule for the Two-Hour
   Gathering per Week 122
  Assessing the Class Activities 125
  Observation 125
  Focus Group Interviews 126
  Member Checking 130
  Documentation of Data 131
  Revisions of the Research Procedures 132
 Research Hypothesis 133
 Operational Definitions 134
  Children 134
  Narratives/Stories 134
  Spiritual Formation 134
  Christian 134
  Perception 135

Informed Consent 135
Sample Selection Procedures 137
Seeking Permission from the Seminary Authorities 138
Recruiting and Training the Research Assistants 138
Pilot Study 139
    Summary 143
Developing an Interview Protocol 143
Data Analysis Procedure 146
    Review the Data 146
    Transcription 147
    Coding Data and Developing Categories 147
    Connecting Categories to Identifying Themes 148
Children as Research Participants: Challenges and Response 149
    Children's Stand about the Topic 149
    Data Collection 150
    Unfamiliarity with the Research Team and
        Other Participants 151
    Participation and the Balance of Power 151
    Spaces of Research 152
    Listening to Children 152
    Inability of Children to Verbalize Their Experience of
        Transcendence 153
    Objectivity 154
    Dissemination 155
Chapter Summary 155

Chapter 5 157
Results
Context of Study 157
    Antioch 158
    Colosse 159
    Ephesus 159
    Jerusalem 159
    Philippi 160
    Rome 160
    Thessalonica 161
Brief Summary of the Research Activities 161
Data Analysis 162
    Stories and Settings 164
    Storytellers of Biblical Stories 164
    Types of Stories 168

  Children's Perceptions: Reasons for Communicating
    Biblical Stories 169
  Recalling Biblical Stories – Intellectual Dimension of Faith 177
  Favorite Biblical Story: Evidences of Maturing Spirituality.......180
  Recollecting Biblical Stories: Linking Stories to Life 189
  Listening to Biblical Stories...198
  Biblical Stories and Awareness of God 201
  Biblical Stories and Awareness of Self.......................................208
  Biblical Stories and Awareness of Others..................................219
 Chapter Summary..220

Chapter 6.. 223
 Conclusions
  Major Findings 224
   Research Question One 224
   Research Question Two 225
   Research Question Three 228
   Research Question Four..230
   Research Question Five...232
   Main Research Question...235
  Implications..238
  Limitations 240
  Recommendations for Future Research 241
  Concluding Remarks 242

Appendix A 245
 Information Leaflet for Pastors and Parents

Appendix B 247
 Information Leaflet for Children

Appendix C 249
 Information Leaflet for Research Assistants

Appendix D 251
 Informed Consent Forms
  Informed Consent Form 1 251
  Informed Consent Form 2 253

Appendix E 255
 Permission Letter to Use the Textbook, God Our Security

Appendix F 257
    Tables Displaying Demographic Information about Participating Churches and Demographic Information of Children from Seven Churches with Respect to Age and Gender

Appendix G... 259
    Children's Expression of Their Awareness of God through Poems, Pictures, and Testimonies

Bibliography.. 265

List of Tables

Table 1: Goldman's Stages of Religious Thinking.............................25

Table 2: The Schedule of the Weekly Class Activities 124

Table 3: The Demographic Details of Children in the Pilot Study................140

Table 4: Categories Derived from Analysis of Children's Responses 163

Table 5: Stories from the Old Testament Part A.............................179

Table 6: Stories from the Old Testament Part B.............................179

Table 7: Stories from the New Testament Part A 180

Table 8: Stories from the New Testament Part B............................180

Table 9: Deconchy's Three Stages of the Idea of God 182

Table 10: Awareness of God: The Relational God............................183

Table 11: Awareness of God: The Positive God..............................184

Table 12: Awareness of God: The Potent God................................184

Table 13: Awareness of God: The Punishing God 185

Table 14: Awareness of Self: Existential Individuating 187

Table 15: Awareness of Sin: Something to Avoid 188

Table 16: Awareness of Others: Appreciating Others' Action 188

Table 17: Children's Understanding of Characteristics of God from Biblical Stories 203

Table 18: Children's Awareness of Self from Biblical Stories..............210

Table 19: Awareness of Self: Being a Change Agent 218

Table 20: The Participating Churches......................................273

Table 21: Distribution of Twenty-Nine Children 274

List of Figures

Figure 1: "God saved me as a car was about to hit me." 278

Figure 2: "God saved me from falling into a ditch. The moral lesson: God saves us from danger." 279

Abstract

This research is to explore children's perceptions of the role of biblical narratives in their spiritual formation. The Judeo-Christian faith has had a keen interest in children's spiritual formation even before the recent emergence of the interest in children's spirituality. Stories are seen as central to the Judeo-Christian worldview. The significance of the topic in the context of this research – Kerala, India – is that Sunday schools are seen as a crucial and exclusive ministry with children where children are spiritually nurtured primarily through telling the stories of the Bible.

This research involved 9- to 11-year-old children from seven Pentecostal/Charismatic churches in and around the town of Adoor, Kerala, India. As children are a vulnerable population, ethical concerns of research with children were considered in the study. The researcher was assisted by three seminary students. Class activities, focus group interviews, and member checking provided ample opportunities to listen to children's verbal and non-verbal expressions about their perceptions. The data was analyzed using established qualitative data analysis methods. Categories developed through data analysis summarizes children's perceptions on this topic.

This research facilitated an opportunity for children to express the following aspects: storytellers of biblical narratives, reasons for communicating biblical stories, life situations in which they remember stories, their experiences when listening to or remembering biblical stories, and I-Thou, I-self, I-other, and I-world understanding generated from biblical narratives.

The researcher hopes to challenge the view that adult's experiences and perceptions are the norm to evaluate children's spirituality. It is a fact that India has the highest number of children in the world. In such a context, time has come for theological institutions and churches in India to value issues of children at par with other areas of study and ministry.

Acknowledgments

With heartfelt gratitude . . .
- to God, to you I owe my life.
- to my parents and my husband's parents (three of them are cheering me from heaven). Thank you for being my parents.
- to my husband and my children, you give me unconditional love and acceptance. I am truly blessed.
- to my sisters, brothers, nieces, nephews, uncles, and aunts, you are truly God's gifts.
- to my friends, my church family – Adoor Vineyard Church, my students, and faculty at Faith Theological Seminary, you have enriched my life.
- to my committee members Dr Lawson, Dr Carr, Dr Tally, you have equipped and enriched me with your wisdom and humility.
- to the faculty, staff, and friends at Talbot School of Theology, you have showed me the meaning of what Jesus' words, "love your neighbor as yourselves."
- to many children whom God has entrusted me to teach in Sunday school since 1987, you have helped me to realize your love for God is deep and colorful.
- to the research team and research participants and participating churches, you helped me to make sense of what I was trying to explore.
- to the Abrahams, in your house I again witnessed God's orchestration in my life.
- to those who have ministered in my life in various times, I am blessed by your kindness.

"I stand in awe of your deeds, O Lord! Renew them in our days, In our time make them known"

CHAPTER 1

Introduction

Even though there is a recent interest in storytelling, storytelling is an ancient phenomenon. Morris Olper, an anthropologist among the Apache of southern New Mexico, noted that a person who had acted unethically within the tribe would be confronted with questions such as, "How could you do that? Didn't you have a grandfather to tell you stories?"[1] As "the oldest all-ability teaching device in the world,"[2] major religions like Buddhism, Islam, Hinduism, Judaism, and Christianity use stories to "assure ongoing generational conversation."[3] The Egyptian Westcar Papyrus, dated 2000–1300 BCE, contains the oldest written description of storytelling.[4] Recent resurgence in storytelling affirms that narrative thought is a major form of cognition even though it is qualitatively different from abstract propositional or scientific.[5]

Along with storytelling, children's spirituality has become an area of exploration in academia as a multidisciplinary field in many countries.[6] The exploration of various dimensions of children's spirituality from the field of

---

1. S. Sasso, "The Role of Narratives in the Spiritual Formation of Children," *Journal of Family Ministry* 19, no. 2 (2005): 24.

2. T. Copley, "The Power of the Storyteller in Religious Education," *Religious Education* 102, no. 3 (2007): 297.

3. T. Steffen, *Reconnecting God's Story to Ministry: Crosscultural Storytelling at Home and Abroad* (Waynesboro, GA: Authentic, 2005), 32.

4. S. May et al., *Children Matter: Celebrating Their Place in the Church, Family and Community* (Grand Rapids, MI: Eerdmans, 2005), 173.

5. P. C. Vitz, "The Use of Stories in Moral Development: New Psychological Reasons for an Old Education Method," *American Psychologist* 45, no. 6 (1990): 711.

6. B. Hyde, *Children and Spirituality: Searching for Meaning and Connectedness* (London: Jessica Kingsley, 2008), 9.

psychology, education, philosophy, neuroscience, theology, and medicine shows the emergence of interest in children's spirituality. Hyde presents the specific reasons for the increasing interest in developed countries: (1) the emphasis on the holistic development in children, (2) the interest in the well-being and resilience of children, and (3) the recognition of the need to develop inner strength and inner resources in children to grow up in the "toxic environment" in which they live.[7] This is evident in the publication of the *International Journal of Children's Spirituality*, the organization of the ChildSpirit Institute, and the triennial conference "Children's Spirituality–Christian Perspectives."[8] Boyatzis noted the increased number of publications in the forms of handbooks, encyclopedias, books, and articles. He also graphically demonstrates the scholarly attention to this topic in terms of the rise in the number of dissertations since the 1990s.[9] This research touches these two areas of interest by exploring children's perceptions of the role of biblical stories in their spiritual formation. Having identified the focus of the research, the discussion on the following pages involves a brief description of the significance and background of the topic.

Description of the Problem

The Old and New Testaments affirm the significance of the mighty acts of God in the lives of the hearers. Transmitting the sacred story to children and grandchildren was of importance in the Torah (Deut 6:1–2). The central affirmation of the *Shema* (Deut 6:6–7) is to tell the revelation of God to children. This commandment involves the following aspects: (1) to tell their children about the deeds of God among them (Deut 4:9–10) and (2) to continuously and deliberately recite or read the law to them at

---

7. Ibid., 16–17.

8. M. J. Bunge, "The Dignity and Complexity of Children: Constructing Christian Theologies of Childhood," in *Nurturing Child and Adolescent Spirituality: Perspective from the World's Religious Traditions*, ed. K. M. Yust et al. (New York: Rowman & Littlefield, 2006), 56.

9. C. J. Boyatzis, "Children's Spiritual Development: Advancing the Field of Definition, Measurement, and Theory," in *Nurturing Children's Spirituality: Christian Perspectives and Best Practices*, ed. C. A. Allen (Eugene, OR: Cascade, 2008), 44.

regular intervals (Deut 31:12–13).[10] Thus the adults were the custodians of the traditions and God wanted children to be part of God's action among Israelites. Brueggemann stresses the importance of the story in the life of Israel. As Sinaic covenant is in the context of exodus, he notes that the story has to be believed for the Law to have any significance for the life of Israel.[11] If the exodus story is not believed, the covenant and the commandment have no value because the context of the law was the Exodus event.

The biblical perspective of telling and listening to stories was not for entertainment but to touch the lives of hearers. Fishbane notes that storytelling enabled children to become "spiritual contemporaries" with their parents.[12] Even though children are not the intended audience in the epistles, the purpose of presenting many characters and episodes from Jewish scripture and traditions was for instruction, warning, and examples in the lives of readers (Rom 15:4; 1 Cor 10:1–13).

Even now stories have an immense power in the religious sphere.[13] Storytelling is a common method to communicate family and religious traditions as it is perceived as an important tool for teaching children. This is evident in the abundance of religious and secular storybooks in the market. The significance of stories in congregations is that biblical stories are the major content of teaching and storytelling is the primary method of teaching children.[14] Stories play an important role in the content of religious education as they can provide access to ideas which cannot be clarified by any other.[15] Brueggemann sees the use of stories in churches as a continuation of the practice found in the Torah.[16]

Indian churches use stories as a primary mode to educate children. The secular world may use stories for entertainment, but churches, however,

---

10. P. D. Miller, "That the Children May Know: Children in Deuteronomy," in *The Child in the Bible,* ed. M. J. Bunge (Grand Rapids, MI: Eerdmans, 2008), 49.

11. W. Brueggemann, *The Creative Word: Canon as a Model for Biblical Education* (Philadelphia, PA: Fortress, 1982), 23.

12. M. Fishbane, *Text and Texture* (New York: Schocken, 1979), 82.

13. Copley, "Power of the Storyteller," 296.

14. M. A. Crain, "Reconsidering the Power of Story in Religious Education," *Religious Education 102,* no. 3 (2007): 244.

15. P. Burt, "'Thus Says the Lord . . .' God's Communication and Children's Understanding," *Journal of Beliefs and Values* 24, no. 3 (2003): 330.

16. Brueggemann, *Creative Word,* 22.

use biblical stories with children to facilitate their spiritual formation. If spiritual formation is the primary aim for sharing biblical stories with children, it is significant for churches to comprehend children's perceptions of the stories in their spiritual formation. How often do educators and teachers ask children about how biblical stories help them to strengthen their relationship with God and others? What is their awareness of the role of the stories in their spiritual formation? Investigating children's perceptions of the role of stories is to find children's understanding of how the stories facilitate their spiritual formation.

This qualitative research explores children's perceptions of the role of biblical stories in their spiritual formation. I believe it is important for adults to comprehend children's perceptions because of the following reasons: (1) The stories are the primary content of Sunday schools for children. (2) Sunday schools are the primary ministry in churches that is focused exclusively towards children. (3) Storytelling is the primary method of teaching the stories to children in congregations. (4) The shared belief in Pentecostal/Charismatic churches is that the Bible brings transformation. (5) It can empower educators to improve their skills of delivering stories, modify their approach to children, confidently arrange the materials and activities for children. (6) It can equip parents and the faith community in using stories more effectively with children. This research is an opportunity to listen and hear what children have to express through verbal, written and non-verbal clues about the role of stories in their spiritual formation.

Background and Significance of the Study

Following the developmental theory of Jean Piaget, Goldman focused on the role of intellect and emotions in religious understanding of biblical narratives,[17] which resulted in neglecting some important aspects of the spirituality of children. His focus on mystical extraordinary spiritual experience negated the "very ordinary aspect of young children's everyday

---

17. R. Goldman, *Religious Thinking from Childhood to Adolescence* (New York: Seabury Press, 1968), 2–3.

experience."[18] Young children's experience of God was overlooked due to religious educators placing emphasis on cognition. Yet the innate spirituality of children is now widely supported. Cavalletti in her twenty-five years of experience of catechesis with 3- to 11-year-old children noted that even young children experience deep belief in the creator God.[19] Coles' research with 8- to 12-year-old children led to the following findings: Children are seekers, they ask deep and intense questions about God much more than adults realize and they integrate their understandings with their own wonderings and conclusions.[20] Recently the study of Hay and Nye affirmed, "children's spirituality is rooted in universal human awareness."[21] They defined children's spirituality as "relational consciousness" with I-Thou, I-self, I-other, and I-world dimensions.[22]

The following section further explains the background and importance of the research with a brief description of spirituality of children in the Bible and in academic discussion.

Children's Spirituality – A Brief Overview

The Bible presents children as spiritual beings. Children have the capacity to ponder spiritually significant matters (Deut 6:20–21) and have the capacity to relate to God. In the Old Testament, they had a place in the reading of the Law at the Sanctuary (Deut 31:9–12). In the New Testament, the Synoptic Gospels show how Jesus radically portrayed children as spiritual beings.[23]

The Bible portrays the activity of nurturing children's faith as a religious duty. God commanded Israel to communicate his commandments to their children and grandchildren so that they will fear the Lord (Deut 6). Stories

---

18. D. Hay and R. Nye, *The Spirit of the Child*, rev. ed. (London: Jessica Kingsley, 2006), 50.

19. S. Cavalletti, *The Religious Potential of the Child*, 2nd ed., trans. P. M. Coulter and J. M. Coulter (Chicago, IL: Liturgy Training, 1993), 31–33.

20. R. Coles, *The Spiritual Life of Children* (Boston, MA: Houghton Mifflin, 1990), 192–193.

21. Hay and Nye, *Spirit of the Child*, 18.

22. Ibid., 109.

23. J. M. Gundry-Volf, "The Least and the Greatest: Children in the New Testament," in *The Child in the Christian Thought*, ed. M. J. Bunge (Grand Rapids, MI: Eerdmans, 2001), 37–47; May et al., *Children Matter*, 39–42.

of God's mighty acts were one of the primary vehicles by which parents and the faith community provided a space to enhance children's spirituality. The stories became a tool which enabled the Israelites to express and communicate their history to their children.[24] Stories children heard developed deep convictions, which became the foundations of their faith.

There have been several empirical studies which have considered how children understood biblical stories and other literature. Children can comprehend stories and interpret the stories based on their life experiences.[25] "They do draw meaning from stories but their hermeneutic is highly individual and reflects their own life experience or their received (but unreflected) personal nurturing environment."[26] Yust noted the importance of exposing children to religious stories as they can create a long-lasting framework for children's perceptions of reality.[27] Cavalletti observed 3- to 11-year-old children for more than twenty-five years in "specially prepared centers of catechesis."[28] Following the liturgical year, four major themes were presented to the children: Christ the Good Shepherd, the Eucharist, Christ the Light, and the Kingdom of God,[29] highlighting various aspects of the life of Christ. Her experiences affirmed that the presentation of these themes created a "mysterious religious bond" between children and God from a young age.[30]

There are conceptual discussions which describe adults' experiences of the use of stories with children: Stonehouse emphasizes that biblical

---

24. D. G. Lawrie, "Old Testament Perspectives on Religious Education," *Scriptura* 43 (1992): 5.

25. H. Worsley, "How Children Aged 9–10 Understand Bible Stories: A Study of Children at a Church-Aided and a State Primary School in the Midlands," *International Journal of Children's Spirituality* 9, no. 2 (2004): 212; A. M. Trousdale and J. S. Everett, "Me and Bad Harry: Three African-American Children's Response to Fiction," *Children's Literature in Education* 25, no. 1 (1994): 11.

26. Worsley, "Children Aged 9–10," 212.

27. K. M. Yust, *Real Kids, Real Faith: Practices for Nurturing Children's Spiritual Lives* (San Francisco, CA: Jossey-Bass, 2004), 28.

28. Cavalletti, *Religious Potential*, 21.

29. Ibid., 24.

30. Ibid., 21–22; see also S. Cavalletti, *The Religious Potential of the Child: 6 to 12 Years Old* (Oak Park, IL: Catechism of the Good Shepherd, 2002), p. x.

stories help children to love Jesus and experience God's presence.[31] She notes that abstract presentation does not carry any meaning to children but stories help children to know God and experience him.[32] By hearing and owning the stories, children can develop their faith. Wangerin notes, "the experience of a good story is always profoundly spiritual" as children can connect to "the deeper truths and ultimate meanings in life" through stories.[33] Hearing the stories of God's character and action is important in the process of confirming and confessing the relationship with God as "He is my Lord." This is because the story of God's character and action is the language of faith.[34]

Christian parents believe that spiritual formation is vital in nurturing their children towards maturity in life. Educators in churches support this vision and the primary purpose in working with children is towards their spiritual formation. In churches in Kerala, India, Sunday schools are seen as a crucial and exclusive ministry with children as there are no adult Sunday schools. In Sunday schools, biblical stories are shared and storytelling is primarily focused towards the spiritual formation of children.

Besides the emphasis given by biblical scholars and educators on stories, there is a cultural significance to the use of stories in India. India is a high-context communication culture.[35] Storytelling has significant implications in such cultures. A message is communicated through stories, proverbs, fables, metaphors, similes and analogies.[36] In high-context cultures, communication is indirect where as in low-context cultures communication is straight forward, concise, and uses precise words. Thus, in high-context

---

31. C. Stonehouse, *Joining Children on the Spiritual Journey: Nurturing a Life of Faith* (Grand Rapids, MI: Baker, 1998), 161.

32. Ibid.

33. Wangerin as cited in D. Ratcliff and S. May, "Identifying Children's Spirituality, Walter Wangerin's Perspectives, and an Overview of This Book," in *Children's Spirituality: Christian Perspectives, Research, and Applications*, ed. D. Ratcliff (Eugene, OR: Cascade, 2004), 12.

34. W. Wangerin, *The Orphan Passages* (Grand Rapids, MI: Zondervan, 1986), 52.

35. A. Hendel, W. Messner, and F. Thun, eds. *Rightshore!: Successfully Industrialize SAP Projects Offshore* (Capgemini, Germany: Springerm, 2008), 112.

36. R. K. James, *Crisis Intervention Strategies*, 6th ed. (Belmont, CA: Thomson Brook/Cole, 2008), 28.

cultures stories are seen not as merely illustrations, but as vehicles that carry the truth.

In such a context, this research has investigated children's perceptions of the role of biblical stories in their spiritual formation. As stories are the primary content of education in churches and storytelling is the primary method of communicating the Bible to children, the current research can have a significant contribution in educating our next generation which determines the future of our churches. In order to explore children's perceptions on this topic the following questions are pondered: Who tells biblical stories to children? What do children perceive as the reasons for sharing biblical stories with them? When do they recall the stories? What are the life situations that lead them to recall the stories? How does the recalling of the narratives impact the life situations they face? How do they perceive the association between stories and their spiritual formation? I believe that comprehending how children perceive the role of stories in their spiritual formation can also benefit teachers and educators who work with children. Educators can improve their skills of delivering stories, modify their approach to children, confidently arrange the materials and activities for children, and further equip parents and the faith community in better using stories with children. The researcher also hopes that this research will spark further interest in the study of children's spirituality.

Retrospection

My present interest in stories is in part a reminiscence of my uncle, Jacob Mammen, who told a variety of stories to my sister Susan and me in our early and late childhood years. Even as an adult, I recall many details which have shaped my understanding of the world around me. While hearing the stories, I imagined the plot and characters as if I was witnessing it happening right then. One day after a long stretch of telling stories to us, my uncle framed one:

> Once upon a time a family had seven children. They were Catholics and the parents took all the children together to their church to get them christened. The priest inquired about the names of children. The father said, "First one is '*ka*', the

second is '*da*', the third '*pa*', the fourth '*ra*', the fifth '*nju*', the sixth '*thir*',and the seventh '*nnu*.'"

My uncle then turned around and asked me to say all the names together. Immediately I said, "*kadaparanjuthirnnu*" which meant "storytelling is over." We laughed together then, even though I was sad that I had to wait until later to hear more stories. I listened to the story purely for entertainment yet as he finished his story I understood his intention – he was tired and he did not want to tell anymore stories. This is an example of inner persuasiveness of stories. Concepts and feelings can be intentionally but indirectly communicated through stories which can lead to a change in behavior.

I have shared stories with my children since they were toddlers. I read to them children's story books and various versions of the Bible for children. In their late childhood during one of their summer holidays, I told them age appropriate biblical stories from the Old Testament. I also read stories of missionaries, moral stories and novels so that they can grow "in wisdom and in favor with God and man."

My involvement in teaching Sunday school since 1999 gave me opportunities to teach juniors (9- to 11-year-old children). The primary content of lessons was stories, and storytelling has been the primary method. I personally enjoy teaching this age group as there are a lot of firsts in this stage: Readiness to comprehend justification by faith, enjoyment of participating in worship, formulation of questions about faith, evaluation of different points of view in search of their own convictions, loyalty to one's church, and openness to spirituality. I also noticed their need to strengthen their self-image as children of God as they begin to accept peer group values over those of adults. This age is considered as "being a more spiritual period in the lifespan."[37] Yoder notes that junior children are limited in their religion yet they are capable of praying, experiencing forgiveness, and the presence of God. Thus he notes that the junior age is an important age for children's

---

37. Worsley, "Children Aged 9–10," 205.

future religious development.[38] This explains the reason for my selection of this age group for research.

Through this study, the researcher hopes to kindle further research and ministry among children in academia and congregations in India. Dan Brewster, Director of Child Advocacy for Compassion International in Asia, has been urging seminaries in India to address the issues of children through their academic disciplines. India with the largest number of children in the world,[39] spirituality of children, and other issues of children are yet to be a topic of priority in theological institutions in India. This highlights the significance of the study in the Indian-subcontinent. The following section highlights the life of children in India.

Children in India

India has the largest child population in the world numbering more than 375 million.[40] It is challenging to describe a typical Indian child. Apart from the diverse languages, cultures, and religions in India, there is a wide gap between the rich and poor. Indian industrialists have found their place among the richest people in the world. Indian youths have secured places in international beauty contests. However, movies like *SlumDog Millionaire* depict the life of the poor children. The following section is an attempt to shed light on the children before and after Indian independence.

Children in Pre-Independent India

Indian classics in regional languages have recorded accounts of children. In some they were at "the center of admiring adults."[41] However, in other cases the status of the Indian child was at the lowest in society.[42] Historically, the mother was the primary caretaker of children, followed by the immediate family, extended family, and caste relationships. Ancient epics gave more

---

38. G. Yoder, *The Nurture and Evangelism of Children* (Scottdale, PA: Herald, 1959), 95.

39. Thukral, Ali, and Mathur, "Children: Background & Perspective," 2009.

40. Ibid.

41. S. Bhakhry, "Children in India and Their Rights" (New Delhi: National Human Rights Commission, 2006), 14.

42. Ibid., 13.

importance to heredity than nurture; however boys of ruling upper-castes were educated by reputed teachers called *gurus*. Children were severely disciplined with beatings. They were expected to respect and obey elders.

It is believed that life begins with conception rather than at birth. The five stages of childhood in the Indian tradition are as follows: (1) *Garbha*, or the fetal period; (2) *Ksheerda* (0–6 months), (3) *Ksheerannada* (6 months–2 years) (4) *Bala* (2–5 years) and (5) *Kumara* (5–16 years).[43] Transition from one stage to another was marked by major rites and rituals. Parents longed to have children; a boy child was preferred to a girl child.[44] Girls were married at an early age, which ended their childhood.

Along with the Indian struggle for independence in the nineteenth century, various social reforms originated focusing on children; the most prominent one was the abolition of child marriage.[45] National leaders like Mahatma Gandhi and Jawaharlal Nehru taught the importance of nurturing children. Thus many laws were passed and various charitable organizations emerged to improve the status of children. Indian children benefited from international organizations like the League of Nations after the First World War and the United Nations Children's Fund after the Second World War.[46]

Children in Independent India

Independent India views the family unit as the primary venue for children's socialization.[47] The Indian constitution and subsequent Five-Year Plans ensure protection of Indian children in the areas of health, nutrition, and education.[48] Children are considered as the nation's most "precious asset"

---

43. D. Sinha, "Indigenizing Psychology," in *Handbook of Cross-Cultural Psychology: Theory and Method Vol 1*, 2nd ed., eds. J. W. Berry, Y. H. Poortinga, and J. Pandey (Needham Heights, MA: Allyn & Bacon, 1997), 149.

44. D. G. Mandelbaum, *Society in India: Continuity and Change*, vol. 1–2 (Los Angeles, CA: University of California Press, 1970), 93.

45. S. Jain, *Encyclopedia of Indian Women through the Ages: Modern India*, vol. 4 (New Delhi: Gyan Publishing, 2003), 127.

46. Bhakhry, "Children in India," 16–17.

47. Ibid., 20.

48. Ibid., 36, 39.

by the National Policy for Children in 1974 and their "nurture and solicitude" is the responsibility of India.[49]

In 2006 a controversial poll listed India as the sixth most dangerous place for children.[50] In spite of India being the third largest producer of food and third largest defense spender, her children live in poverty and are deprived of their childhood.[51] According to the National Sample Survey Organization, 16.4 million 5- to14-year-old children are involved in child labor, which makes India the country with the largest number of child laborers.[52]

Problems faced by urban, middle-class Indian children are different from poor children. Under academic pressure, they face negative emotions which is reflected in their "low affect state, low activation level, low experience of choice, and high experience of social anxiety."[53] Certain problems faced by girl children are as follows: abortion of unborn daughters, child prostitution, pornography, sexual abuse, and social oppression.[54]

Regardless, India has made some leaps in terms of ensuring basic rights of children. Thus infant mortality rates are down, child survival is up. Literacy rates have improved and school dropout rates have fallen in recent years.[55] There is a change in perception of the girl child now compared to the 1970s and 1980s. Many government incentives like free education have opened up new horizons for girl children. They are no longer considered a disadvantage in urban and semi-urban areas.[56]

---

49. S. N. Tripathy, *Girl Child in India* (New Delhi: Discovery Publishing, 2003), 1.

50. H. Suroor, "A Controversial Survey on India," *The Hindu*, 19 July 2006. Online edition of India's National Newspaper.

51. Ibid.

52. K. Damodaran, "Child Labor: An Unresolved Issue," *The Hindu* (8 February 2009), 14.

53. S. Verma, D. Sharma, and R. W. Larson, "School Stress in India: Effects on Time and Daily Emotions," *International Journal of Behavioral Development* 26, no. 6 (2002): 505.

54. A. Sherwani, *The Girl Child in Crisis* (New Delhi: Indian Social Institute, 1998), vii.

55. Thukral, Ali, and Mathur, "Background & Perspective."

56. P. Umman, "W(h)ither the Girl Child?" *The Hindu*, 25 April 2010, 14.

The Locale of the Proposed Research

The locale of this proposed research is in a semi-urban town of Adoor, Kerala, India. The state of Kerala has some perplexing demography. It has both the highest literacy rate – 90.86 percent and the highest female literacy – 87.86 percent among Indian States.[57] The government of Kerala's commitment to promote education, health and other social amenities has resulted in rapid social development compared to other states in India.[58] Yet, Kerala ranks highest in suicide rate – 25.2 per one hundred thousand when the national average was 11.2 per one hundred thousand.[59] Family murder suicide is increasing in the state – one of the parents kills the children and spouses, and then commits suicide.[60] Other issues in Kerala that affect children are as follows: the increasing divorce rate, single-parent households due to employment away from home, alcohol consumption, alcohol related psychiatric and physical problems among youths and middle adults, consumerism, competitive lifestyle, rapid social change, and gender role change.[61] Recently media brought attention to various alarming social evils among children in Kerala. This includes incest, rape, sex trafficking, theft, drug and alcohol abuse, and pornography.

Explanation of Key Terms

The explanation of the following key terms is significant to comprehend the research in its entirety. These terms are used throughout this paper.

Children

The UN Conventions on the Rights of the Child defines children as every human being under the age of 18 years unless the legal age of majority in

---

57. Government of Kerala (Kerala: Education, 2005), accessed 3 April 2009.

58. V. B. Nair, *Social Development and Demographic Changes in South India: Focus on Kerala* (New Delhi: M. D. Publications, 1994), 2.

59. C. Maya, "Suicide Rate Is Down in State." *The Hindu* – the Online Edition, 12 September 2009.

60. C. J. John, "Family Murder Suicides in Kerala," 2000, accessed 3 April 2009, 1.

61. Ibid., 1–2.

a county is lower than eighteen.⁶² The Census of India defines children as those boys and girls below the age of 14 and social scientists include 15- to 19-year-old females in the girl-child demographic data.⁶³

Narratives/Stories

Narratives are stories. A story can be fictional, historical, or a combination. Garland lists the characteristics of stories: They tell a sequence of events which are connected to one another by a plot, or causal connectives. These events are experienced by characters that are making choices in an attempt to influence those events. There is a beginning, middle and an ending, and there is an audience for the story.⁶⁴ For this research, the stories used are only biblical stories. The term "narratives" and "stories" are used interchangeably.

Spiritual Formation

Christian spirituality is defined as "achieving and sustaining a relationship with God" which is reflected in actual Christian life.⁶⁵ Thus it is living out the encounter with Jesus by fostering and sustaining this relationship.⁶⁶ Blair saw spirituality as a process of growing in the awareness of God, self, and others and of acting upon that knowledge.⁶⁷ The goal of spiritual formation is a maturing faith and a deepening relationship with Jesus Christ, through which we become more like Jesus in our daily lives.⁶⁸ Our relationship with Christ and the process of sanctification, which results from the relationship are the two sides of spirituality.⁶⁹ Allen noted the role of the

---

62. United Nations Committee on the Rights of the Child United Nations Children's Fund and Bernard van Leer Foundation, *A Guide to General Comment 7: Implementing Child Rights in Early Childhood*, 2006, accessed 2 November 2009.

63. Thurkral, Ali, and Mathur, "Background & Perspective."

64. D. Garland, "Family Stories: Resources for Nurturing Family Faith in Congregational Life," *Journal of Family Ministry* 18, no. 3 (2004): 30.

65. A. E. McGrath, *Studies in Doctrine* (Grand Rapids, MI: Zondervan, 1997), 2.

66. Ibid., 2–3.

67. C. E. Blair, "Women's Spirituality Empowered by Biblical Story," *Religious Education* 87, no. 4 (1992): 534.

68. Stonehouse, *Joining Children*, 21.

69. K. Issler, *Wasting Time with God: A Christian Spirituality of Friendship with God* (Downers Grove, IL: InterVarsity, 2001), 252.

Holy Spirit and the community of believers that nurture this relationship and "the child's understanding of, and response to, that relationship."[70]

Christian

The word "Christian" is found only three times in the New Testament (Acts 11:26; 26:28; 1 Pet 4:16). It means one who is "an adherent of Christ."[71] Christians worship together in denominational churches and non-denominational churches. There are differences in beliefs and practices among denominations, but they all adhere to the Bible as the Scripture. In this research, the sample is selected from Pentecostal and Charismatic Christian churches.

Pentecostal/Charismatic Churches

Pentecostal/Charismatic churches in India emphasize the reliability of the Bible and the need for the transformation of an individual's life through faith in Jesus. Pentecostals generally adhere to the doctrine of Biblical inerrancy believing that the Bible has definite authority in matters of faith. They believe in the baptism of the Holy Spirit as the second blessing and speaking in tongues as the initial, physical evidence.

Perception

The word "perception" is from the Latin words *perceptio*, or *percipio*. Perception is "the process of becoming aware or conscious of a thing or things in general; the state of being aware."[72] Perception is different from sensation. Sensation occurs in sense organs, yet perception is an activity of mind.[73] Sensation helps us to interpret and label the information received through our senses.[74] For perception to occur, sensory information is integrated with memories, emotions, and expectations. The process of

---

70. C. A. Allen, "Exploring Children's Spirituality from a Christian Perspective," in *Nurturing Children's Spirituality: Christian Perspectives and Best Practices*, ed. C. A. Allen (Eugene, OR: Cascade, 2008), 11.

71. J. Dickle, "Christian," in *The International Standard Bible Encyclopedia*, vol. 1: A–D, ed. G. W. Bromiley (Grand Rapids, MI: Eerdmans, 1979), 657.

72. Oxford English Dictionary, 2009 edition.

73. J. R. de J. Jackson, ed., *The Collected Works of Samuel Taylor Coleridge: Logic*, Bolligner Series, 2nd ed., vol. 75 (Princeton, NJ: Princeton University, 1981), 309.

74. H. Looy, "Sensation and Perception," in *Baker Encyclopedia of Psychology and Counseling*, eds. D. G. Benner and P. C. Hill (Grand Rapids, MI: Baker, 1985), 1092.

perception consists of three stages: selection, organization, and interpretation.[75] In the selection stage, we select stimuli to which we attend through our sense: sight, sound, smell, taste, and touch. Organization happens when stimuli are mentally arranged so that one can grasp or understand the stimuli. The last stage interpretation is involved when meanings are attached to stimuli. This is usually based on our values, needs, beliefs, experiences, expectations, involvement, self-concept, and other personal factors.

Statement of the Research Questions

Growing out of my interest in stories and children, this study focused on the primary research question: what are children's perceptions of the role of biblical narratives in their spiritual formation? In order to understand their perceptions, the following questions are considered:

1) Who tells biblical stories to children? Where do they hear stories?
2) Why do others tell biblical stories to children?
3) When do children recall the stories?
4) Does recalling or listening to biblical stories impact the life situations they face? If so, how?
5) How do these children's perceptions of the role of biblical stories in their spiritual formation compare with the dimensions of relational consciousness in Hay and Nye's study in the United Kingdom: I-Thou, I-self, I-other, and I-world? Are there other important insights from the proposed study that challenge or go beyond the model developed by Hay and Nye?[76]

Population and Sample

The population of this research is 9- to 11-year-old children in semi-urban Kerala, India who are part of Pentecostal/Charismatic churches and have opportunities to hear biblical stories at church and home. The sample consists of twenty-nine 9- to11-year-old children who were selected by a purposeful sampling technique from seven Pentecostal/Charismatic

---

75. M. Brignall, "The Process of Perception," (n.d.) accessed 23 February 2010.
76. Hay and Nye, *Spirit of the Child*.

churches in and around the town of Adoor, Kerala, India. A minimum of two children and a maximum of eight children were recruited from one congregation. The initial plan was to have twenty-five children. However, twenty-nine children were selected for the sample in order to compensate for possible absentees. All children did not participate in the weekly activities or member checking. The minimum number of participants for class activities was twenty-five and the maximum was twenty-nine. Care was taken to include children representing both genders and a range of socio-economic strata. Inclusion of both genders is not primarily to examine gender differences but to hear from both genders. The following criteria were used in selecting the sample:

1) Those who have been part of Pentecostal/Charismatic churches for at least two years.
2) Those who regularly attend worship and other weekly meetings along with at least one of their parents.
3) Those who regularly (at least three times a month) attend Sunday schools.
4) Those who have the opportunity to listen to biblical stories at home and church.

The researcher was assisted by three students of Faith Theological Seminary, Kerala, India. They were selected in the month of March and their training was an ongoing process from April to July. Thus the research team consisted of four members: two males and two females.

Once a week children were gathered to a common place, the conference room of Faith Theological Seminary, Manakala, Kerala, India for two hours of class activities for six weeks in the months of April and May, 2010. This was an opportunity to hear several biblical narratives and do story-related activities based on the six lessons from *God Our Security*, a textbook published by India Sunday School Union, Konoor, India. Assessing written, oral, and group activities of children during the two-hour gathering each week for six weeks, and observing the classroom, are two methods of research associated with the classroom activities.

Focus group interviews and member checking were other methods of data collection in this research. Focus group interviews were conducted two weeks after the six weeks of activities with children in the months of

June and July. There were six focus group interviews, with a minimum of three and a maximum of six children, which were moderated by two research team members. Nine-year-olds were in two same gender groups. The other four groups were also same gender groups with 10- and 11-year-old children. Informal member checking happened throughout the focus group interviews as moderators asked follow-up questions and paraphrased children's responses to accurately comprehend the meanings of children's responses. Five follow-up focus group interviews were in the month of July with four children in a group. These consisted of same gender groups. A selected group of children participated in formal member checking to evaluate findings of this research. The findings were also discussed with the research assistants, four faculty members of Faith Theological Seminary, and sixteen students of the seminary who have been involved in children's ministry for a minimum of two years.

Assumptions of the Study

1) Children are actively in search for meaning.[77] They try to make sense of the world and integrate the information they gain through experience or otherwise. The processes by which children make interpretations of their experiences, alter, and order the interpretations are called assimilation and accommodation according to Jean Piaget.[78]

2) Children are innate spiritual beings. Regardless of the cultural context of the child, children have spiritual potentiality. The Bible presents children as possessing the capacity to ponder spiritually significant matters (Deut 6:20–21; Matt 21:14–16). They are a blessing from God (Pss 113:9; 127:3–5; 128:3–4) and were required to follow the obligations of the covenant (Exod 20:8). In the Gospels, Jesus acknowledged the spirituality of children.[79]

---

77. R. A. Gobbel, and G. G. Gobbel, *The Bible, a Child's Playground* (Philadelphia, PA: Fortress, 1986), 18.

78. S. K. *Mangel, Advanced Educational Psychology* (New Delhi: Prentice-Hall of India, 1999), 81.

79. Gundry-Volf, "Least and the Greatest," 37–47; May et al., *Children Matter*, 39–42.

Cognitive development theories, which depict childhood religion as inadequate have been challenged by others.[80] Children's spirituality is rooted in a universal human awareness. It is "really there," not just a culturally constructed illusion.[81] They saw that spirituality is "something biologically built into the human species."[82]

3) The context plays a vital role in nurturing the innate spirituality of the child. Many studies have commented on the importance of context in nurturing spirituality in children.[83] Spirituality can be nourished by daily paying formal attention to "aspects of human experience that brings spiritual awareness to light."[84] Further, a context where spiritual insight can be expressed helps in the concrete expression of spiritual insight.[85] Caregivers can provide a space to enhance something that is developing and "already there."

4) Children can share their insights, feelings and opinions with caring adults in a non-threatening environment. Hay and Nye and Coles are some research studies where children reveal that they are willing to share their insights and questions with others. The Bible witnesses the inquisitiveness of children by the phrase, "When your children ask" (Exod 12:26; 13:14; Deut 6:20–21; Josh 4:6, 21) as the beginning point of discussions with children about the significance of the law and lifestyle.

5) Telling stories has the potential to impact children's relational consciousness, which is patterned in I-Thou, I-Others, I-Self, and I -World.[86] Hay and Nye stated that relational consciousness is

---

80. Gobbel and Gobbel, *Child's Playground*, 5–10; K. E. Hyde, "A Critique of Goldman's Research," *Religious Education* 63, no. 6 (1968): 429–435; Hay and Nye, *Spirit of the Child*.

81. Hay and Nye, *Spirit of the Child*, 18.

82. Ibid., 63.

83. Hay and Nye, *Spirit of the Child*, 60; Hyde, *Children and Spirituality*, 20; L. Duff, "Spiritual Development and Education: A Contemplative View," *International Journal of Children's Spirituality* 8, no. 3 (2003): 235.

84. Hay and Nye, *Spirit of the Child*, 145.

85. Ibid.

86. Ibid., 109.

in the "rudimentary core of children's spirituality" from which originate "meaningful ascetic experience, religious experience, personal and traditional responses to mystery and being, and mystical and moral insight."[87]

Delimitations of the Study

1) The empirical study concentrates on 9- to 11-year-old children from Pentecostal/Charismatic churches. The impact of stories on children in other age groups is beyond the scope of this research. Children's perceptions of biblical stories in other Christian denominations is thus beyond the scope of this research.
2) Geographical limitation and a small sample are other delimitations. All children in the sample are from the vicinity of one town in Kerala. The sample consisted of twenty-nine children. As the research is in a town in Kerala, generalizing the findings of the research to other states in India is not recommended.
3) This research focuses only on the relationship between biblical stories and spiritual formation. It does not deal with how songs help in spiritual formation.
4) This research does not consider how prayer enables spiritual formation.
5) This does not investigate how children's participation in various programs and activities in church fosters their spiritual formation.
6) Further, it is not in the scope of the research to argue for or against the concerns raised about the appropriateness of sharing biblical stories with children.[88] Goldman argued for "drastic reduction of Bible material" below the age of 12.[89] Crain noted

---

87. Ibid.
88. Goldman, *Religious Thinking*; Crain, *Power of Story*.
89. Goldman, *Religious Thinking*, 70.

that stories are powerful in transmitting faith, yet it can be an oppressive tool if used uncritically.[90]

7) Finally, this research does not address the use of narratives in postmodernism.

Summary

The proposed research explores how 9- to 11-year-old children in Pentecostal/Charismatic churches in the town of Adoor, Kerala, India perceive the role of biblical stories in their spiritual formation. This qualitative study uses observations, class activities, focus group interviews, and member checking to listen to children about how they do or do not connect stories to their spiritual formation.

Indian children have benefited from the commitment of missionaries and national and international organizations like Compassion International, Operation Mobilization, World Vision, and Viva Network. Theological institutions and churches in India have a great responsibility as India has the largest number of children in the world. The time has come for Indian Christians to consider the issues and needs of children if churches are to continue in their efforts to build a better future for Indian children.

Chapter 1 has identified and described the research problem, background, significance of the topic, sample, and research procedure. Chapter 2 critically surveys conceptual and empirical studies addressing various aspects of the spirituality of children and storytelling with children. Chapter 3 explains the biblical and theological basis of the topic with a special emphasis on Psalm 78:1–8. Chapter 4 discusses the research design and procedures for collecting and analyzing data, bearing in mind the ethical consideration while doing research with children. Chapter 5 presents the analysis of the data and chapter 6 discusses the findings and implications for children's ministry and recommendations for future research.

---

90. Crain, *Power of Story*.

CHAPTER 2

Review of Relevant Literature

Spirituality is now recognized as a core dimension of the lives of children. However, the Judeo-Christian faith has had a keen interest in children's spiritual formation even before the recent emergence of interest in children's spirituality. Simultaneously stories of God's mighty deeds and wonders are seen as central to its worldview.[1] This is evident in the long storytelling tradition presented in the Bible. The recital of stories of God's mighty acts to the Israelite children made the generation of parents and the generation of children "spiritual contemporaries" with their parents.[2]

In Kerala, India, Sunday schools are seen as a crucial and exclusive ministry with children where children are spiritually nurtured primarily through telling biblical stories. This shows the significance of the research topic of this proposed study – children's perceptions of the role of biblical narratives in their spiritual formation. The focus of this research necessitates a closer look at the spirituality of children and the practice of storytelling in religious and general education.

Rationale for the Domain of the Research

This proposed research has explored perceptions of children regarding the role of stories in their spiritual formation. This entails the discussion of this chapter to focus on two domains: (1) spirituality of children and (2) stories and storytelling in general and in religious education. The first domain considers empirical and conceptual studies in children's spirituality. The

---

1. N. T. Wright, *The New Testament and the People of God* (London: SPCK, 1992), 41.
2. Fishbane, *Text and Texture*, 82.

second domain reviews the conceptual and empirical research which deals with various dimensions of telling stories to children in general and in religious education.

Children's Spirituality Domain

Social science research examining children's religious and spiritual life has a history of more than one hundred years.[3] The first half of the twentieth century saw a shift from a "holistic, integrated perspective of children" to a decreased emphasis on experience.[4] The second half of the twentieth century witnessed a shift from a cognitive approach in understanding religious and spiritual development to a more comprehensive understanding of spirituality. Goldman's developmental framework dominated the research of religion among children in the beginning second half.[5] The focus on thinking and reason led to the questioning of the religious dimension in children's lives. Yet, the inadequacy of developmental theory in explaining religious nurture is now widely discussed.[6]

The research of Fowler[7] falls under the category of developmentalism yet they had a role in igniting a new appreciation for faith in childhood. Unlike Fowler and Westerhoff, Coles and Hay and Nye with their primary focus on children, have contributed to the understanding of spirituality as an essential part of children's development. The following section describes these and other research studies and reflections which focused on the characteristics of children's spirituality.

---

3. D. Ratcliff, "The Spirit of the Past: A Century of Children's Spirituality Research," in *Nurturing Children's Spirituality: Christian Perspectives and Best Practices*, ed. C. A. Allen (Eugene, OR: Cascade, 2008), 21.

4. Ibid., 22.

5. Goldman, *Religious Thinking*.

6. C. Dykstra, "Faith Development Issues and Religious Nurture," in *Changing Patterns of Religious Education*, ed. M. J. Taylor (Nashville, TN: Abingdon, 1984), 85–86.

7. J. W. Fowler, *Stages of Faith: The Psychology of Human Development and the Quest for Meaning* (Victoria, BC: Dove Communications, 1981); J. W. Fowler, *Becoming Adult, Becoming Christian: Adult Development and Christian Faith* (San Francisco, CA: Harper & Row, 1984).

Ronald Goldman

The research of Goldman was an attempt to understand "the modes and patterns of thinking" of children on religious teaching they hear in school, church, and family. Thus the focus of the research was on the intellectual understanding of children in their attempt to understand religious teachings.[8] His study is based on Piaget's structure of developmental thinking[9] and Harms' series of religious stages.[10] He employed a clinical interview pattern using three religious pictures and three Bible stories.[11] The sample consisted of two hundred British children from various state schools.[12] There were twenty children with an equal number of boys and girls from the 6- to 14-year age group and there were twenty 15- to 17-year-old children.[13] They represented children from various churches and non-church backgrounds.[14]

Based on the research, Goldman explained religious thinking of children in stages of concepts. The three stages of religious thinking and corresponding age boundaries based on the analysis of the response of the children[15] are given in the following table.

Table 1: Goldman's Stages of Religious Thinking

Stage	Age
Pre-operational thought	Up to 7/8 years
Concrete operational thought	7/8 to 13/14 years
Formal operational thought	13/14 onwards

The sample of this proposed research falls within Goldman's concrete operational stage. The characteristics of children in this stage are given as follows: (1) The thinking of children are limited to concrete, visual, and

---

8. Goldman, *Religious Thinking*, 2.
9. Ibid., 19.
10. Ibid., 24.
11. Ibid., 36–37.
12. Ibid., 40, 43.
13. Ibid., 34, 40.
14. Ibid., 42.
15. Ibid., 64.

tangible elements. (2) They are not capable of generalizations. (3) Their interpretations of verbal problems are based on the content and their experiences.[16] (4) Intellectually they are in between childhood fantasy and adult logic.[17] He noted individual differences with two characteristics: differences in maturational level among children of the same age group and an individual child's inconsistent response to various problems.[18] The important factors that cause the first difference are as follows: church or Sunday school attendance, habits of prayer or Bible reading, and parents' attitudes to religion.[19] Familiarity with the stories and experience and motivation of children are factors that caused the second difference.[20]

Goldman noted that modes and methods of religious thinking is the same as in other fields. This research supported the concept that "theologic and logic are closely related" as faith is related to experience.[21] The theological outlook of the world of a child at a particular age corresponds to the mental age of the child.[22] He concluded that religious thinking of children is also "childish and immature" as children have an immature and childish form of thought.[23] As religious immaturity continues till adolescence, he suggested avoiding education based on a critical and rational approach to religion before adolescence.[24] Propositional thinking is possible for children only after the age of 13 years. This research confirmed an earlier research that children may merely describe the story before the age of 13 but they do not have the capacities to "set up possibilities to account for events in a story."[25] Thus he showed an inhibition towards spirituality of young children.

Goldman's research has attracted many criticisms and replication studies. The positive elements of the research are notable. His stress on the

---

16. Ibid., 56.
17. Ibid., 234.
18. Ibid., 64.
19. Ibid., 65.
20. Ibid.
21. Ibid., 66.
22. Ibid., 67.
23. Ibid.
24. Ibid.
25. Ibid., 22.

importance of mental age in the development of religious thinking has brought a new dimension to the understanding of child development and a new thinking about religious education. His findings have influenced curriculum construction in religious education ever since.

However, some aspects of the implications of his research need to be applied to religious education with caution: (1) It needs to be noted that the miraculous element in the three stories that Goldman used might have influenced the findings. (2) The focus only on religious thinking might have caused him to overlook religious experience and feelings. He had acknowledged that "the sensitive world of feeling, wonder and unique personal experience" is at the "heart of all religious knowledge."[26] (3) It is a fact that children may not fully understand biblical passages, but how many adults can fully understand the Bible?[27] (4) Instead of merely telling or reading the stories, the use of audio-visual tools and various activities may help children to find the relevance of the stories in their lives.

Referring to children's religious thinking as immature and childish contradicts the biblical view of children. In the Old Testament, children were obliged to observe the commandments (Exod 20:10). God commanded the Israelites to tell God's might acts to children (Deut 6). Gundry-Volf gives a detailed study of how Jesus welcomed children and their spirituality.[28]

James Fowler

Enlightened by the development theories of Piaget, Erikson, and Kohlberg, Fowler's research[29] focused on the pattern of faith development. He interviewed approximately 359 people with religious and secular orientation in ten years over a variety of settings.[30] The sample represented male and female participants involving an age span from 4 years to the early 80s.[31]

---

26. Ibid., 3.
27. J. M. Lee, "How to Teach: Foundations, Process, Procedures," in *Handbook of Preschool Religious Education*, ed. D. Ratcliff (Birmingham, AL: Religious Education Press, 1988), 160.
28. Gundry-Volf, "Least and the Greatest," 37–47; May et al., *Children Matter*, 39–42.
29. Fowler, *Stages of Faith*; Fowler, *Becoming Adult*; J. W. Fowler, "Faith Development at 30: Naming the Challenges of Faith in a New Millennium," *Religious Education* 99, no. 4 (2004): 405–421.
30. Fowler, *Stages of Faith*, 313.
31. Fowler, "Faith Development," 414.

He incorporates cognition, emotion, imagination, and moral sense in describing the stages of faith development.[32] He defines faith as "the most fundamental category in the human quest for relation to transcendence."[33] Even though interviews with children were brief, the interviews of adults and adolescents were two to two and one-half hours. The interview had four parts: life review, life-shaping experiences and relationships, present values and commitments, and religion.[34]

Fowler's analysis of the interviews showed that faith develops through seven recognizable and sequential stages: primal faith, intuitive projective faith, mythic-literal faith, synthetic-conventional faith, individuative-reflective faith, conjunctive faith, and universalizing faith. A child's faith is different from adults in content and in "the inner patterned structure of operation by which the child has faith."[35] The primary goal of religious education is not to promote stage advancement rather it is just a "byproduct" of teaching and the practices of faith.[36]

The age group of the children in the present research, 9- to 11-years, falls within the mythic-literal stage. The characteristics of this stage are as follows: Children consciously join the immediate social group and their stories and can take the perspectives of others. Faith involves reliance on the stories, rules and values of the family or the larger community.[37]

Faith development theory has received both negative and constructive criticisms. Fowler was willing to dialogue with both critics and supporters, thus developing a "'common' language, so as to allow experiences to be shared, validated, and questioned."[38] It has inspired a number of empirical and conceptual research studies. It has influenced religious education and

---

32. Ibid., 412.
33. Fowler, *Stages of Faith*, 14.
34. Ibid., 307–312.
35. T. H. Groome, *Christian Religious Education* (San Francisco, CA: Harper and Row, 1980), 67.
36. Fowler, "Faith Development," 417.
37. Fowler, *Stages of Faith*, 149.
38. G. Durka, "Through the Looking Glass: Reflections on a Gift to Religious Educators," *Religious Education* 99, no. 4 (2004): 424.

pastoral care.[39] An important question that has been raised is about the relevance of Fowler's definition of faith in the context of Christian education.[40]

One particular implication of this research has relevance to the research topic of this study. Fowler pointed out the need for providing opportunities to engage children in the sacred practices and texts of a community of faith to enrich their imaginations, will, knowledge, and moral development. Even when children may not intellectually comprehend the meaning and concepts, they can apprehend the meanings of the teachings through the emotions, the images, and the practices of faith thus nurturing the spiritual imagination of children.[41]

John Westerhoff

Faith, according to Westerhoff is "a way of behaving which involves knowing, being, and willing."[42] As faith is action, faith is expressed through our action which can transform others. Thus he unveils the inadequacy of schooling and the instruction-training paradigm to nurture children's faith.[43] He proposes faith formation or a community of faith-enculturation as the alternate model[44] of religious education. Such a community is to encourage meaningful intergenerational interaction to enrich the community.

Based on Westerhoff's experiences and reflection, he explains four distinctive styles of faith: experienced faith, affiliative faith, searching faith, and owned faith.[45] Each style is complete and whole in itself but one can expand into new styles and reach one's faith potential.[46] The second stage "affiliative faith" falls within the age group of the children in this proposed research. Characteristics of this stage are as follows: (1) a need to participate in the community activities, (2) dominance of religious affections which necessitates opportunities to attend to the religion of heart and religious

---

39. H. Streib, "Faith Development Research at Twenty Years," 2003, 18.
40. T. P. Jones, "The Basis of James W. Fowler's Understanding of Faith in the Research of Wilfred Cantwell Smith: An Examination from an Evangelical Perspective," *Religious Education* 99, no. 4 (2004): 353.
41. Fowler, "Faith Development," 412–414.
42. Westerhoff, *Will Our Children*, 87.
43. Ibid., xv.
44. Ibid., 21, 45.
45. Ibid., 88.
46. Ibid.

affections, and (3) a sense of authority which implies the need to tell and hear the story of the community and internalize it as one's own story.[47]

Even though his observations are based on his own experiences, Westerhoff's contributions to Christian education are highly respected. The primary object of the observations was not children, yet he appreciated faith in children as complete in itself. His definition of faith as action has brought the attention of actions of faith rather than just knowing the content of faith. As his understanding of faith is not in terms of cognitive categories he proposed the faith-enculturation model.[48] His evaluation of schooling-instruction model in developing faith is highly appreciable. If the faith-enculturation model has to be effective, the faith community has to see the need and value of nurturing children through various intergenerational activities. Then it calls to forgo the narrow understanding and practice of nurturing the faith in children through classroom activities[49] to a broader understanding of the community of faith as the nurturing environment.

Robert Coles

The intention of Coles' two-year research was to learn from children's "exquisitely private sense of things that nurtures their spirituality."[50] He was interested to know what children think about God, about the Bible, and about going to church.[51] He described his work as "phenomenology and existential" rather than "psychopathology" in nature.[52] The variables in research were as follows: age, gender, social background, race, and nationality. The sample represented children from different continents: North and South America, Africa, Europe, and Middle East. The sample of five hundred represented 8- to 12-year-old children even though children as young as 6 and as old as 13 were included in the sample. The children were from various religious backgrounds: Christian, Islam, Jewish, and less religiously

---

47. Ibid., 93.

48. B. Miller-McLemore, "Whither the Children? Childhood in Religious Education," *Journal of Religion* 86, no. 4 (2006): 643.

49. Westerhoff, *Will Our Children*, 85.

50. Coles, *Spiritual Life*, 36–37.

51. Ibid., 28.

52. Ibid., 39.

inclined groups.⁵³ They represented various national, religious, and cultural backgrounds. Yet the major part of the research happened in Concord, the hometown of Coles and in the city of Lawrence, where there were poor and working class families.⁵⁴ He focused his research more on children even though he talked with parents and teachers.

Coles described his role and the role of the children in research: Children became the authority – the teacher and his role besides enabling children to reveal their experiences, was to listen, record, and to find a "sense of what I have heard and seen."⁵⁵ Following the advice of Dr William, Coles stayed with a number of children for a long time to earn their trust before he could learn from them.⁵⁶ Conversations with individual children and with groups of children about their religious and spiritual experiences were tape-recorded and were presented in the book. The presentation style of this book is not an "abstract or analytic" form, but a narrative form.⁵⁷

Coles noted that "the entire range of children's mental life can and does connect with their religious and spiritual thinking."⁵⁸ He identified various psychological themes that recurred in children's talk: Their desire, ambitions, hopes, worries, fears, and moments of deep and terrible despair. These were connected in idiosyncratic ways "with biblical stories, or with religiously sanctioned notions of right and wrong, or with rituals such as prayer or meditation."⁵⁹ He recognized that religious tenets can be a vital and convincing part of conscience in children⁶⁰ and the consistency and explicit nature of religious practice in homes play a key role in affirming spiritual values in children.⁶¹ Christian children emphasized the coming of Jesus, Islamic children stressed the surrender and obedience to Allah, and Jewish children focused on righteous living. He saw that even children

---

53. Ibid., 36.
54. Ibid., 37.
55. Ibid., 27.
56. Ibid., 37.
57. Ibid., 39.
58. Ibid., 108.
59. Ibid.
60. Ibid., 119.
61. Ibid., 127.

from a non-religious background struggled to find the meaning of life and religious and non-religious children ask questions about life and faith.

Coles' clinical experiences might have enabled him to listen to the verbal and non-verbal signals of children from different backgrounds. His efforts to listen to children are evident in verbatim of children's conversation which he offered as evidence to his findings that children are spiritual beings. Besides, various paintings and drawings of children portrayed their understating of God, biblical figures, or their concept of the sacred and the profane. The narrative style of the book helps the readers to hear voices of children and their inner dialogue. Yet the narrative style of writing can disappoint readers who are used to an analytical style of writing. This research has not only kindled research on various aspects of children's spirituality but also brought attention to the importance of listening to children as subjects not objects of study.

David Hay and Rebecca Nye

In their groundbreaking book, *The Spirit of the Child,* Hay and Nye[62] described their three-year research with eighteen 6- to 7-year-old and twenty 10- to 11-year-old children. The sample represented children from both genders and different religious affiliations and no religious affiliations. The random sample had equal number of boys and girls of which twenty-eight had no religious affiliation. Nye met with each child three times during the research. She also observed children during school assemblies and in class and had conversations with them. Her conversations can be classified as "casual chatter, religious discourse, and implicitly spiritual discourses."

Hay and Nye argued that "children's spirituality is rooted in universal human awareness"[63] and proposed three interrelated themes or categories of spiritual sensitivity or awareness in children and adults: (1) Awareness-sensing includes here and now, tuning, flow, and focusing on the felt sense, (2) Mystery-sensing includes wonder and awe, imagination, and (3) Value-sensing includes delight and despair, ultimate goodness, and meaning. Children "reach out towards the mystery which lies outside of their

---

62. Hay and Nye, *Spirit of the Child.*
63. Ibid., 18.

control."[64] These three themes are related as "relational consciousness" which is the core category of spirituality.[65] The term "consciousness" describes children's spirituality as a distinctive property of mental activity and it is "relational" in the sense of I-thou, I-others, I-self, and I-world. Child-God consciousness has to do with how children talked about their concept of God and the meaning and emotions associated with it. Child-people consciousness refers to children's interpersonal relations which reflect their spiritual life. Child-world consciousness indicates "children's sense of relationship with the natural world." Child-self consciousness relates to children's relationship with their own identity and mental life.[66]

Conversations with children in Hay and Nye's research revealed certain characteristics of their spirituality. (1) Even though they found some general qualities of children's spirituality, researchers noted a "personal signature" to the spirituality of each child.[67] (2) The primary influence on the spirituality of children flows from their personalities. Age and gender only have a secondary influence. (3) The research suggested a continuum by which children express their perspectives: those who perceive spiritual matters in terms of questions or principles, those who make unconscious and conscious association with traditional spiritual religious language, and those who have experienced their spirituality directly and personally in the form of religious insights.[68]

Since spirituality is biologically built it cannot be taught, yet teachers can help children to become "aware of this awareness."[69] Spirituality can be nourished or sustained by daily paying formal attention to "aspects of human experience that brings spiritual awareness to light"[70] and providing a context where spiritual insight can be expressed concretely – "context of ritual, communal narrative, doctrine and social teaching which both focuses attention on and gives concrete expression to spiritual insight."[71]

---

64. Ibid., 65.
65. Ibid., 108.
66. Ibid., 115–117.
67. Ibid., 94.
68. Ibid., 106–107.
69. Ibid., 143.
70. Ibid., 145.
71. Ibid.

This research received wider attention probably due to many reasons: the emerging interest in children's spirituality, the attempt to address spirituality in educational institutions, excellence in research, and the superiority in the theory they proposed. Research studies that followed this study see this as a "key reference point" and it is viewed as the best research so far in the area of children's spirituality.[72]

Brendan Hyde

Children and Spirituality presents Hyde's research[73] among thirty-six 8- to 10-year-old children that represented both genders and various religious backgrounds from three inner-city, suburban, and rural Catholic schools in Melbourne, Australia.[74] Consequently he looks at the characteristics of children's spirituality so that those who work with children can identify it when they encounter it and nurture it.[75] Constructionism was central to this qualitative research.[76] Hermeneutical Phenomenological approach allowed producing a fusion of text and prior understanding of the author. After spending two-hour sessions in the classrooms assisting teachers, Hyde met with groups of children in three semi-structured meetings which focused on awareness-sensing, mystery-sensing, and value-sensing. Video recording enabled him to have a "more holistic picture – a more complete text."[77]

Hyde used the four lifeworld existentials of Van Manen as lenses to interpret the texts.[78] The four lifeworld existentials are: lived space, lived body, lived time, and lived human relations. These "permeate the lived experiences of all human beings, regardless of their social, cultural or historical contexts."[79] The four criteria of Lincoln and Guba – credibility,

---

72. Ratcliff, "Spirit of the Past," 31, 35.
73. Hyde, *Children and Spirituality*.
74. Ibid., 72.
75. Ibid., 9–10, 18, 20.
76. Ibid., 63.
77. Ibid., 71.
78. Max Van Manen, *Researching Lived Experience: Human Science for an Action Sensitive Pedagogy*, quoted in Hyde, *Children and Spirituality*, 74.
79. Hyde, *Children and Spirituality*.

transferability, dependability, and conformability – helped Hyde to maintain the trustworthiness in research.[80]

Hyde is aware of the multiplicity of diverse meanings of the term spirituality. Subsequently children's spirituality is understood as an ontological reality which involves a path towards the realization to the true Self.[81] The four qualities of children's spirituality he identified are as follows: felt sense, integrating awareness, weaving the threads of meaning, and spiritual questing.

The research found two factors that inhibit children's expression of their spirituality: material pursuit and trivializing.[82] The recommendations for nurturing spirituality in children are given with three foci: space, pedagogical framework, and relativism. Parents and teachers have the responsibility to create a space for nurturing spirituality and to allow children to create such a space. He proposes a pedagogical model that comprises the cognitive, the affective, and the spiritual dimensions. He argues that although spiritual questing seems to promote relativism, it is the genuine search for making meaning in relating authentically to Other.[83]

Hyde relied upon prior understanding as this was a qualitative research with a hermeneutic phenomenological approach, yet the trustworthiness was established by the four criteria of Lincoln and Guba: credibility, transferability, dependability, and conformability.[84] Methodology is clear except for two aspects: (1) the criteria in forming groups of children in three schools – whether the groups are based on schools, age, or gender. (2) The use of Catholic schools as a Christian framework to enrich spirituality in children might have impacted the spirituality of the sample even though they represent various religious backgrounds.

Hyde's expertise and acquaintances have also enhanced the research: the opportunity to engage in critical discussion with his university colleagues,[85]

---

80. Y. S. Lincoln, and E. G. Guba, *Naturalistic Inquiry* (Beverly Hills, CA: Sage, 1985) quoted in Hyde, *Children and Spirituality*, 76.
81. Hyde, *Children and Spirituality*, 44.
82. Ibid., 141.
83. Ibid., 170.
84. Lincoln and Guba, *Naturalistic Inquiry*, 76.
85. Ibid., 18.

and his wide experiences in various capacities in Catholic primary schools.[86] He has clearly stated his case that young children can have spiritual experiences and that they can be suppressed and damaged by the environment.[87] This builds into the aspect of providing guidelines to parents and teachers in recognizing and nurturing the spirituality of children. The extensive suggestions and implications given in the book can be applied not only in developed countries but also in developing countries as children growing in the cities of developing countries have common elements with children in developed countries.

Sofia Cavalletti

In her 2002 book, *The Religious Potential of the Child: 6–12 Years Old*, Cavalletti presents her experience of Catechesis of Good Shepherd with younger and older children for more than forty-five years. The questions that this book considers are as follows: "Who is the human being in the phase of life between 6 and 12 years of age? How is the older child's relationship with God built? How does he or she live this relationship with the transcendent?"[88] By portraying the relationship between God and 6- to 12-year-old children, she challenges the impression that the religious life of adults is the measuring rod for the religious life of children.[89]

Cavalletti and Gianna Gobbi developed Catechesis of Good Shepherd to nurture the religious potential of children within the church. Grounded in Montessori's pedagogy, it assumes that children are already in deeper relationship with God and need a space and language for the relationship to grow. Atrium is the name of the environment created to develop this relationship. Here both catechist and child acknowledge Christ as the only Teacher. It is different from the traditional model of religious education as younger children are immersed in the image of the Good Shepherd and the older children work with the image "the Vine and Branches."[90] Various themes presented in this model are viewed with reference to the covenant,

---

86. Ibid., 19.
87. Ibid., 59–60.
88. Cavalletti, *6 to 12 Years Old*, 10.
89. Ibid., xiii.
90. Ibid., xi.

which is the underlying theme of the Bible. This is to bring a unity to the various discussions. For older children, the covenant reality is expressed in the context of sacred history, which is the history from creation to *parousia* and the history of all people.[91]

The key moments of salvation history which are constantly referred to in the liturgy are the primary focus of the catechesis.[92] For example creation, the flood, and the crossing of the Red Sea are a few of the studies of the catechesis. After briefly introducing the text and posing one or two meditative questions based on the text, the catechist proclaims the Scripture passage without explaining the text or paraphrasing it. It allows the Inner Teacher, the Holy Spirit, to speak to the children.[93] Following this, children work with materials based on biblical texts to help them to derive meaning of the particular events in threefold dimension: past, present and future fulfillment.[94] The catechists' role is to prepare and maintain an environment by paying attention to their attitude towards children and the serenity in the physical environment so that children can respond to the Christian message.

Cavalletti worked with children from different countries, cultural setting, and socio-economic backgrounds. Regardless of these differences, she found some "constants" in the responses of older children to the Christian message: (1) Their "capacity to grasp the Mystery" and the pace at which they move with "ease and spontaneity" into the world of Mystery quickens.[95] (2) Even though older children need more themes than younger children, they are interested in going deeper into the themes through personal work. (3) They are interested in time and history. The orientation to biblical time/history helps to respond to "spiritual and psychological needs of the child" and to "find oneself at home in reality."[96] (4) Children saw the link between Old Testament events and the New Testament events, for example, the link between crossing of the Red Sea and baptism and between Manna and

---

91. Ibid.
92. Ibid., 44.
93. Ibid., 48.
94. Ibid., 50.
95. Ibid., x.
96. Ibid., 19.

Eucharist.[97] Children saw the link between the biblical events and the present as they noted the similarities between past and present events.[98]

The focus of the present research – children's perceptions of the role of stories in the spiritual formation of children – Cavalletti's work brings out the importance of reading biblical stories and allowing children to do hands-on activities. Her reflections of her experiences of working with children in a ministry setting show that children can link the biblical events to the present and see the future fulfillment. This affirms the assumption of this proposed research that children try to make sense of the world and integrate the information they receive. Various pictures drawn by children and their conversations presented in the book assert that the religious potential of children is more than what adults imagine. Cavalletti's assumptions that children have deep relationships with God and the importance of context to nurture spirituality are also two assumptions of this proposed research.

Gretchen Wolf Pritchard

Offering the Gospel to Children describes how Pritchard[99] encouraged children to encounter biblical narratives through arts, symbols, rituals, and liturgies instead of just telling stories to them. Rather than following the practice of presenting a few themes like prayers and moral issues, which makes faith a private and personal matter, she creatively shares the whole story of the Bible. She strongly states that children are part of the worshiping community[100] and baptized children are Christians who need to be included in the life of the community.[101]

Pritchard laments over the neglect shown to Christian education in Episcopal churches and critically evaluates the practices of educational activities with children. She disagrees with the practice of adults coming to attend worship and children coming for Sunday school to acquire information. Then the unspoken assumption is that children learn how to be Christians in an academic setting before they can begin to do any of

---

97. Ibid., 46.
98. Ibid.
99. G. W. Pritchard, *Offering the Gospel to Children* (Lanham, MD: Cowley, 1992).
100. Ibid., 144.
101. Ibid., 142.

the things that Christians do together in the community of faith.[102] Even though the Sunday morning class has an important role in nurturing the spirituality of children, it is insufficient for nurture. There is a need to create new structures where children can live out what they learn. Thus their lessons can last beyond the class and activities and become part of their deepest selves.[103] The creative approach she developed incorporated not only Sunday classes but also activities in the intergenerational setting which allowed children to spend extended time in the church with other children.

The pattern Pritchard created incorporates education with liturgy and it intertwines the imaginative and emotional lives of children. Along with telling biblical stories and presenting them through audio and video form, she provided opportunities for children to encounter the stories through the arts, symbols, rituals, and liturgies. As children are liturgical beings, each year they repetitively celebrate different festivals. Thus they learn through participation. Anticipation and preparation are involved in celebrating holidays and festivals. Memories of past celebrations create anticipation in children. The liturgical year for children can emerge by considering the needs of children and the history of the church. The stories of children she presented in the book supports the spirituality of children and she urges adults and church leaders to take the spiritual life of children seriously.

Donald Ratcliff and Brenda Ratcliff

Based on their experiences in teaching and working with children and adults, Ratcliff and Ratcliff explain the spiritual growth and experience of children. They affirm that spirituality is integral to children[104] and emphasize the spiritual sensitivity of children.[105] Children' spiritual growth varies because of different rates of development and differences in training.[106] It can be subtle and gradual compared to adults who undergo rapid change after their conversation experience. They encourage their readers not to

---

102. Ibid., 140–141.
103. Ibid., 145.
104. D. Ratcliff and B. Ratcliff, *Childfaith: Experiencing God and Spiritual Growth with Your Children* (Eugene, OR: Cascade, 2010), 17.
105. Ibid., 9.
106. Ibid., 7.

limit spirituality to intellectual knowledge but to see the importance of relationship with God.

A desire to change and a degree of contentment with their spiritual growth are the two important aspects of spiritual growth that children require in their spiritual journey.[107] The authors propose ten areas of spiritual growth in children. (1) A movement towards God followed by salvation or conversation. (2) Through the learning of biblical content the child knows more about God and faith. (3) Children's view of God becomes more consistent with the Bible as they advance in years. (4) Children move in the direction of becoming more like Jesus in the sense of portraying godly attitudes and actions. (5) Children's eagerness to have spiritual depth in the sense of loving God, praising God, and desiring more of God. (6) An increased sensitivity to the Holy Spirit as children listen to God's voice and obey accordingly. (7) Children become aware of sanctification which is characterized by recognizing and confessing sin, receiving forgiveness and turning away from sin. (8) Children's faith develops as they grow in Christ. (9) Children make moral decisions and act accordingly as their conscience become more sensitive to biblical standards of life. (10) Children give more time to serve others in various ways.[108]

There are general spiritual experiences in terms of awe and wonder. Yet, Christian children can experience distinctively Christian spiritual experiences which are directed towards God.[109] Salvation is such a distinct Christian spiritual experience. Spiritual discipline can lead to spiritual experience. They discuss some ways to encourage spiritual discipline in children: (1) teach about God, (2) affirm spiritual experiences without coercion thus allowing the Holy Spirit to draw children to such experiences, and (3) expose children to age appropriate spiritual disciplines.[110]

This discussion on ten areas of spiritual growth enables educators to have some standard of expectation to which children can be encouraged to grow. Portrayal of God as the initiator and the relationship with him as the focal point of spiritual growth enables teachers and educators to assess

---

107. Ibid., 9
108. Ibid., 9–12.
109. Ibid., 19.
110. Ibid., 19–23.

the extent to which their involvement facilitates spiritual growth in children. The authors do not completely negate stage development theories yet proposes them as one perspective of spiritual development.[111] Adults thus are encouraged to see the significance of children's thinking and experience and to value immaturity of children as a step towards maturity. Even when the role of spiritual disciplines in spiritual experiences of children is discussed, educators are warned not to take the role of the Holy Spirit who draws children to the disciplines.

Summary

This section presented certain extremes in the discussion of children's spirituality from Goldman to Hay and Nye. Goldman viewed children's religious quest as immature and childish while Coles, Hay and Nye, and Hyde observed spirituality as a core dimension of children's lives. Ratcliff and Ratcliff's presentation of different areas of spiritual growth in children gives certain tangible targets for spiritual growth in children. Fowler and Westerhoff not only formulated patterns of faith development but also observed the value of children knowing the story of the faith community.

However, the environment of children is a key aspect in the above discussions. Spirituality can be nurtured by deliberately attending to those experiences that enlightens spirituality.[112] Material pursuit and ignoring inner feelings can hinder spirituality.[113] Cavalletti's and Pritchard's ingenious methods created an environment to nurture the spirituality of children. Cavalletti's atrium, the environment where children can have spiritual experiences and Pritchard's intergenerational setting and incorporation of education with liturgy are unique elements of the environment they created. One aspect of the environment that this present study attempts to focus on is the impact of storytelling on spiritual formation of children. The following section sheds light on certain aspects of storytelling in religious and general education.

---

111. Ibid., 7.
112. Hay and Nye, *Spirit of the Child*.
113. Hyde, *Children and Spirituality*.

Storytelling in Religious and Secular Traditions

Various scholars have noted the use of stories for teaching children from theological, psychological, intellectual, and philosophical dimensions of faith formation. This is the rationale for reviewing the conceptual studies related to stories and spiritual formation. The studies discussed below look at the role of stories and storytelling in the following dimensions: worldview formation, religious education, character formation, faith formation, and spirituality. Even though no research has been focused on the children's perceptions of stories in their spiritual formation, some empirical studies have focused on children's understanding of stories.

Formation and Transformation of Worldview

Narratives have a role in the formation, maintenance, and transformation of worldview. Bartholomew and Goheen argue that human beings have some basic story that they embrace "through which we understand our world and chart our course through it."[114] Unknowingly or knowingly people make meaning in their lives and order their lives based on some story. Hesselgrave insists that not only the substance of biblical narratives is important in worldview transformation but also the story form is vital for the transmission of worldview from one generation to another.[115] Furnish notes that as storytelling touches our feelings it can render a change in worldview.[116] Evans expresses the significance of story as it can enter the heart and cause change without intellectual assent or intentional behavioral change.[117] Wright addresses some misconceptions about story to depict its role in worldview change and cultural transformation. Even though the popular notion is that stories illustrate the propositional point, he sees that human life is "grounded in and constituted by the implicit or explicit

---

[114]. C. G. Bartholomew and M. W. Goheen, *The Drama of Scripture: Finding Our Place in the Biblical Story* (Grand Rapids, MI: Baker, 2004), 19.

[115]. D. J. Hesselgrave, *Scripture and Strategy: The Use of the Bible in the Postmodern Church and Mission* (Pasadena, CA: William Carey Library, 1994), 51.

[116]. D. E. Furnish, *Experiencing the Bible with Children* (Nashville, TN: Abingdon, 1990), 94.

[117]. S. A. Evans, "Matters of the Heart: Orality, Story and Cultural Transformation – The Critical Role of Storytelling in Affecting Worldview Change," *Dharma Deepika* 12, no. 1 (2008): 74.

stories which humans tell themselves and one another."[118] Story is not a "poor people's substitute for the real thing." It is the most characteristic expression of worldview and provides answers for the basic questions of human existence.[119]

Stories can covertly modify and subvert the worldview of the hearers which they might hesitate to reveal. Thus people can be less defensive in listening and sharing stories even when it is intended to bring change in hearers. Steffen notes that recitation of myths and stories are vital for the survival of worldview and the transformation of worldview.[120] This according to him is the non-threatening and inoffensive way of challenging basic beliefs and behavior.[121]

Ann M. Trousdale

The significance of stories, according to Trousdale is that in every culture children's perceptions of the world are shaped by the stories they hear.[122] Every spiritual leader sees the relationship with stories.[123] Eloquent sermons or authoritative discourses do not have the power of "inner persuasiveness" that a story holds.[124] The power of the story is that while reading or hearing a story, the audience rewrites the story in their imagination by "making inferences."[125] The inferences hearers make after perceiving "the connections between motivations, actions, and consequences" make the story "relevant and authentic" in their lives[126] and thus shapes their outlook.

Henry A. Corcoran

In relation to worldview, Corcoran notes that narratives in general and biblical narratives in particular enable people to "'try on' a new community

---

118. Wright, *People of God*, 38.
119. Ibid., 123.
120. Steffen, *Reconnecting God's Story*, 39–40.
121. Ibid., 34.
122. A. M. Trousdale, "Using Children's Literature for Spiritual Development," in *Spirituality and Ethics in Education: Philosophical, Theological and Radical Perspectives*, ed. C. A. Alexander (Brighton: Sussex Academic, 2004), 132.
123. Ibid.
124. Ibid., 133.
125. Ibid., 132.
126. Ibid., 133.

and a new worldview."[127] Biblical stories invite the listeners into a "biblical world."[128] In the postmodern context, the church as the narrative community holds resources to change lives. He asserts that biblical narratives center in the great meta-narrative of Jesus. The church is the repository of this great meta-narrative which he describes as the "central meta-narrative of human existence.[129] Jesus beckons the hearers of the story to enter into his story thus re-forming and re-creating the character and intellect of the hearers. As the faith community is being re-formed, it in turn transforms communities through biblical narratives.[130]

Summary

From the above discussion it is obvious that human beings derive meaning of their lives based on some story. Stories have a role in maintaining and transforming their worldview.[131] Stories have the power to touch the heart and mind of the readers/hearers and transform their outlook even when they do not intend such change.[132] The inner persuasiveness of a story touches the imagination of the hearers and they derive inferences about the plot and characters which makes the story relevant in their lives.[133] It is important for children to hear biblical stories so that their worldview can be shaped and transformed by the meta-narrative of Jesus. In the postmodern context, sharing of the stories is the key to transform lives and to transform communities.[134]

Religious Education

The discussion of stories and religious education swing between two arguments: Goldman's cautionary note to the early presentation of biblical stories to children to others who laudably promote stories and

---

127. H. A. Corcoran, "Biblical Narratives and Life Transformations: An Apology for the Narrative Teaching of Bible Stories," *Christian Education Journal* 4, no. 1 (2007): 36.
128. Ibid.
129. Ibid., 37.
130. Ibid., 41.
131. Steffen, *Reconnecting God's Story*.
132. Evans, "Matters of the Heart."
133. Trousdale, "Using Children's Literature."
134. Corcoran, "Biblical Narratives."

storytelling in order to engage children in self-reflection and in enriching the I-Thou relationship.

Ronald Goldman

Based on the findings of his research, Goldman suggested some implications for religious education, pointing out the dangers of teaching stories in the Bible to children. (1) Early presentation of biblical stories may create misconceptions of their meanings in children which may retard later insights and cause to reject religion as "intellectually untenable."[135] This may have a regressive effect on religious thinking. (2) Familiarity because of constant retelling of the story may impede the freshness, enjoyment, and awe, thus generating boredom among children.[136] One general implication that influenced the curriculum of younger children is that the selection of materials needs to be based on the conceptual thinking of children.[137] His suggestions regarding the use of biblical narratives have found its reflection in the focus of religious education and the focus became the basic needs of children.

Jordan stresses the role of story in Christian education by stating that story and Christian education are made for each other.[138] Boys affirms that traditions have its place in religious education as it is the memory which is foundational for personal relationship and building of a civilization.[139] Biblical stories "narrate, instruct, regulate, inform, and interpret" the experience of the people.[140] She presents narration as one of the modes of religious education by which the teller and the hearers are "mutually immersed in the stories and symbols" which are crucial for their identity.[141] As the message of Scripture is "filled in" by stories, the religious educator needs to fill in the "fundamental faith claims" by stories.[142]

---

135. Goldman, *Religious Thinking*, 222.
136. Ibid., 223–224.
137. Ibid., 224.
138. C. R. Jordan, "Education and Story," *Theological Educator* 33 (1986): 62.
139. M. C. Boys, *Tradition and Transformation in Religious Education* (Birmingham, AL: Religious Education Press, 1979), 16.
140. Ibid., 17.
141. Ibid., 28.
142. Ibid.

Pamela Mitchell

Mitchell[143] proposes the use of stories in religious education based on the work of Kierkegaard,[144] Booth,[145] and Coles.[146] Religious education cannot be an opportunity to impart a certain body of knowledge as Christianity is more than a body of knowledge. If Christianity is to change the lives of people, religious education is to be a place where self-reflection can happen. She presents narrative as the best mode of communication to enable subjective appropriation of Christianity through the process of self-reflection. With respect to children, she claims that stories enable children to engage in self-reflection from a very early age even before they can intellectually understand the claims of the Bible.[147]

Sandy E. Sasso

Because of the centrality of story in relating to God and learning to speak about God, Sasso stresses that "story ought to be at the heart of all religious education."[148] The reasons for her conclusion are as follows: (1) Spiritual life is about experiencing God and story is the language to express the encounter with God.[149] (2) Stories enable the hearers to evoke a sense of wonder and to make connections with the characters of the narratives.[150] (3) Stories are the best vehicle to address their theological concerns rather than using abstract language.[151] As a writer of children's literature, she sees

---

143. P. Mitchell, "Why Care about Stories? A Theory of Narrative Art," *Religious Education* 86, no. 1 (1991): 35.

144. Søren Kierkegaard, *Søren Kierkegaard's Journals and Papers,* vol. 1, no. 657, trans. H. and E. Hong (Bloomington, IN: Indiana University Press, 1967–1975).

145. W. Booth, *The Company We Keep: An Ethics of Fiction* (Berkeley, CA: University of California Press, 1988).

146. R. Coles, *The Call for Stories: Teaching and the Moral Imagination* (Boston, MA: Houghton Mifflin, 1989).

147. Mitchell, "Why Care about Stories?," 42.

148. S. E. Sasso, "When Your Children Ask: A Jewish Theology of Childhood," in *Spiritual Education, Cultural, Religious and Social Differences: New Perspective for the 21st Century,* eds. J. Erricker, C. Otta, and C. Erricker (Brighton: Sussex, 2001), 180.

149. Ibid.

150. Ibid., 181.

151. Ibid., 182.

children as spiritual beings and believes they can understand theology in a story even though they cannot articulate theology in its abstract form.[152]

Theodore Brelsford

Brelsford proposes a "mythical realist" approach to religious education where intuitive and counter-intuitive understandings are held together. The goal of Christian education is to "nurture strong and healthy Christian faith" which must include the ability to perceive/experience/understand the world in Christian "mythical" and "realistic" terms.[153] This is because healthy religious beliefs have two understandings: mythic (counter-intuitive) and scientific (intuitive). Overemphasizing counter-intuitiveness can lead to "dangerous fanaticism and lunacy" and over-commitment to intuitive understanding can lead to "artless dispirited existence."[154]

Pedagogical implications to this approach show the importance of stories in religious education: (1) The way to nurture mythical realism is to nurture appreciation for stories and nurture "wonder, awe, and imagination." (2) Learning the stories of Christianity helps to connect one's life story to the larger story so that one can faithfully live the life through Christian myth.[155] (3) Stories help in nurturing wonder, awe and imagination in children.[156]

Henry A. Corcoran

Corcoran criticizes that a large segment of the church focuses on developing only one facet of faith: propositional knowledge. However, they neglect developing qualities like courage, virtue, emotional development, and responsibility to the social world.[157] In order to develop these qualities, he argues, "the teaching of biblical narratives aimed at transforming lives

---

152. Ibid., 185.
153. T. Brelsford, "A Mythical Realist Orientation for Religious Education: Theological and Pedagogical Implications of the Mythical Nature of Religious Study," *Religious Education* 102, no. 3 (2007): 265.
154. Ibid., 274.
155. Ibid., 276.
156. Ibid.
157. Corcoran, "Biblical Narratives," 34.

should become an intentional activity in a Christian educator's repertoire for individual, small group, and congregational spiritual development."[158]

Others have stressed the inclusion of biographies along with biblical stories in Christian education. Jordan proposes that biographies have a place in Christian education as biographies describe personal encounters with Christ.[159] Wallace presents the importance of personal stories of faith, as she claimed that such stories continue to live as it were in storytelling.[160] Telling stories which reveal the encounter with God in daily life can lead to spiritual formation.

Margaret Ann Crain

Crain observes, "story is both the content and the method of religious education."[161] Further she describes the power of stories: (1) They can surpass differences and build compassion.[162] (2) They are the primary carrier of meaning for people. (3) They contain the accumulated experiences which determine one's identity.[163] She brought up another aspect of the importance of knowing individual stories as religious educators. It is important for religious educators to come to know their own stories and the stories of others. If the stories of others are unknown to religious educators, they can assume their stories as normative and in turn can use them to oppress others.[164] On the other hand, knowing and recognizing their own stories enable religious educators to appreciate others' stories.

Hosffman Ospino

The revelatory power of biblical narratives and biographies according to Ospino is that they can unveil what is human and what is divine.[165] He

---

158. Ibid., 36.

159. Jordan, "Education and Story," 56.

160. C. M. Wallace, "Storytelling, Doctrine, and Spiritual Formation," *Anglican Theological Review* 81, no. 1 (1999): 41.

161. Crain, "Power of Story," 244.

162. Ibid., 248.

163. Ibid., 245.

164. Ibid., 247.

165. H. Ospino, "Unveiling the Human and the Divine: The Revelatory Power of Popular Religiosity Narratives in Christian Education," *Religious Education* 102, no. 3 (2007): 328.

calls biblical stories as "Sacred/Classic stories" and stories of people's everyday experience as "sacred/popular" or "popular religiosity stories."[166] The former focuses on stories of how God met with the people in the past. The latter highlights how people encounter God in their every day life within the particular socio-historical and cultural context and in "*lo cotidiano*" (usual situation).[167] He notes the significance of popular religiosity stories in education: (1) They can inspire hearers to "understand, embrace, and live their faith with conviction and faithfulness,"[168] and (2) they express the diversity of ways in which people encounter God in their day-to-day lives.[169]

Mike Newby

Looking at spirituality from a non-religious context, Newby defines spiritual development as development of self-identity in education. He presents "the desire for a meaningful life-narrative" and engagement with authoritative cultural narratives as prerequisite for spiritual development.[170] Thus he identifies the significance of relating to "story-forms" as a fundamental or "food" to the development of personal identity as well as for spiritual maturity. Story-forms provide models, corrective lessons, goals and philosophies of life, and challenge to adventure.[171]

Newby laments at the loss of "master-stories" which is a characteristic of post-modernity. The sacred stories which provided "ideals, norms, patterns and destinies" in people's search for meaning have been abandoned. Thus the influence or role a priest or preacher had on the spiritual maturity of individuals has also disappeared with the neglect of sacred stories. However, only by personally engaging in these master-stories can children and adults develop spiritually. This brings to attention the importance of acknowledging and communicating the Bible as the "meta-narrative."[172] Goheen

---

166. Ibid., 329.
167. Ibid., 331.
168. Ibid., 337.
169. Ibid., 338.
170. M. Newby, "Towards a Secular Concept of Spiritual Maturity," in *Education, Spirituality, and the Whole Child*, ed. R. Best (London: Cassell, 1996), 92.
171. Ibid., 101.
172. F. B. Craddock, "The Letter of the Hebrews," in *The New Interpreter's Bible: A Commentary in Twelve Volumes*, vol. 12 (Nashville, TN: Abingdon, 1998), 13.

affirms that the Bible is "one cosmic story of the world" and the significance of comprehending our place in the story.[173] The implications of this to Christian educators are as follows: They are to present the Bible as the "master-story" and engage children in it so that their personal identity and spiritual maturity can be developed with respect to the ontological meaning that the Bible teaches.

Summary

Even though Goldman's research has faced several criticisms, he has rightly voiced the need of comprehending the conceptual thinking of children in education. This has been reflected in teaching and curriculum designing ever since. However, in working with children, stories and storytelling have been recommended as the content and method of Christian religious education respectively.[174] Children are fascinated by stories. They can understand the nature of God and his creation through stories rather than through propositional statements.[175] Stories help them to develop awe, wonder, and imagination in children. Thus not only adults often recite "let me tell you a story," but also children ask "can you tell me a story?"[176] However, Newby[177] laments the neglect of "master-stories" and argues that only by personally engaging in master-stories that children and adults can develop spiritually. Christians believe the Bible as the meta-narrative or master-story. Thus Christian educators have the responsibility to present the Bible as the meta-narrative and to engage children in the stories of the Bible.

Character Formation

Character formation is one of the concerns of Christian educators. How do stories contribute in character formation? How do educators see this association?

---

173. Goheen, "*Reading the Bible as One Story*," 7.

174. Jordan, "Education and Story"; Boys, *Tradition and Transformation*; Corcoran, "Biblical Narratives."

175. Sasso, "When Your Children Ask."

176. J. L. Seymour, "Editorial," *Religious Education* 102, no. 3 (2007): 237–239.

177. Newby, "Secular Concept."

E. D. St John

St John notes how great teachers of the past valued the significance of stories in building character in their hearers.[178] Ancient cultures like the Hebrews, Chinese, Indian, Arabian, Japanese, and Roman used stories to mold each generation.[179] He presents two classifications of stories in the realm of moral and religious education: idealistic which are fictional in origin and realistic which are factual stories.[180] He notes that the power of stories lies in the element of emotional appeal it holds.[181] There is an entertainment value in stories, but the message which is embodied in the story cannot be ignored.[182] The story becomes an effective tool in character formation when the hearers are permitted to make their own inferences out of the content of the story.[183]

Paul C. Vitz

Vitz presents the psychological and educational rationale for using stories as a method of teaching morality to children. The educational rationale for the use of narratives in moral education is as follows: the human need of narratives which is evident in the popularity of narratives in every culture and the use of stories to transmit moral and cultural heritage to children.[184] This is presented in the context of increasing moral problems among youths in the USA. Kohlberg's cognitive development model proposed moral education as propositional thinking and verbal discussion of abstract moral dilemmas. Vitz pointed out the limitation of Kohlberg and Piaget's cognitive model: (1) It only focused on the paradigmatic thought and ignored the importance of narrative thought which focuses on concrete human and interpersonal situations.[185] (2) It overlooked the context of personal narratives by which people interpret moral issues. So he argues that next to actually placing children in various situations, the effective

---

178. E. D. St John, *Stories and Story-Telling* (New York: Pilgrim, 1901), 1.
179. Ibid., 2–3.
180. Ibid., 8.
181. Ibid., 88.
182. Ibid., 33.
183. Ibid., 37.
184. Vitz, "Moral Development," 717.
185. Ibid., 710.

way to introduce children to moral life is to have them hear, read, or watch morally challenging narratives.[186] This is because narratives provide a life-like and detailed description of the moral dilemma rather than "abstract, juiceless quality" of principles.[187]

Kieran Egan

Egan notes the role of imagination in inculcating social virtues. He sees stories as a means to inculcate social virtues as it develops imagination. Stories communicate information and at the same time touch the emotions of hearers or readers. Stories describe a range of human qualities and hearers are invited to make these qualities part of their lives.[188] It enables the hearers to imagine what happens when they have these qualities. He encourages teachers to use the right kind of stories with children and a variety of stories so as to stimulate the imagination of children.

Summary

Stories have been used in many cultures to instill values in children.[189] The popularity of stories implies that human beings need stories.[190] Paradigmatic thought in Kohlberg's and Piaget's model can develop morality by presenting principles but narratives can touch emotions and provide the necessary content.[191] By presenting a range of virtues, stories invite hearers to own them. Stories develop character by enabling children to imagine various life situations before they face such situations.[192] In developing character, either the storyteller can directly list the values underlined in stories or the hearers can be allowed to make their own inferences through group discussion or individual reflection.

---

186. Ibid., 716.
187. Ibid., 717.
188. K. Egan, *Imagination in Teaching and Learning: The Middle School Years* (Chicago, IL: University of Chicago Press, 1992), 55.
189. St John, *Stories*.
190. Vitz, "Moral Development."
191. Ibid.
192. Egan, *Imagination*.

Faith Formation

Even though character formation is a concern of Christian educators, faith formation is their primary concern. The following section explains how educators describe the role of stories in faith formation.

James Fowler

The research of Fowler[193] supported the development of faith through several stages. He affirmed that children's perceptions of God are less mature compared to adults yet it is not an argument against introducing the Bible to children. They need to be encouraged to construct mature images of God as they grow. The children's age group in this proposed research falls within Fowler's Mythic-Literal Stage of the Faith Development. The characteristics of this stage in association with stories are as follows: (1) Children of this age group can bind their "experiences into meaning through the medium of stories"[194] and hearing the stories of their community is crucial to the development of mature faith. (2) "The new capacity or strength of this stage is the rise of narrative and the emergence of story, drama and myth as ways of finding and giving coherence to experience."[195] (3) As children can understand the perspective of others and understand relations and consequences, narratives are the "favored and most powerful way" to generate and express personal and shared meanings.[196] (4) Children can retell stories once heard or seen and create self-generated stories. (5) Stories are a major way to find coherence to their experiences. (6) The symbolic and dramatic materials affect children of this age group deeply and powerfully.

John Westerhoff

The four styles of faith proposed by Westerhoff can be understood in the light of narratives and spiritual formation.[197] His second style "affiliative faith" falls within the age group of the children in this research. The following characteristics of the affiliative faith are related to stories: (1) Learning the community's story is essential for faith during this stage. (2) Narratives

---

193. Fowler, *Stages of Faith*; Fowler, *Becoming Adult*.
194. Fowler, *Stages of Faith*, 136
195. Ibid., 149.
196. Fowler, *Becoming Adult*, 56.
197. Westerhoff, *Will Our Children*, 92.

help to provide identity and authority during this stage of faith. (3) He presents the importance of the intuitional and intellectual mode of consciousness.[198] Thus he affirms the significance of activities encouraging "religion of heart" such as storytelling and drama.[199] Storytelling needs to be "a natural and central part of church life."[200] (4) He observes that children can internalize the story only when the church constantly tells and acts the story.

Westerhoff notes the four kinds of stories in the Bible and their unique functions: (1) Myths which explain "the way life is in spite of any evidence to the contrary."[201] Lives are guided by myths, giving meaning and purpose. (2) Apologetic stories are biographies that defend myths. (3) Narratives are those stories that explore the world which myths affirm and apologetic stories defend. It searches the contradictions and finally reconfirms the myths. (4) Parabolic stories function to "subvert the world and the way our culture sees life" so that our perceptions of the world are consistent with the myths.[202] The heart of the Bible is the Christian myth, which has to be "known, owned, and lived"[203] if one has to be Christian. He encouraged the faith community to return to telling biblical stories that enable us to discover the greatest human need, the meaning of our lives.[204]

Bonnie Miller-McLemore

Miller-McLemore stresses that oral and written stories can nurture faith in children.[205] As a "deeply spiritual practice," storytelling can enrich the spiritual life[206] of children as they connect the stories to their lives. Based on John 1:1, "the Word was with God, and the Word was God" she argues

---

198. Ibid., 70.

199. Ibid., 92.

200. Ibid., 71.

201. J. Westerhoff III, *Bringing Up Children in the Christian Faith* (Minneapolis, MN: Winston, 1980), 37.

202. Ibid., 38.

203. Ibid.

204. Ibid., 39.

205. B. Miller-McLemore, *In the Midst of Chaos: Caring for Children as Spiritual Practice* (San Francisco, CA: Jossey-Bass, 2007), 154.

206. Ibid., 153.

that reading or telling biblical stories has rich potential for faith.[207] She brings to attention the biblical references – Ezekiel 3:1–3, Psalm 119:103 – to describe the sweetness of the Word like honey.[208] As food brings shape to the body, books can form the soul. Hearing stories brings pleasure and a "deeper moral and intellectual relationship with ourselves, others, our world, and God."[209] This is the formative aspect of hearing or reading stories. The transformative aspect is that stories help to shape us morally and intellectually.[210]

Roberta Louis Goodman

Goodman states the advantage of stories in nurturing faith in children. He notes that stories explicitly present the relationship between God and his people and the relationship among individuals.[211] The entertainment nature of stories presents the worldview and values embedded in them in a non-didactic way.

Peter W. Macky

Stories can lead us to respond to God in faith more than theological propositions. Macky presents story theology which is speaking of God by telling a story, as an excellent way to achieve relational speech. Stories kindle personal relationships as they invite hearers to be personally involved with the plot.[212] They express the interpersonal reality of humanity in cognitive and affective fullness. So he notes that the best way to engage people to live in their relationship with God is through stories about God's involvement with humanity.[213]

---

207. Ibid.
208. Ibid., 156.
209. Ibid., 161.
210. Ibid., 166.
211. R. L. Goodman, "Nurturing a Relationship to God and Spiritual Growth: Developmental Approaches," in *Teaching about God and Spirituality: A Resource for Jewish Settings*, eds. N. R. Levy, R. L. Goodman, and S. H. Blumbert (Denver, CO: A.R.E. Publishing, 2002), 78.
212. P. W. Macky, "Biblical Story Theology," *The Theological Educator* 33 (1986): 24.
213. Ibid., 29.

Children's Perceptions of the Role of Biblical Narratives in Their Spiritual Formation

Karen Marie Yust

Yust discusses five activities of "story-linking" in relation to the faith formation in children. This is based on the Wimberly's and Brueggemann's works.[214] The Bible is a book of stories that portrays the activity of God in the world. Children can be enabled to see the connection between their lives and the lives of the biblical characters. Parents and religious leaders have the task of helping children to embrace biblical stories so that they can see that the Bible becomes the story of individuals and the community's story. For this to happen in children, first adults are to value the stories in the lives of children. Second, stories of the religious tradition need to be made accessible to the children.

The five activities of "story-linking" are receiving, hearing, celebrating, telling, and becoming.[215] Receiving the story is the basic aspect of parenting and care giving. It involves sharing our own experiences of the sacredness of life and God's love through compassionate care for our children.[216] Since children associate their caregivers with God, the influence of early human relationships communicate to children how God's love is present in the world of the child. Through godly actions, religious communities share with parents the responsibilities to help children to receive the faith story.

The second activity happens when adults tell religious stories to children so that they are hearing the story of God's love.[217] Through reading, storytelling, looking at the pictures, preaching, teaching, playacting, and singing, parents and faith communities can invite children to hear the story of the Scripture. Celebrating the story, the third activity, happens when story is integrated in the community through their personal engagement with their faith community's stories.[218] For the fourth activity to happen, children need to put the story in their own words so that the story can be part

---

214. W. Brueggemann, *Belonging and Growing in the Christian Community* (Atlanta, GA: General Assembly Mission Board, Presbyterian Church in the United States, 1999; A. S. Wimberly, *Soul Stories: African American Christian Education* (Nashville, TN: Abingdon, 1994) quoted in Yust, *Real Kids*, 42.

215. Ibid.
216. Ibid., 43.
217. Ibid., 49.
218. Ibid., 60.

of their understanding of the world.[219] This helps them to move beyond memorization and to express them in their own words. In the fifth activity, becoming the story, children walk in faith when their lives are transformed by the encounter with the God of the story. This means to learn to engage in a way of life that links spiritual awareness with their daily practices.[220]

Sandra M. Levy

Levy touches the various aspects of imagination and faith journey. Faith formation happens through the opportunity that stories provide for imagination. Stories and storytelling are popular because of two reasons: (1) A sense of security that the happy endings of stories can provide.[221] (2) The spiritual impact and personal growth that stories can provide when the readers read how various characters of the story "develop and change across the time frame of the plot."[222] The plots and characters of the story can enable the readers to imagine various choices that they might make before they face similar situations in life. This helps the hearers/readers to comprehend meanings that are implicitly expressed,[223] thus bringing transformation in them. She explains the process behind transformation: our imaginations get engaged with the symbols and metaphors in the stories to understand the truth beneath them.[224]

Walter Neidhart

The importance of adults in the faith community to live out the biblical stories is the focus of Neidhart. Only when adults in families and the faith community live by the standard that biblical stories portray, children will see the effect of story.[225] He gives the psychological and theological value of biblical stories for children:

1) The telling of stories is a call to faith, not just reporting of facts.

---

219. Ibid., 64.
220. Ibid., 66.
221. S. M. Levy, *Imagination and Faith Journey* (Grand Rapids, MI: Eerdmans, 2008), 75.
222. Ibid.
223. Ibid., 80.
224. Ibid.
225. W. Neidhart, "What the Bible Means to Children and Adolescents," *Religious Education* 53, no. 2 (1968): 115.

2) Stories attract even un-churched children.
3) Stories deal with different walks of life, which help the children to think of basic questions of life without any initiation from adults: "Who am I? What am I here for? What is my true support? What do I have to do?"[226]
4) Identification of children with the principal person or group in a story through imagination helps in the development of the child.[227]

Regardless of children's identification with stories, Neidhart notes a gap between children enjoying biblical stories and the distance adults in the faith community show to the Bible. This leads to the question raised by many educators of whether it is good to tell biblical stories to children.[228] Or does the love for adventure and play in children lead to a premature understanding of the truth the Bible witnesses? Neidhart stresses that it is not the wearing out of childish interest of biblical narratives that cause this disregard when children become adults. The reason is the dearth of role models in the community. Unless the adults in the faith community live out the stories, the Bible becomes *terra incognita* (an unexplored region) to children.[229] When adults live out biblical stories, it is an active confrontation for children by which they experience the truth even before they hear the stories. Children are thus enabled to see the difference between the stories and fairy tales when they visualize the relation between the Scripture and the community of faith.

However, Neidhart notes the urgency in adults to get children acquainted with the Bible by telling stories considering the mental age of children. He sees it is an "erroneous belief"[230] to give importance to the quantity of material presented to children. He also stress that critical understanding of biblical stories at an early age can develop an indifference to faith. He

---

226. Ibid., 113.
227. Ibid., 114.
228. Ibid.
229. Ibid., 115.
230. Ibid., 119.

affirms that it is not the intellectual interpretation of the texts but the living witness who passes on the story to the children.[231]

Summary

The research of Fowler recommended the use of stories with children in developing faith in the mythic-literal stage. Westerhoff's presentation of the styles of faith, also stresses the importance of using stories with the second style, the affiliative faith. The sample in this proposed research falls in these categories. When Goldman's recommendation cautioned the use of Bible stories with younger children, these religious educators affirmed the use of stories with children. Miller-McLemore calls storytelling as a spiritual practice which has the potential to develop faith in children. The importance of stories in enriching I-Thou and I-other relationships is the focus of Goodman and Macky. Levy brings in the concept of faith and imagination: stories enable faith formation as it touches the imagination of hearers.

Yust presents "story-linking" with its five activities and gives practical suggestions of how to use stories with children in developing faith. Here she brings in the importance of not only telling biblical stories but also valuing the stories of the children. Adults in the faith community are to tell stories to children and model the stories through their lives.[232]

We have been observing some key concepts in stories and children with respect to their faith formation. Adults are obliged to tell stories and live out the stories. At the same time, they are to value the stories of children. With respect to the research procedure of this proposed study, sharing biblical stories to children is an important aspect. The conceptual and empirical studies beginning with Fowler provide credibility to the particular research procedure of telling stories to children.

Spirituality

Spirituality of children is an important topic of discussion and focus among educators. Below we will look at what practitioners and researchers have shared about the role of stories and spiritual formation in children.

---

231. Ibid.
232. Neidhart, "What the Bible Means."

Sandy E. Sasso

Sasso affirms that written and oral stories influence the spiritual and religious lives of children. She laments that in the effort to transmit knowledge and information about rituals, customs, and history, religious education neglected the "deeper questions of faith" that children were asking.[233] The understanding of the Jewish tradition is that the ritual telling of the stories of faith at the same time every year will change the world.[234] She affirms that narratives provide content and language for children to express their spiritual lives. Further stories are the first language of sacred experience.[235] Her experience and literature survey affirm the innate spirituality of children.[236] With the absence of language for expression, the spiritual lives of children remain dormant and unable to grow. In the story, children meet God and they have a unique understanding of sacred biblical narratives.[237] The stories help them to recognize the abstract concepts, and express their feelings. As a Jew, she saw the invitation of *Midrash* as a way to nurture the spiritual growth of children. When stories of *Midrash* are told it provides a meeting place for the person's life story and the community's story. She acknowledges that the act of storytelling and listening to stories are spiritual exercises.[238]

Sasso brings the Hebrew word *Haggadah* (telling) as a pedagogic model in developing spirituality in children. Affirmatively, she recognizes how Judaism sees storytelling as integral to the spiritual journey.[239] Family narratives mark the beginning of the Torah and the book of Exodus presents the story of the covenant people. The reading of the Torah was central to Sabbath worship, and the *Midrashim* (rabbinical commentaries) gave a new meaning to the text.[240]

---

233. Sasso, "Role of Narratives," 13.
234. Ibid., 19.
235. Ibid., 21.
236. Ibid., 14.
237. Ibid., 25.
238. Ibid., 19.
239. Sasso, "When Your Children Ask," 27.
240. Ibid., 26.

The Jewish practice of ritual telling of the Passover event not only emphasizes the centrality of the child among the Jewish community but also the centrality of telling the story of God's mighty acts in spiritual formation. The questions that the child asks mark the beginning of the celebration of the Passover which is the core story for the Jewish community. In the dialogue between child and father, the answer the father provides is not "a single, absolute answer but a story."[241] Here the story is recited, lived out and finally celebrated with a song.[242] As the exodus story provides an alternate reality to children it provides an "impetus for action," and basis for societal change. Thus *Haggadah* aims to help Jewish children to connect their story with the story of Israel.[243]

The implications of this Jewish celebration on spiritual development of children are twofold: (1) Spiritual nurture happens in a community, (2) spirituality develops when children encounter other people and when the community encounters the sacred story.[244] It is clear that the encounter with God's story is the key to spiritual nurture.[245]

Steven M. Rosman

Rosman remarks that storytelling has been "rediscovered" in professionals of all disciplines.[246] Stories can touch the soul[247] and the I-Thou experience between the storyteller and the listener leads to experience the Eternal Thou, God.[248] He describes the relationship between storytelling and spirituality: storytelling cultivates the innate spirituality in children.[249]

---

241. Ibid.
242. Ibid., 28.
243. Ibid., 27.
244. Ibid., 25.
245. Ibid., 32.
246. S. M. Rosman, "God Dwells in the Story," in *Teaching about God and Spirituality: A Resource for Jewish Settings*, eds. N. R. Levy, R. L. Goodman, and S. H. Blumbert (Denver, CO: A.R.E Publishing, 2002), 204.
247. Ibid., 205.
248. Ibid.
249. Ibid.

Howard Schwartz

The Jewish view of children, according to Schwartz is that they are spiritual beings and can be spiritually developed largely by telling biblical stories and post-biblical Jewish literature.[250] The stories instill trust in God which enriches the I-Thou relationship in children and this relationship is the basis for spirituality in Judaism.[251] Storytelling is central to Judaism as hearing the stories "creates a powerful link to the mythic past and a desire, on the part of children, to develop their own spirituality."[252]

Sonja M. Stewart

Stewart sought to find how young children can experience God when they are enabled to know God through biblical stories in the context of worship. She chose "worship perspective" over "schooling educational perspective" as she believed that "worship, not teaching about God, is the entry point of the Christian faith."[253] Her research involved providing an opportunity for children to indirectly experience the essential parts and stories of worship by working directly with biblical stories and liturgical symbols in some material forms.[254] The environment offered an opportunity for children to encounter and worship God and to abide in God's love as expressed in the Bible and liturgies. The fourfold order of worship she organized was as follows: the approach to God, the proclamation of God's Word, giving thanks to God, the Eucharist, and going in God's name to love and serve the world.[255] The greeter prepares the children to the first order of worship, "approach to God." They quietly sit in a circle with awe as the room becomes a special place to be with God. Stories, parables, and liturgy are presented to children through materials and indirect method of communication. This follows a time of response through either "a communal wondering

---

250. H. Schwartz, "Narrative and Imagination: The Role of Texts and Storytelling in Nurturing Spirituality in Judaism," in *Nurturing Child and Adolescent Spirituality: Perspectives from the World's Religious Traditions*, eds. K. M. Yust and E. C. Roehlkepartian (Lanham, MD: Rowman & Littlefield, 2005), 191–193.

251. Ibid., 192.

252. Ibid., 197.

253. S. M. Stewart, "Children and Worship," *Religious Education* 84, no. 3 (1989): 351.

254. Ibid., 352.

255. Ibid., 352–353.

together" or "personal work with story and art materials."[256] Then a story from the Bible is read to children, followed by a prayer of thanksgiving and snack time which is referred to as joyful feast and departure. Stories follow the themes of the church year from a worship perspective to provide a context and meaning for a day of worship, places of prayer and worship, and ways of expressing gratitude.[257]

The findings can be summarized as follows: Engaging children in stories is significantly different from other modes of religious instruction. Through indirect communication children were able to "enter and experience" God, not just hear about him.[258] Stories are not merely illustrations or a moral lesson, yet children can naturally enter into biblical stories. The environment of worship transformed the room into a sacred place to meet God. The research affirmed the ability of young children to love and worship God as they experience God through the stories.[259]

The strengths and weaknesses of this research need to be considered. The two theoretical bases – Cavalletti's and Berryman's storytelling method and Loder's transformational logic – enabled her to combine storytelling with a worship perspective.[260] The opportunity for children to learn about God and to meet God in the worship environment instead of the schooling paradigm is appreciable. In this qualitative research, the hypothesis, purpose, research questions, and fourfold order of worship are clearly stated. Clarification of the term "indirect communication"[261] and defining the sample in terms of age and gender instead of using the general term "young children" would have improved the comprehensibility of the research.

Karen Marie Yust

The three-year research of Yust[262] allowed her to see how children's spirituality is understood and nurtured in mainstream Protestant congregations in the USA. She intended to propose various theoretical suggestions

---

256. Ibid., 354.
257. Ibid., 356.
258. Ibid., 361.
259. Ibid.
260. Ibid., 351.
261. Ibid., 354.
262. Yust, *Real Kids*.

towards developing children's spirituality. Her primary tools of research were site observations and semi-structured interviews with parents, church professionals, and children's ministries volunteers.

Yust noted that one of the easiest ways to cultivate spirituality in young children is to expose them to religious stories and provide opportunities to reenact the stories in play.[263] Stories create a long-lasting framework on the perception of reality in children,[264] and enable them to use religious terminologies and verbalize God-concepts. Adults have a responsibility to create contexts where children can share stories and their spiritual experience. Just like children are familiar with the different characters of various TV shows, children need to develop a relationship to the characters and images of their faith tradition.[265] They need to see them and hear of them frequently. The spiritual characters need to have names and personalities – for example "what would Moses do?" Or "What was David's uniqueness or what were the words of Jesus?" As children begin borrowing ideas from their environment to make meaning of their world even before they can express beliefs or evaluate them as appropriate or inappropriate, adults can create an environment to nurture the spirituality of children even at a young age.[266]

Yust relied upon her extensive research with various congregational children's ministries and her experiences as a pastor, educator, and mother. She presented the alternative approach in nurturing children's spirituality: "something you do with your children,"[267] not "for" children. She illustrated her approach with numerous examples from her professional and personal life. The article is silent about the research procedures. However, inclusion of such details would have helped others to replicate the research in other contexts and cultures.

Barbara Kimes Myers

The significance of sharing stories with children in a caring environment is the focus of Myers. Stories that are shared with children in families help

---

263. Ibid., 37.
264. Ibid., 28.
265. Ibid., 24.
266. Ibid., 26.
267. Ibid., xii.

children to derive meaning of how their families extend care for each other. She sees stories as a means to discuss spirituality.[268] It helps children to see what adults think about various matters. The stories we share show who we are. Thus stories have an "ontological purpose."[269] Stories connect us to that which "lies outside" of us and in the process we seek the meaning of our existence. This shows the importance of sharing biblical stories with children in the caring environment of the family so that children can understand what is important to the family. And children and adults together can search the meaning of their existence in this world.

Diana Garland

The research of Garland allowed her to see the characteristics of faith and spirituality in family life and the lives of families in the Christian congregation.[270] The study involved thirty-two congregations in four regions of the USA out of which she selected two congregations in each of the four denominations: Southern Baptist, National Baptist, United Methodist, and Presbyterian.[271] In addition to using surveys to comprehend the demographic and interpersonal processes of families in the congregation, she conducted two-hour interviews with 110 families in the congregations. The selection of the families was based on the suggestions of pastors and church committees. The families varied in their structure: two parent families, remarried families, single parents, single adults without children, childless families, empty nesters, senior adult singles and couples.[272] Another characteristic of the families was their involvement in the church: active families, those in the fringes, and occasional attendees. Her conversations with the families after the interview enabled her to see whether she has understood what the families had told her.

---

268. B. K. Myers, *Young Children and Spirituality* (New York: Routledge, 1997), 18.
269. Ibid.
270. D. Garland, *Sacred Stories of Ordinary Families: Living the Faith of Daily Lives* (San Francisco, CA: Jossey-Bass, 2003), xiv.
271. Ibid., xv.
272. Ibid.

In her search for the dimension of faith in families, Garland found that family faith is "embedded in family stories"[273] and families need to share stories with one another in the family and to others in the congregation.[274] Families share stories to explain how they live out their faith, how they find meaning and purpose in life, and how they experience God in their ordinary lives.[275] Telling stories often presents opportunities for exploring and deepening the faith experiences of families. She asserted that the church has an effective language for its purpose: "language of faith, the language and narratives of Scripture."[276] These are stronger than the language of the social science and clinical practice even though the latter has helped in understanding family dynamics. She noted that there are various kinds of family stories: stories of beginnings, and new beginnings, stories of loss and endings, stories of heroes and ancestors, stories of survival, cautionary tales, funny tales, and sacred stories.[277] Sacred stories explain how they experience God in the family life. Family stories are accounts of shared history which explain "the defining moments" that have changed the course of the family.[278] Thus family stories define their unique identity. They share the stories during special occasions which tie the events in the past to the present and hold the foundations for the future. Only by telling a story can the full extent of the meaning be grasped and when hearing the stories, children feel a sense of belonging to the family.[279]

Families need a community to hear these stories. The faith community with grand narratives helps its members to connect their smaller stories to the truth that is larger than themselves.[280] Thus the congregation plays a unique role in confirming and affirming stories that families share and to remind them that there is a truth much larger than these stories which families need to own. The faith community becomes a community of stories.

---

273. Garland, *Ordinary Families*, 27; D. Garland, "The Sacred in Family Stories," *Journal of Family Ministry* 19, no. 2 (2005): 57.

274. Garland, *Ordinary Families*, 199.

275. Ibid., 27–28.

276. Garland, "Family Stories," 26.

277. Garland, *Ordinary Families*, 19–28; Garland, "Sacred," 51–57.

278. Garland, *Ordinary Families*, 11.

279. Garland, "Sacred," 43.

280. Garland, "Family Stories," 29.

This community is not about social status of individuals but based on stories which have shaped these individuals and which ultimately connect to the grand narrative of faith.[281]

In the pages of this book one can find stories of joys and sorrows, laughter and tears from families she interviewed. This made it a book full of sacred stories of faith from the ordinary life of families. Her argument is clear: it is the telling of stories that brings families closer and strengthens their relationship with God.

Catherine Stonehouse and Scottie May

Stonehouse and May[282] presented the findings of multiple research exploring children's spirituality. Stonehouse's Listening to Children Study was a seven-year longitudinal study with an equal number of children from two churches in the same area. Five- to 17-year-old children from two churches participated in three sets of interviews, which were three-and-a-half years apart from each other. The first interview with forty 5- to 10-year-old children was two hours in duration. Nineteen children participated in the second interview. Twenty-one children participated in the third interview. Her second study, Adult Reflection Study was with 25- to 45-year-old adults from three suburban evangelical churches of a large metapolis. Both churches have different approaches to children's ministry. One church has no curricular plan for its children's worship. Schedule, content, and pattern of delivery were under the discretion of person leading the children's worship for any particular Sunday. In the second church, followed a curricular plan and biblical stories were shared in a "Reflective Engagement."[283]

The second study, Adult Reflection Study[284] involved twenty-seven, 24- to 45-year-old adults who have been Christians since childhood. They represented three evangelical churches from different denominations. They were interviewed regarding their feelings and memories of their childhood faith experiences.

---

281. Ibid., 29.
282. C. Stonehouse and P. May, *Listening to Children on the Spiritual Journey: Guidance for Those Who Teach and Nurture* (Grand Rapids, MI: Baker, 2010).
283. Ibid., 75.
284. Ibid., 3.

The third study, Good Shepherd Research,[285] involved a two-year research with eighteen preschoolers. With the help of three graduate students, Scottie developed a reflective, scared space based on the principles of Berryman, Cavalletti, and Stewart. For ten weeks a curriculum that introduced Good Shepherd was used. They carefully observed children and listened to them as they talked about their life with the Good Shepherd. In the first interview after two months, twelve out of fourteen of these children remembered activities of the project. After two years, nine out of twelve children could remember the activities of the project.

Good Shepherd Family Research,[286] the fourth project was a ninety-minute section with children and adults from six families for six weeks. Twelve 3- to 10-year-old children and their parents were engaged in the parable of the Good Shepherd. The environment of the Good Shepherd Research was adapted for this research by adding a journaling response area and a few adult books in the reading area.

Certain aspects of Listening to Children Study are relevant to the current research. Children believed that God is their creator, the Trinity, the ever-present protector and Good Shepherd.[287] Children listed the following attributes of God: loving, expected obedience, great and good God.[288] Children expressed their experiences of closeness with God and their conversations with God in their everyday lives.[289] Analysis of content of prayers of children shows that there is praise, adoration, and thanksgiving.[290] They pray for others and themselves.[291] Children expressed that they hear God's voice in their heart and mind.[292] Children receive moral guidance and sense that God is interested in their future and vocation.[293] They experienced God in their home, church, and in other places like supermarkets, restaurant and enjoy peace and joy in God's presence.

---

285. Ibid., 4.
286. Ibid., 5.
287. Ibid., 31.
288. Ibid., 35.
289. Ibid., 41.
290. Ibid., 45.
291. Ibid., 45–46.
292. Ibid., 47.
293. Ibid.

Both congregations in the Listening to Children Study valued the Bible and teach the Bible to the young. Families also gave importance to teaching the Bible in homes. Parents shared biblical narratives in such a way that the children could meaningfully engage in them.[294] In the three interviews in the study, children shared facts of biblical events and found pleasure as they recalled those narratives and derived meanings from them.[295] The meanings children derived from the stories are connected to their life experiences.[296] Children who are part of Reflective Engagement form of worship significantly engage with the story and expressed pleasure and positive comments about their experiences in children's worship.[297] Children continue to find pleasure in stories as they grow older and find the value of the stories in their formation.

The uniqueness of reflective methodology in sharing biblical stories are as follows:

1) Concrete visuals in the room that represented people and items in the story helped children to find pleasure and derive meanings from the story.[298]
2) The opportunity to be quiet and to reflect on the story after storytelling encourages children to talk to God and hear from God.[299]

Stonehouse and May noted that God's story in the Bible is one of the factors that brings spiritual formation in children.[300] The richness of complex influences they receive in families and churches provide many opportunities for meaningful relationships and experiences. They expressed the importance of God's story as it is meta-narrative that gives a frame of reference to life. They explained the power to bring spiritual formation in children using the following concepts: "know the whole story of God, meet God in the story, and make God's story their story."[301]

---

294. Ibid., 75.
295. Ibid., 76.
296. Ibid., 78.
297. Ibid., 77.
298. Ibid., 80.
299. Ibid., 81.
300. Ibid.
301. Ibid., 83.

Children's faith stories and adults' retrospective faith stories of their coming to Jesus and following him were unique from person to person. Children's voices expressed an increased sense of awareness of the relationship with Jesus as they grow older. Church and parents' involvement in congregations have played a significant role in empowering children to enter into relationship with God.[302] Children expressed other key issues regarding their relationship with Christ: (1) it is significant to know that Jesus loves them, (2) opportunities to have conversations about faith, and (3) opportunities to nurture faith of children through prayer, blessings, Bible reading.[303]

This literature is unique among its own kind as multiple research studies by two different authors are integrated to express children's spiritual potential, their experience of God, and how they attempt to weave together pieces of theological understanding.[304] They hesitate to claim that listening to biblical story as the only factor that facilitate spiritual formation.[305] Thus they emphasis the role of adults in nurturing or hindering children's sensitivity to God. They suggest reflective methodology[306] as the conducive environment for children to experience God and listen to God. Their discussion of the view of children from the time of Jesus to the present day given in the first chapter provides the readers a context to meaningfully engage in the discussion of children's voices about their experiences of God. This book has relevance to the current research: (1) Children understand the role of death of Jesus in removing their sins.[307] (2) Children's God-concepts emerged out of interviews with children. (3) Children could recall biblical narratives and express how they derive meanings from the stories for their life situations. (4) Children expressed their experience of listening to God's voice in their mind and heart.

---

302. Ibid., 98, 102.
303. Ibid., 102–106.
304. Ibid., 6.
305. Ibid., 82.
306. Ibid., 6–7.
307. Ibid., 78–93.

Summary

This section provided some valuable insights to this research as educationists discuss the significance of stories in the spiritual lives of children. The discussion begins with the assumption of the innate spirituality of children.[308] Sasso and Schwartz bring in the Jewish worldview of storytelling and children. Many centuries after Moses, Jews continued to practice the telling of God's mighty acts to children. Children do not have the language to express their spirituality but stories provide a means to overcome this limitation which is vital for their spiritual growth. Stewart's ingenuity is evident in the worship perspective she presented as an alternative to the schooling model in presenting the biblical story to children. Yust's research showed that stories have a long-lasting influence on the outlook of children. Thus she recommended to tell stories and to empower children to live out the story as the easiest way to cultivate spirituality in children. Stonehouse and May noted that telling of the biblical narratives is one of the factors that facilitate spiritual formation in children. Other factors are the activities in the church, involvement of parents in the church, and the experiences and relationship. They proposed Reflective Engagement form of worship as the conducive environment to facilitate spiritual sensitivity in children.

Even though Garland is not focusing on biblical stories, she identified that dimension of faith is embedded in telling their stories to one another in families and in the faith community. As families share how they experience God in their daily lives, children can comprehend how others live out their faith, find meaning in life, and experience God in their daily lives. The faith community can be another venue in which these stories are shared. The faith community has a unique role of affirming stories of families. It provides a community to hear families' stories yet at the same time reminds the families of the truth and the grand narratives of faith which they need to own.

Children's Perceptions of Stories

The following discussion focuses on four empirical studies that investigated how children understand stories and how they respond to stories.

---

308. Sasso, "Role of Narratives."

Howard Worsley

Worsley explained an initial pilot study by the Bible Story Project (BSP) to examine children's understanding of stories in two schools in urban priority area of Nottingham in Britain.[309] One school was church aided from a Roman Catholic foundation and the other a county primary school. The target group included children in Year 5 of ages between 9 and 10. The sample represented children from various ethnic groups and both genders. In the first lesson, two stories, one from the Old Testament and another from the New Testament were told using godly play method. Then children were given an opportunity to retell the story. Certain conceptual concept questions were asked to check whether the narrative outlines were followed. Next, the class could depict the stories either through art, drama or words. In the second lesson, children were given an opportunity to tell a story. They could choose either their favorite Bible story or a story of their choice from their memory or religious tradition using a four-box cartoon. Children gave the explanation to the research team based on their work with box cartoons. Team members used puppetry to introduce and conclude both lessons. The five procedures for research were godly play, puppetry, choice of art, drama, or verbal feedback, cartoon-style feedback, and individual feedback.[310]

Children from both schools liked the stories they heard.[311] The stories children retold were compiled and analyzed. Even though children cannot fully understand the meanings of stories they can "engage with the feeling aroused from the nurturing environment in which they encountered the story"[312] or they have "little personal understanding of the intended meanings of their favorite stories."[313] The meanings they derive from stories are based on a "personal hermeneutic" which reflects their life experience and nurturing environment.[314] Children from Roman Catholic schools told significantly more stories from the Bible compared to county schools

---

309. Worsley, "Children Aged 9–10," 205, 215.
310. Ibid., 207.
311. Ibid., 209.
312. Ibid.
313. Ibid., 212.
314. Ibid.

(97% as opposed to 57%).[315] The faith tradition of the home influenced the meaning children derived from the stories they heard. He identified the challenge within the Christian tradition to affirm the authority and meaning of biblical narratives on the one hand and on the other hand "release the prophetic insights of the child to offer new meaning as the child engages with scripture."[316]

These findings illuminate the present research as this deals with the 9- to 10-year-old children's understanding of stories which include stories of the Bible. Children may not understand the intended meaning of the story yet they are touched by the feelings of the environment in which they heard the story. The various procedures like godly play, puppetry, and various methods to receive feedback employed in the research seem beneficial to the present study.

The dialogue with various literature from Goldman to Hay and Nye shows the in-depth understanding in the field of study. The only subgroup was the two schools, however the subgroup based on gender would have enhanced the study. The detailed explanation of the various teaching techniques used in the two lessons is helpful for the present research.

Paul Burt

Aware of the criticisms against Goldman's findings, Burt replicated Goldman's research with a small sample. The sample included ten boys from Year 3 to Year 8 who attended Pilgrim's School, Winchester, UK.[317] Thus sixty boys of age 7–13 heard stories of Moses and the burning bush, the crossing of the Red Sea, and Jesus' temptations. They were interviewed to know their ideas about God, the demands of divine justice and love, means of God's communication with people, understanding about Jesus, and authority and relevance of the Bible.[318] The article particularly deals only with three topics: relevance of the Bible, means by which God communicates, and the visualizing of God.[319]

---

315. Ibid., 210.
316. Ibid., 214.
317. Burt, "Thus Says the Lord," 331.
318. Ibid.
319. Ibid.

There were differences between Goldman's findings and the present research.[320] As early as 10 years of age, children can comprehend stories from different historic-cultural contexts and apply them to their own context[321] which Goldman noted as an achievement only for children beyond 12 years of age. In terms of visualizing God, there was a general agreement with Goldman's research "in terms of types of answers given and the existence of rough boundaries between visualization, intermediate, and abstract conceptions."[322] Yet Burt's research supported the view that the ability for abstract thinking in terms of God's visibility and his way of communication was present in children at an earlier age than that was set by Goldman.[323] A very high proportion of the respondents had "an advanced conceptual approach."[324] He suggested, "the religious stories yield their sense more satisfactorily when the contexts of worship and study coexist in a complimentary way, rather than existing separately and perhaps antagonistically."[325]

Burt's is an additional study to critique Goldman's research recommending very little biblical material before the age of 12.[326] However, the researcher was aware of the school environment which nurtured the relevance of the Bible[327] and communication to God through prayer.[328] He has also noted the influence of modern translations of the Bible on children's understanding of stories. Another reason for the difference in findings might have been because children are exposed to modern means of communicating biblical stories involving multiple senses. This can not only lead to better comprehension of the story but also improve the mental capacities of children. Besides, the environment of 1960 in which Goldman did the research is different from to the twenty-first-century environment.

---

320. Goldman, *Religious Thinking*, 334, 338.
321. Ibid., 334.
322. Ibid., 336.
323. Ibid.
324. Ibid., 338.
325. Ibid.
326. Ibid., 67.
327. Ibid., 334.
328. Ibid., 338.

Ann. M. Trousdale and Jane S. Everett

The focus of Trousdale and Everett's research is to see how African-American children respond to fiction. Three 7-year-old African-American children from a lower-income housing area were the sample of the research. All three children enjoyed reading books.[329] Three stories were read aloud to the children in Everett's classroom in "an intimate and informal atmosphere."[330] She wrote three humorous stories around "the theme of a child's birthday."[331] Thus she was in a better position to compare the children's interpretations of the story with the authors' intended meaning.[332] Three stories were read aloud and she individually worked with the children a week after they heard the story.[333] The children were asked to retell the story to see if there was any alteration in the retelling. She used open-ended questions about the story as another way to comprehend how children derived meanings of the story.[334]

The retelling of the story showed children's comprehension of the plot of the stories, events of the stories and their relations to each other.[335] They filled in the characters' motivations and emotional reactions which were only implicit in the story. The author's intended meaning matched at "the level of physical causality" and "psychological causality" but not in the "level of theme or message" of the story.[336] Only one child found the abstract lesson that the author intended while the other two saw the lessons related to the particular situations in the stories.[337] One child focused on the child protagonist in the story as her hero, while the other two named the adult figures as the hero. Their interpretation of the events and characters reflected their life experiences and situations. Retelling the stories revealed

---

329. Trousdale and Everett, "Me and Bad Harry," 2.
330. Ibid.
331. Ibid., 5.
332. Ibid., 6.
333. Ibid., 2.
334. Ibid.
335. Ibid., 6.
336. Ibid.
337. Ibid., 7.

that children are capable of "higher and more complex thought processes than a mere accurate retelling of the story."[338]

The authors show inhibition in generalizing the findings to all African-American children.[339] However this research alerts adults to value children's ability of comprehension beyond mere memorization of facts. A certain level of children's understanding of the intended meaning of the author encourages teachers and adult caregivers to read and/or tell stories to children. However the stories used were age-appropriately written specifically for the research. This implies that when reading or telling biblical stories to children, the age-appropriateness in terms of content, theme, and language are matters of concern. The clarity in explaining the research procedures and findings is an advantage of this research as it helps in replication of the research with different samples representing various age groups, gender, and socio-economic backgrounds.

Ann. M. Trousdale and Sally McMillian

In their longitudinal study, Trousdale and McMillian focused on a young girl's response to feminist and patriarchal folktales.[340] They chose three feminist tales and one patriarchal tale "for the purpose of contrast and to highlight any differences in response to feminist or patriarchal heroines."[341] The girl, Nikki, was selected on the basis of "criterion-based selection."[342] She was a vivid reader and was part of a white middle-class family. At the age of 8 and 12, Trousdale read four stories to Nikki. At both ages, they met informally five times at Trousdale's living room. Each session was one week apart.[343] While reading the stories, the researcher asked many open-ended questions to Nikki. She was encouraged to ask questions or share comments about the story. At the end of each session, Nikki retold the story and the succeeding session began by her retelling the last story. At

---

338. Ibid., 13.
339. Ibid., 14.
340. A. M. Trousdale and S. McMillian, "'Cinderella Was a Wuss': A Young Girl's Response to Feminist and Patriarchal Folktales," *Christian Literature in Education* 34, no. 1 (2003): 1.
341. Ibid., 4.
342. Ibid., 7.
343. Ibid., 9.

the final session, Nikki answered summative questions about the stories and characters of the story. A tape recorder recorded all the sessions of storytelling and conversations. At the end of the sessions, the researcher interviewed Nikki's mother.

The analysis of the data showed developmental differences in how Nikki made meaning of the stories. At the age of 8, she accepted the magical elements in the tale, yet at the age of 12 she found it unrealistic.[344] Her focus of the story was not primarily on the protagonist, yet showed concern to the secondary characters of the story. At the age of 8 she valued characters that showed concern to others and at the age of 12 she valued those with inner strength and self-confidence.

Nikki's perception of the themes of the fairy tales also changed as she grew older which supports earlier research. Yet her divergence from being a pro-protagonist contradicts earlier findings that the egocentric nature of children leads to the centrality of the protagonist of the fairy tales.[345] Her analysis of the feminine characters of the story at the age of 12 was influenced by societal expectation of women. Other findings include how the perspective of gender roles changed as she matured[346] and how "girls gain maturity in the context of caring relationship."[347]

Generalizing the findings to a larger population was not the intention of the authors,[348] yet it raises some keen observations. There was no comparison with the authors' intended meaning and the meaning Nikki deduced from the stories. This article calls attention to the role of gender in making meaning[349] and constantly dialogues with previous research findings. These are two unique components of this research. The varied interpretation of the same story at two different stages of the child leads to consider the importance of repeatedly telling the stories to children. Even though children make meaning of the stories at each stage of their lives, it is not fixed, rather rehearing of the story generates a different meaning at different age levels.

---

344. Ibid., 10.
345. Ibid., 23.
346. Ibid., 25.
347. Ibid., 23.
348. Ibid., 22.
349. Ibid., 23.

Does it imply that hearing biblical stories at an early age will not cause redundancy? Or do the misconceptions if any were formed in an earlier age, be replaced by mature perceptions as the child develops?

Summary

Worsely's research dealt with children and the Bible. The age of the sample is similar to the sample of this proposed research. He noted that children can retell the stories they hear. They can derive meanings but may not fully understand the meanings of stories. This shows that retelling of the stories may not always mean that children have grasped the meaning of the stories. The role of the environment influences the meanings they develop.

Burt's and Trousdale and Everett's research studies supported the view that children can comprehend stories and abstract thinking is possible in children before the age suggested by Goldman. Burt replicated Goldman's study but affirmed the use of stories with young children. He recommended the presentation of stories in an environment of worship. Trousdale and Everett noted that children's derivation of the physical and psychological causality of stories is similar to the author's intended meaning, yet there was inconsistency in the theme or message of the story of children and the author.

Trousdale and McMillian noted the developmental differences in the inferences children make from the stories they hear and the gender tints the meaning children infer from stories they hear or read. This challenges the notion of egocentrism of young children. It also shows how the societal expectation influences the meaning children derive from stories.

Chapter Summary

The focus of this chapter was on the empirical and conceptual understanding of children's spirituality and storytelling in religious and general education. Goldman proposed the notion that children's spirituality is immature and childish. Yet now innate spirituality of children is valued and cherished by many scholars and educators. The contributions of Coles and Hay and Nye in this perspective are highly admirable as they presented the spirituality of children as a core dimension of their development. Fowler and Westerhoff have brought an appreciation of the faith in children. Cavalletti and Pritchard noted the religious potential in children. They used creative methods to present the Bible to children based on the liturgical year and based on certain themes. This helped children to understand biblical stories, metaphors, and symbols at a deeper level.

Stories and storytelling are widely used with children in churches and in schools. Discussion of the second domain, storytelling in religious and general education has various dimensions: worldview transformation, character, faith, and spiritual formation. This section discusses how various educators have seen the relation between stories and these dimensions. As stories shape, sustain, and transform one's worldview[350] children need to hear stories in the Bible so that their worldview can be formed accordingly. Goldman proposed that earlier presentations of stories of the Bible to children can lead to misconceptions in children. Yet, Fowler's faith development theory also recommended the role of stories in the faith formation of children. Westerhoff and Fowler proposed the importance of telling the biblical story with children which reversed the suggestion of Goldman. Other educators also recommend the use of biblical stories with children.[351]

Storytelling is viewed as a means to develop character[352] and enrich spirituality in children.[353] Jewish celebrations profess how stories of God's mighty acts can be used to nurture children's spirituality.[354] Based on their research, Yust, Stewart, and Garland encourage the telling of religious stories with children to promote their spirituality. Garland identifies the congregations as a venue to share stories of families and to remind families of the grand narratives of the faith.

Research with children shows that they can retell and comprehend the stories they hear even though they may not be able to fully grasp the meaning.[355] Burt noted that some abstract thinking is possible for children even

---

350. Steffen, *Reconnecting God's Story*; Trousdale, "Children's Literature."

351. Mitchell, "Why Care about Stories?"; S. E. Sasso, "Tell Me a Story about God," in *Teaching about God and Spirituality: A Resource for Jewish Settings*, eds. N. R. Levy, R. L. Goodman, and S. H. Blumbert (Denver, CO: A.R.E Publishing, 2002); Brelsford, *Mythical Realist*.

352. John, *Stories*; Vitz, "Moral Development"; Egan, *Imagination*.

353. Sasso, "Role of Narratives"; Rosman, "God Dwells."

354. Sasso, "When Your Children Ask."

355. Worsley, "How Children Aged 9–10."

before the age proposed by Goldman. Children's inferences of the stories change as they grow and gender has an influence in the meanings they derive.[356] They can relate to plots, characters, and events and derive meaning based on their experiences and environment.[357] Biblical stories help children to experience God and listen to God, thus become one of the factors that enable spiritual formation in children.[358]

The above discussion of these empirical and conceptual studies reveals the benefits of stories with children to promote worldview transformation, character formation, faith development, and spiritual formation. The empirical studies reveal that children can comprehend stories and interpret stories based on their life experiences. In Indian churches, biblical stories are the major content and storytelling is the primary method of teaching children in Sunday schools. The primary purpose in using stories with children in congregations is to nurture children's spirituality in the Christian faith tradition. This obliges the educators to comprehend perceptions of children about the stories they hear. However, how often do teachers and other adults pause to ask children about their perceptions of the role of stories in their spiritual formation? This research deals with children's perceptions of the role of stories in their spiritual formation. What is children's understanding of how biblical stories help in their spiritual formation? According to children, what is the significance of the stories in their spiritual formation? This research is an opportunity to listen and hear what children have to express through verbal, written and non-verbal clues about the role of stories in their spiritual formation.

---

356. Trousdale and McMillian, "Cinderella Was a Wuss."

357. Trousdale and Everett, "Me and Bad Harry"; Trousdale and McMillian, "Cinderella Was a Wuss."

358. Stonehouse and May, *Listening to Children.*

CHAPTER 3

Christian Worldview: Integration and Synthesis

This research sought to explore the perceptions of children about the role of biblical stories in their spiritual formation. Accordingly, the goal of this chapter is to look at children's spirituality and storytelling from a biblical perspective to enrich the understanding generated from the literature review. The discussion has three domains: (1) The Bible as the story that needs to be told, (2) The Old Testament and New Testament use of stories, and (3) spirituality of children. After the discussion of these domains, the exegesis of Psalm 78:1–8 presents the significance of intergenerational transmission of divine truth.

The Bible – the Story that Needs to be Told

This section explains the first domain by briefly exploring two aspects: the Bible as a story and the Bible as a story to be told. Emphasizing the Bible as story is neither to ignore the various genres in the Scripture nor to devalue the role of propositional thought in the Bible. It also does not neglect the historicity of the events. The historicity of the events and places in the Bible is real just like the world we live in.[1] Biblical stories are not considered in this research as vehicles of propositional truth but the truth of God.

---

1. Bartholomew and Goheen, *Drama of Scripture*, 9.

The Bible – the Story

The insight that the Bible is the story of God has gained acceptance in various disciplines. Barr states that "all of the Bible counts as 'story'."[2] He continues to argue that in the Hebrew Bible, legal materials appear as part of the story of Moses and Poetic books can be generally connected with the narratives in Samuel, Kings, and Chronicles. In the New Testament, the Epistles and Revelation "form part of the story" like the Gospels and Acts. Thus he notes that even though all parts of the Bible are not narrative, "the narrative character of the story elements is a better framework" to understand the non-narrative parts than any framework based on the non-narrative to comprehend the story elements in the Bible.[3] Wright also sees that story links "together the three enterprises of literary, historical and theological study of the New Testament."[4]

Beck presents God as the storyteller because story is the primary literary form of the Bible.[5] He notes the reasons for God's choice of this form of communication: to entertain, to build communities between God's people of the past and present, to challenge the faith and thinking, and to teach by touching their mind, heart, and imagination.[6] He points out some important aspects for understanding the stories of the Bible: "As a storyteller, God imbues the stories in the Bible with meaning. By carefully selecting content and managing the form of communication, the events of the past are turned into stories with an enduring meaning."[7]

---

2. J. Barr, *The Concept of Biblical Theology: An Old Testament Perspective* (Minneapolis, MN: Fortress, 1999), 356.

3. Ibid.

4. Wright, *People of God*, 139.

5. J. A. Beck, *God as Storyteller: Seeking Meaning in Biblical Narrative* (St Louis, MO: Chalice, 2008), 1.

6. Ibid., 3.

7. Ibid., 7.

Gerkin, the practical theologian,[8] Hauerwas from the field of theological ethics,[9] Newbigin,[10] and Goheen[11] from the field of mission, also affirm the importance of viewing the Bible as narrative in their respective field of scholarship. Peterson notes that "the Bible is basically and overall a narrative, an immense, sprawling, capacious narrative."[12] He affirms that the Bible is a "vast, over-reaching, all encompassing story – a meta-story."[13]

However, Goheen laments over the trend of fragmenting the Bible into bits – "oral bits, systematic-theological bits, devotional bits, historical-critical bits, narrative bits, and homiletical bits."[14] Based on the work of Wright,[15] Bartholomew and Goheen present the Bible as one unfolding story with six acts – creation, sin, Israel, Christ, church, and new creation.[16] It is important to present the whole story so that people know the thread of the whole story. Narrating various biblical episodes with constant reference to the "big picture of salvation history" can help in reducing the "risk of breaking down one rich history of God" into bits and pieces.[17]

Practical theologians have emphasized the significance of stories in their field of study. (1) Macky stresses that propositional theology has a place in Christianity, yet it can never replace stories as the meaning of it lies in the story itself.[18] (2) Discussing the engaging power of narratives over creeds and dogmas, Groome notes that the "practical languages of the narratives" can be more "accessible" and "engaging" than "metaphysical languages of creeds and dogmas of Christian faith."[19] (3) In a multi-faith context like

---

8. C. V. Gerkin, *Widening the Horizons: Pastoral Responses to a Fragmented Society* (Philadelphia, PA: Westminster, 1986), 49.

9. S. Hauerwas, *The Peaceable Kingdom: A Primer in Christian Ethics* (Notre Dame, IN: University of Notre Dame Press, 1983) 25.

10. L. Newbigin, *A Word in Season* (Grand Rapids, MI: Eerdmans, 1994), 204–205.

11. Goheen, "Reading the Bible," 4.

12. E. Peterson, *Living into God's Story*, 2006, accessed 12 June 2009.

13. Ibid., 2.

14. Goheen, "*Reading the Bible,*" 5.

15. Wright, *People of God*, 139–142.

16. Bartholomew and Goheen, *Drama of Scripture*, 13.

17. Cavalletti, *6 to 12 Years Old*, 20–21.

18. Macky, "Biblical Story Theology," 24.

19. T. H. Groome, *Sharing Faith: A Comprehensive Approach to Religious Education and Pastoral Ministry* (Eugene, OR: Wipf and Stock, 1998), 141.

India, Newbigin's statement has great implications. In his discussion on relationship of Christians to other faiths he noted that "telling the story, the story of Jesus, the story of the Bible," is the crucial contribution of Christians to dialogue.[20]

Establishing the Bible as "a single unfolding narrative"[21] is not to discredit the propositional discussions of the Bible. Bausch sees that creed and story need to be affirmed as each has a different function.[22] Greeley describes the importance of creed and story in a belief system:

> A belief system without creed may be too amorphous to survive in a propositional culture like our own…Story is nothing more than an attempt to resonate and represent that experience, while creed, far removed from experience, is a result of philosophical refinement and purification and distillation of the experience.[23]

Thus stories translate creed to the real life situations of people while creed presents the truth in systematic, abstract, and conceptual form.

The Bible – the Story to be Told

Goheen stresses not only the importance of viewing the Bible as "one cosmic story of the world" but also the significance of comprehending our place in the story.[24] Knowing the story is vital for each generation in perceiving their place in the story of God. In the Bible we read how God met the people in the realities of their lives and thus gave meaning in the lives of the people who received the revelation. Thus in each generation God's revelation was intertwined with the life story of that generation along with what was handed down to them.

Strong evidence for the fact that Patriarchs successfully transmitted God's revelation is found in certain specific incidents in the book of Genesis and Exodus. Joseph knew about God's promise of the land which was given

---

20. L. Newbigin, *The Gospel in a Pluralist Society* (London: SPCK, 1992), 182.

21. Bartholomew and Goheen, *Drama of Scripture*, 22.

22. W. L. Bausch, *Storytelling: Imagination and Faith* (Mystic, CT: Twenty-Third Publications, 1984).

23. A. S. Greeley, *Religion: A Secular Theory* (New York: Free Press, 1982), 103.

24. Goheen, "Reading the Bible," 7.

to his great-grandfather Abraham. Thus, Joseph entrusted his descendants to bury his bones in Canaan when God delivers them from Egypt to inherit the Promised Land (Gen 50:24). Storytelling was not the intention of Joseph but in essence his descendants transmitted and preserved his story. When the Exodus happened several centuries after his death, they took his bones and safely carried them and buried them in Canaan (Josh 24:32). This shows that not only Joseph but also his descendants believed in the promise given to the Patriarchs and their lives and became part of the story the Bible. In another incident, the Hebrew midwives Shiphrah and Puah did not obey Pharaoh's order to kill the newborn Hebrew boys because they feared God (Exod 1:15–16). Even being in slavery for many generations they knew God and they feared God. Their knowledge of God would have come from people telling them the story of God's revelation to their forefathers.

With respect to children and stories which is the focus of this research, the Law of Moses with its central affirmation of the *Shema* (Deut 6:4–9) establishes the importance of telling and listening to God's revelation. This became the practice of the Jewish people. Certain rituals and festivals were opportunities to communicate their story to children. Moses and Joshua used a similar formula "when your children (son) ask(s) you . . . then tell them" (Exod 12:26; 13:14, 18; Deut 6:20–21; Josh 4:6, 21). This prescribed reply shows the importance of the recitation of events associated with the inheritance of the Promised Land. The repeated instructions to tell children of these incidents imply God's initiative in communicating his revelation to a new generation so they might love and fear the Lord who brought them out of Egypt to the Promised Land.

Maintaining the covenant relationship with God was essential for the continual occupation of Israel in Canaan. For this each generation needs to obey the commandments and meaningfully participate in the rituals and feasts. Unless one generation transmitted God's revelation, their descendants would have neither known their past events nor the requirements of God. The transmission helped to assert their history to the next generation so that they can commit to the obedience of the laws and commandments. The covenantal relationship between God and his people in each generation depends on the obedience to the law which was the outcome of acknowledging the stories of God's might and power in the past.[25] Thus telling and remembering became integral for the existence of Israel. Or in other words, the preservation and transmission of the story of Israel determined the future of their nation.[26]

The social structure of the Old Testament showed a strong intergenerational relationship, which included the older generation's responsibility to transmit the biblical story to the next generation. The regular reading of the Law, and observation of festivals and feasts and various symbols were to remind and recollect Israel's past. Israelites were "experts in the use of story, symbol, and ritual to maintain their distinctive identity in a very diverse and often oppositional world."[27] Brueggemann explains this practice of intergenerational transmission which inculcated in children what is foundational for the community: The passages in Exodus, Deuteronomy, Joshua (Exod 12:26; 13:14, 18; Deut 6:20–21; Josh 4:6, 21) expected a time when children would be eager and ready to learn the practices of the community. They would ask questions regarding the meaning and significance of these practices and life style. In all the answers the community were to tell "the long deep memory which started with nobodies who were surprised by transformation and became a community through the historical process."[28]

The content of teaching that was transmitted was the Torah, which included the events associated with the lives of the Patriarchs, the possession of the Promised Land and the various laws. In order to differentiate between the events and propositional statements, the content of teaching can be stated as twofold: the law of the Lord and "the story behind the rules."[29] Through transmission children might know the God of Abraham, Isaac, and Jacob and obey the requirements of the Lord.

In the New Testament, the "new Israel" also practiced recounting or narrating the story of God's action. For the New Testament, it is not just

---

25. D. L. Christensen, *Deuteronomy 1–11*, Word Biblical Commentary, eds. D. A. Hubbard and G. W. Barker, vol. 6A (Dallas, TX: Word, 1998), 152.

26. C. Westermann, *Praise and Lament in the Psalms,* trans. K. R. Crim and R. N. Soulen (Atlanta, GA: John Knox Press, 1981), 246.

27. Steffen, *Reconnecting God's Story*, 33.

28. W. Brueggemann, "Passion and Perspective: Two Dimensions of Education in the Bible," *Theology Today* 42, no. 2 (1985): 172–173.

29. Miller, "Children May Know," 50.

telling the story, yet the story is proclaimed. Moreover, the covenantal relationship in the new covenant was no more through the obedience of the law but through believing in Jesus. Subsequently, the apostles saw the importance of proclaiming the good news that Jesus is Christ, the "Christ crucified," who is the fulfillment of the Old Testament. This was an opportunity for Jews and Gentiles to hear the message of salvation.

> For there is no difference between Jew and Gentile – the same Lord is Lord of all and richly blesses all who call on him, for, "Everyone who calls on the name of the Lord will be saved." How, then, can they call on the one they have not believed in? And how can they believe in the one of whom they have not heard? And how can they hear without someone preaching to them?" (Rom 10:12–14)

The proclamation of the gospel has continued for the past twenty centuries revealing the work of God through Jesus. In the present generation, the responsibility of telling and proclaiming the story has been entrusted to us so that those who have not heard can hear and believe in the God of the story. Peterson notes the importance of stories and storytelling for Christians: in revealing God to human beings stories have "a pride of place." Those who communicate God's truth are storytellers. Further he notes that "storytellers in our Christian community carry a major responsibility for keeping us alert to these stories and the way they work."[30] This leads to the discussion of the use of stories in the Old and New Testaments.

The Old Testament and New Testament Use of Stories

Certain passages in the Old Testament instruct the older generation to recite the exodus story and the story of the possession of the Promised Land to children. Discussion of the use of stories in the New Testament reveals that even though the epistles do not present stories as in the Gospels and Acts, the narrative character of the epistles implies that the New Testament church comprehended stories as a method of enriching the spirituality of

---

30. Peterson, *Living into God's Story*, 1.

its members. The following section presents the use of stories in the Old and New Testaments.

The Use of Stories in the Old Testament

Certain passages in the books of Exodus, Deuteronomy, and Joshua exhorted adults to tell the stories of redemption from Egypt and their journey to the Promised Land. In these passages adults responded to the queries of children regarding various practices they observed.

Even though passages from Exodus to Joshua are discussed in this segment, there are other references in the Old Testament where the past events are recited. Josiah (2 Kgs 23:2) and Ezra's (Ezra 8:2–3) reading of the Book of the Law to the people are examples of recounting the past. The prayer of Nehemiah (Neh 1:5–11) and Daniel (Dan 7:4–19), psalms of Israel (Pss 78, 105, 106) are other examples of reciting the events from Israel's history. As the "protectors of Torah"[31] these prophetic messages echoed the Mosaic Covenant. The narration in Chronicles of the history of Israel from Adam to Cyprus to the post-exilic Jews is an "extended redescription of the Jewish past."[32] By presenting the "most extended genealogy" in the Bible, 1 Chronicles 1–9 have not only connected the present to the past but also summarized the past.[33]

The discussion in this section is limited to those passages where parents are instructed to recite these stories to their children. Three passages in Exodus 12 and 13 are in the context of the celebration of Passover, consecration of firstborn and firstlings. Exhortation to instruct the children and grandchildren to obey the statutes of God is the context of the Deuteronomy passage. The context of the Joshua passages is the event associated with the crossing of the Jordan River. The following discussion based on these passages shows how the Bible ensures that the story of the redemption from Egypt be made known to the next generation. This is to

---

31. G. R. Osborne, *The Hermeneutical Spiral: A Comprehensive Introduction to Biblical Interpretation* (Downers Grove, IL: InterVarsity, 2006) 264.

32. W. Brueggemann, *An Introduction to the Old Testament: The Canon and Christian Imagination* (Louisville, KY: Westminster John Knox, 2003), 375.

33. Brueggemann, *Introduction*, 376; J. H. Walton, V. H. Matthews, and M. W. Chavalas, *The IVP Bible Background Commentary: Old Testament* (Downers Grove, IL: InterVarsity, 2004), 414.

instill obedience to the law in children, which was crucial in the covenantal relationship between God and Israel. It also implies that the Bible respond to children's eagerness to enter into the life and belief of adults.

Questions embedded in the rituals as an opportunity to recollect the story: Exodus 12:26; 13:8; 13:14

These passages depict that it is important for the next generation to know the significance of the Passover. The nine plagues leading to the protection of Israel from the tenth plague "becomes a medium of memory and celebration for future generations" which is "attested by the command that it be kept as a requirement in perpetuity."[34] The remembrance shows the significance of preserving and proclaiming the saving acts to the next generation.[35] The rituals, which commemorated various dimensions of the exodus experiences, were pointing towards a single goal. According to Durham the single end was that the generations to come

> may know the exodus, by taste and by feel, by cost and by result, as an experience of their own as equally as an experience of their fathers. And so they await the time, then taste the bread and give Yahweh his due, explain it all to the ones who must remember to those after them, and thus experience the freedom to glorify Yahweh in service that is their heritage.[36]

The recollection, which was a part of the rituals, was an opportunity for adults to "enwrap the children into an empowering narrative"[37] so that children can hear how God worked for his people. The household of Israel "becomes the catalyst by which Israelites connected their children to the larger theological story in progress."[38] The actions of God on behalf of his

---

34. J. I. Durham, *Exodus*, Word Biblical Commentary, eds. D. A. Hubbard and G. W. Barker, vol. 3 (Dallas, TX: Word, 1998), 162.

35. R. A. Cole, *Exodus: An Introduction and Commentary*, Tyndale Old Testament Commentaries, vol. 2 (Downers Grove, IL: InterVarsity, 1973), 111.

36. Durham, *Exodus*, 180.

37. W. Brueggemann, "Vulnerable Children, Divine Passion, and Human Obligation," in *The Child in the Bible*, ed. M. J. Bunge (Grand Rapids, MI: Eerdmans, 2008), 402.

38. D. D. Campbell, "In Pursuit of the Ideal: Parents' Role in the Spiritual Formation of Young People as Reflected in Wisdom Literature and Ancient Near Eastern Cultural Conventions," 2006, accessed 22 August 2009.

people became their story for the generations to come. As Brueggemann noted the telling of these stories affirmed, "there can be no other stories."[39] Thus the reality of the redemptive act was brought into the lives of the children from one generation to another.

Questions by children had become a "deliberate and conscious part" of the Passover celebration[40] to which parents responded by telling the story of their redemption from Egypt. Curiosity of children will naturally lead them to ask questions when they witness the elaborate preparations and different rituals associated with the festival: "When your children ask you, 'What does this ceremony mean to you?'" (Exod 12:26) and "In the days to come, when your son asks you, 'What does this mean?'" (Exod 13:14). Then adults were instructed to tell the deliverance event to their children: "then tell them" (Exod 12:26), "On that day tell your son" (Exod 13:8), and "say to him" (Exod 13:14). This retelling of the story of redemption was a binding responsibility of adults and became a central part of the festivals of Passover and Unleavened Bread.[41] The reciting is not just a report of the event but a "confession to the ongoing participation of Israel in the decisive act of redemption from Egypt."[42] This made the generation of parents and the generation of children to be "spiritual contemporaries."[43]

Questions about the law as an opportunity to recollect the story: Deuteronomy 6:20–25

Deuteronomy frequently and directly presents the prominence of families in telling and instructing the commandments of the Lord to children and grandchildren (Deut 4:9; 6:7–9; 11:18–21). The parents are directed to share the Lord's instruction on special and regular occasions. Parents are to tell God's revelation not only in the time of festivals and feasts but also in the daily activities of life.

---

39. Brueggemann, "Passion and Perspective," 173.

40. Cole, *Exodus*, 110.

41. C. R. M. McGinnis, "Exodus as a 'Text of Terror' for Children," in *The Child in the Bible*, ed. M. J. Bunge (Grand Rapids, MI: Eerdmans, 2008), 38.

42. B. S. Childs, *The Book of Exodus: A Critical Theological Commentary* (Philadelphia, PA: Westminster, 1974), 200.

43. Fishbane, *Text and Texture*, 82.

The lifestyle of Israel reflected their obedience to the laws of God which made children curious about the law and practices among them. Children asked about the significance of commandments and statues of the Lord – "In the future, when your son asks you, 'What is the meaning of the stipulations, decrees and laws of the Lord?'" (Deut 6:20). The prescribed reply of the parents was the story of Israel found in the Torah which guided the present life and conduct of the people.

God placed a higher responsibility upon parents to embody their faith and inculcate the obedience to the law in their children. The prosperity of the people of Israel and their very existence depended on their obedience of the law.[44] "The continuity of faith within the context of a religious community depends on the observance of that faith within individual families."[45]

Apart from the instruction of parents, children were given the opportunity to listen to the reading of the law by priests (Deut 31:9–13) in the congregational setting. The regular hearing of reading of the Torah helped children to understand the necessity of obedience of statutes in the context it was given. Thus a generation who had not seen the might of God could know the significance of the law in the context in which it was given.

The presence of other religions in Canaan demanded Israel to tell their story in the context of families and in the context of the faith community. If the faith is not handed down it will result in "profound decomposition" due to the "intrusions of conceptions from the heathen nature cult."[46] Von Rad understands that this is to fill the generational gap between a generation that has witnessed the deliverance from Egypt and a generation who hasn't experienced what the previous generation has experienced.[47] Hearing the story of their community enabled the children to grasp the reason for their lifestyle which was different from other communities.[48]

---

44. Christensen, *Deuteronomy 1–11*, 152.

45. Ibid.

46. G. Von Rad, *From Genesis to Chronicles: Explorations in Old Testament Theology* (Minneapolis, MN: Fortress, 2005), 93.

47. Ibid.

48. J. A. Thompson, *Deuteronomy*, Tyndale Old Testament Commentaries (Downers Grove, IL: InterVarsity, 1974), 126.

Questions about the stones as an opportunity to recollect the story: Joshua 4:4–7; 21–24

The twelve stones from the middle of the Jordan which were carried by the representatives of twelve tribes were to "serve as a sign among them" reminding them of the miracle they witnessed in the Jordan (Josh 4:4–7; 21–24). The memorial stones were to keep alive the memory of the miracle of crossing the Jordan on dry ground. The Old Testament witnesses stone monuments and piles of stones as common reminders for the future generations (Gen 28:18–22; 31:45–52; Josh 7:25–26; 1 Sam 7:12).

Here also questions were initiated by children – "What do these stones mean?" (Josh 4:6, 21) – and it refers to the significance of the stones. This was the starting point of the recital of the story of God's actions in the life of Israel. This was also a means to transmit their story to those who have not seen the might and power of God so that they will fear the Lord.

There are other passages in the Old Testament where God initiated the use of symbols as testimonies for future generations among Israelites. God asked Moses to keep the Decalogue in the ark of the Lord (Deut 10:4–5). It was a common practice in the ancient Near East to keep treaty documents in sanctuaries of those involved in the contract.[49] Similarly, the jar of manna (Exod 16:32–33) and Aaron's budded rod (Num 17:10) were kept before the testimony. The jar of manna was a sign for the future generations and Aaron's rod was a sign for the rebels among Israelites. Nehushtan, the bronze serpent (Num 21:8) that Moses made, was later stored in the temple. Ahaz's son Hezekiah removed it from the temple as it became an object of worship (2 Kgs 18:4). Eleazar hammered and overlaid the altar with the 250 censers of Korah, Dathan, Abiram, and the elders of Israel who was swallowed up by the earth. This was a sign and reminder to the Israelites that only Aaron's descendants were to burn incense before the Lord (Num 16:36–40). Except for the jar of manna, the purpose of preservation of these symbols was not stated in relation to future generations. However each of these symbols represented a story of God's mighty acts among Israelites. Thus in the context of the Old Testament, even though

---

49. Ibid., 144.

not explicitly stated, preservation of these symbols was to remind the future generation the story of God's might and power.

Summary

In the passages discussed above, reciting the events associated with the entry to the Promised Land followed the children's inquires about the meaning of various rituals and laws. This was used as an opportunity for the Israelite community to assert to its young the stories of their history. Other means of educating the young were listening to the reading of the Torah and participation in festivals and rituals. What they heard as reply from parents enabled children to understand God's revelation and to grasp the deep convictions of the older generations. These recitals can be seen as a primary vehicle by which the historical tradition of Israel reached children.

The Torah was the content which included the events that led to the selection of Israel as a holy nation to the possession of the Promise Land. This explained the significance of the unique lifestyle they have unlike their neighbors who worshipped other gods. Thus telling the events in their past was a method of transmission of God's revelation from one generation to another and an important part of the "curriculum" was also in the form of story.

The Use of Stories in the New Testament

The Old Testament discussion naturally leads to its fulfillment – the New Testament. This segment explains the use of stories in the New Testament writings. The narrative character of the four Gospels is obvious to any reader. Acts continues the tradition by telling the stories of disciples of Jesus. Recently narrative analysis has focused on the texts in the New Testament which are not only in the form of a story but also in the form of letters. Narrative is not embedded deeply in the epistles, but narrative underlying is present in the epistles of Paul and other apostles. They have mentioned many episodes and characters from Jewish tradition in their writings. The epistles utilized three types of stories which might be known to both the Jewish and Gentile readers: (1) the Old Testament, (2) the life of Jesus, and (3) the story of contemporary Christians. By referring to the positive and negative examples, the apostles exhorted the readers to understand their contemporary issues. Yet the gospel of Jesus Christ had the "highly influential role" in their writings and thus became "the foundational 'story' of the early Christian movement."[50] The following section explores the use of stories in the teachings of Jesus and how apostles employed various narrative episodes in their writings.

Jesus the storyteller

Even though Jesus' audience was not exclusively children, the Synoptic Gospels portray storytelling as a primary method of teaching for Jesus the great Master Teacher:[51] "Jesus told the crowds all these things in parables; without a parable he told them nothing" (Matt 13:34; cf. Mark 4:33–34). Even though all parables of Jesus were not stories, narrative parables in the form of stories were one of the categories.[52]

Anderson and Foley refer to Jesus as "a storyteller with bread"[53] as the Gospels portray many table fellowships he had during his life. They note an added dimension of the use of stories in the ministry of Jesus. During meals Jesus not only shared stories but also listened to the stories of the people who had gathered and "brought these two narrative streams into dangerous and transformative proximity to each other."[54]

The reservoir of stories for Jesus was not only the Old Testament, but also the flora and fauna of Palestine. He used a variety of life situations in his times to bring the truth, values and principles of the kingdom to his hearers. Wright noted that Jesus just continued the long tradition of Israel whose theology was expressed through explicit stories.[55] His parables have become a source of theological dialogue. "Jesus' stories packed with theology, caused reason, imagination, and emotions to collide, demanding a

---

50. R. L. Webb, "The Use of 'Story' in the Letter of Jude: Rhetorical Strategies of Jude's Narrative Episodes," *The Journal for the Study of the New Testament* 31, no. 1 (2008): 67.

51. A. J. Hultgren, *The Parable of Jesus: A Commentary* (Grand Rapids, MI: Eerdmans, 2000), 1.

52. Ibid., 3; see also K. R. Snodgrass, *Stories with Intent: A Comprehensive Guide to the Parable of Jesus* (Grand Rapids, MI: Eerdmans, 2008), 11.

53. H. Anderson and E. Foley, *Mighty Stories, Dangerous Rituals: Weaving together the Human and Divine* (San Francisco, CA: Jossey-Bass, 2001), 154.

54. Ibid.

55. Wright, *People of God*, 77.

change of allegiance. Jesus' example forcibly demonstrates that stories can effectively communicate theology."[56]

When God spoke through Jesus, he not only used propositional teaching style but also stories to explain the nature of the kingdom and the character of God and his expectations of humanity in the kingdom.[57] His stories were to challenge the worldview of his hearers to accept the worldview of the kingdom of God. The significance of stories as a method of Jesus can be implied from the following verses: "In many and various ways God spoke of old to our fathers by prophets; but in these last days he has spoken to us by his Son" (Heb 1:1–2) and "without a parable he told them nothing" (Matt 13:34; cf. Mark 4:33–34). The context of these verses indicates that this was a method he used because he wanted his disciples, not the crowd to have the "knowledge of the secrets of the kingdom" (Matt 13:10–11). This is strategic as we see the role disciples played in continuing the mission of Christ.

Paul, the theological commentator of the story

Paul was not considered to be a man of parable or story, or a storyteller.[58] He did not use parables as Jesus did, even though he used narratives in his sermons seen in Acts (Acts 13:17–37; Acts 20, 22 and 23). Now it is widely accepted that reflections and moral discourse in the Pauline epistles are based on scriptural narratives.[59] Roman 6:1 and following, and Philippians 1:27–2:18, refer to the life of Jesus to encourage the readers to have Christian conduct. These passages, two examples of Pauline moral discourse "derive their force and intelligibility from the stories underlying them."[60]

---

56. Steffen, *Reconnecting God's Story*, 38.

57. Snodgrass, *Stories with Intent*, 2.

58. B. W. Longenecker, "Narrative Interest in the Study of Paul: Retrospective and Prospective," in *Narrative Dynamics in Paul: A Critical Assessment*, ed. B. W. Longenecker (Louisville, KY: John Knox Press, 2002), 3; W. A. Meeks, *The Origins of Christian Morality: The First Two Centuries* (New Haven, CT: Yale University Press, 1993), 193; R. B. Hays, "Is Paul's Gospel Narratable?" *Journal for the Study of the New Testament* 27, no. 2 (2004): 221.

59. Longenecker, "Narrative Interest," 4; S. Fowl, "Some Uses of Story in Moral Discourse: Reflections on Paul's Moral Discourse and Our Own," *Modern Theology* 4, no. 4 (1998): 304.

60. Fowl, "Uses of Story," 295.

The epistles of Paul bring christological, ecclesiological, eschatological, and ethical teachings by quoting various episodes and characters. The epistles explain the life and practices of the body of Christ in the light of the revelation through Christ, the Messiah. The typological treatment of events and characters of the Old Testament provided some "explicit link to his readers" and also for the "readers to make their own connections,"[61] thus demonstrating the unfolding plan of God through the ages. Thus, "scriptures" in general (whatever was written in former days, Rom 15:4 NRSV) provide examples, instruction, and warning for contemporary believers (Rom 15:4; 1 Cor 10:1–13).

Different episodes found in Paul's letters are from the stories of creation, Israel, Jesus, his life, and from the life of predecessors and inheritors of the church.[62] Yet, "the story of Jesus paradigmatically shapes the stories of Paul and his converts."[63] Wright notes that Paul used the Old Testament not as "mere proof-texting" – he suggested "new ways of reading well-known stories" to find a "natural climax in the story of Jesus."[64] Hays notes that Paul became "a theological commentator" on the stories of Israel[65] and he is presented as a "revisionary reader"[66] who transforms Israel's story by the life of Jesus. Even though I do not agree with Hays' "revisionary" perspective regarding Paul's writings, I appreciate his treatment of the use of stories in Paul's writings. Hays concludes that in Paul's epistles the message of salvation "is always bound up with the narrative of grace."[67]

Peter and John, the eyewitnesses of the story

The epistles of Peter and John do not have the narrative character like that of the Gospels, yet these epistles affirm the authenticity and historicity of the stories of Jesus as they are the eyewitness of the life of Jesus (2 Pet 1:16–17; 1 John 1:1). Peter refuted the charge of "cleverly invented stories"

---

61. J. P. Sampley, *The First Letter to the Corinthians, The New Interpreter's Bible: A Commentary in Twelve Volumes, vol. 10* (Nashville, TN: Abingdon, 2002), 913.

62. Longenecker, "Narrative Interest," 12–13.

63. Hays, "Paul's Gospel," 231.

64. Wright, *People of God*, 79.

65. Hays, "Paul's Gospel," 221.

66. Ibid., 237.

67. Ibid., 239.

or "myth" (2 Pet 1:16a NIV) leveled against the teaching of apostles when they told the stories of Jesus. The use of "we" (2 Pet 1:16) refers to the apostles in general who were eyewitnesses of the ministry of Jesus even though all did not witness every important event in the life of Jesus.[68] The phrase "we have made known to you" (2 Pet 1:16) signifies the "apostles' preaching of the gospel which included the expectation of the Parousia."[69] This has an apologetic emphasis which refers to the historical basis of the gospel.[70] Peter refers to certain Old Testament characters to emphasize the godly life of Christians: Sara and Abraham (1 Pet 3:6), and Noah (1 Pet 3:20). As we see in the case of other epistles, the foundational story behind his epistles was the life and teaching of Jesus.

John's epistles refer to himself as part of those who "have heard," "have seen with our eyes," and "have looked at and our hands have touched" (1 John 1:1). John declares himself a man who has heard, seen, and felt the Jesus of history.[71] By using "we" (1 John 1:1) he places himself among the others who handed down the "primal testimony" to the recipients of the letter.[72] The validity of the presentation of the revelation of Christ in the epistles of Peter and John is based on the authenticity and historicity of Jesus' story of which they were eyewitnesses.

The anonymous reciter of the story – the author of Hebrews

The book of Hebrews, with the "most extended treatment of the Old Testament" presents the meta-narrative of "the story of God's saving initiative toward humankind" through many "subnarratives."[73] Moses, temple of Israel, old covenant, and the Levitical priesthood found its antitype in the Son, heavenly temple, new covenant and in the priesthood of Jesus respectively. The heroes of faith in chapter 11 celebrate the "faithfulness of men and women who were exposed to persecution, humiliation, and execution"

---

68. R. J. Bauckham, *Jude, 2 Peter*, Word Biblical Commentary, eds. D. A. Hubbard and G. W. Barker, vol. 50 (Waco, TX: Word, 1983), 214–215.

69. Ibid., 214.

70. Ibid., 216.

71. S. S. Smalley, *1, 2, 3 John*, Word Biblical Commentary, ed. D. A. Hubbard and G. W. Barker, vol. 51 (Waco, TX: Word, 1984), 4–6.

72. C. C. Black, "The First, Second, and Third Letters of John," in *The New Interpreter's Bible: A Commentary in Twelve Volumes*, vol. 12 (Nashville, TN: Abingdon, 1998), 383.

73. Craddock, *Hebrews*, 13.

and "the catalogue of martyrs was crowned with reference to Jesus."[74] Thus the book of Hebrews also used many characters and episodes from Old Testament to affirm the significance of the new covenant through Jesus.

Jude, the rhetorical arguer

Jude's use of "story" is integral to his rhetoric argument.[75] Apart from the types of stories found in other epistles, the book of Jude uses stories from later Jewish tradition without any distinction between Old Testament stories. Even though being the shortest letter in the New Testament, Jude uses various plots and characters in his writings.[76] Without any chronological order in his narration of Jewish stories, Jude's rhetorical use of stories was to convince his readers the need for reorientation in their perceptions.

Jude's rhetorical strategy in citing the stories from Jewish scriptures "is to use inductive reasoning by way of examples" from Scripture which has "the authority of Scripture behind them."[77] The examples of the sins of those who were judged are "points of comparison between the scriptural traditions and Jude's opponents."[78] Webb notes Jude's uniqueness in the use of stories – "Jewish scriptural tradition is interwoven with the story of Jesus."[79] He accomplished this by interweaving the story of Jesus, story of the Christian community, and the story from the scriptural tradition.[80]

Summary

The New Testament begins with Jesus who told stories as the primary method of his teaching. With respect to stories and storytelling, his disciples have used narratives in their preaching, yet in their epistles they are not storytellers as Jesus was. Even though the epistles are a different genre when compared to the Gospels, they have employed many characters and episodes from Jewish scripture and traditions to explain the covenant

---

74. W. L. Lane, *Hebrews 9–13*, in Word Biblical Commentary, eds. D. A. Hubbard and G. W. Barker, vol. 47B (Waco, TX: Word, 1991), lvii.

75. Webb, "Jude," 53.

76. Ibid., 55.

77. Ibid., 64.

78. Ibid.

79. Ibid., 69.

80. Ibid., 85.

relationship with God through Jesus. The purpose of mentioning various personalities and episodes was for instruction, warning, and examples in the lives of readers (Rom 15:4; 1 Cor 10:1–13). The Holy Spirit enabled these writers to reveal the contemporary relevance to the past events. This helped the new believers to differentiate their lives from that of Jews who believed only in the Old Testament but not in Jesus.

The use of characters and plots of the Old Testament in the epistles implies that the first readers of both Jewish and non-Jewish Christians knew the Old Testament revelation. The early church might have continued the Jewish practice of recounting God's actions in the past as commanded in the Law of Moses (Deut 6:1–21). Thus storytelling was practiced in the New Testament church in communicating the good news to Jews and Gentiles.

In conclusion, even though there are different genres in the Bible, it is the meta-narrative and it is the story that needs to be told. Storytelling was a practice of the Old and New Testaments in presenting the revelation to others by which people can enter into covenant relationship with God. As the research question of the proposed study is children's perceptions of the role of biblical stories in their spiritual formation, besides storytelling in the Bible, a brief discussion of the biblical perspective of the spirituality of children is needed.

Spirituality of Children

With the emergence of the interest in children's spirituality, scholarly attention has been turned to children in the Bible. The recently edited work *The Child in the Bible* (2008) is an example of the pursuit. The following section briefly discusses the Old and New Testaments passages which address various aspects of biblical references of children.

The Old Testament

The discussion based on the Old Testament pertinent to children's spirituality has the following outline: (1) children as a blessing from God, (2) children and covenant, (3) children and spiritual formation, and (4) Samuel, the child protégé.

Children as a blessing from God

Biblical authors repeatedly affirmed that children are God's blessing to their family. The beginning chapters of Genesis declared this truth. God blessed the first family in the Garden of Eden; "Be fruitful and increase in number; fill the earth and subdue it" (Gen 1:28). Eve viewed her two children Cain and Seth as gifts from God (Gen 4:1 – Cain; Gen 4:25 – Seth).

The Patriarchs believed that children are a blessing from God. (1) One of God's promises to Abram was the blessing of children (Gen 12:2). Apart from this passage, the topic of the promised child was a theme of conversation between God and Abram in six chapters (Gen 13, 15, 17, 18, 21, and 22). (2) Isaac sought the Lord in prayer for a child (Gen 25:21). (3) Leah acknowledged the hand of God in giving her children (Gen 29:32, 33, 35; 30:18, 19, 22–23). (4) Rachel saw God's hand in bearing children (Gen 30:6, 23). (5) Jacob's response to Rachel showed this trust in God: "Am I in the place of God who has kept you from having children?" (Gen 30:2). His response to Esau's question, "Who are these with you?" further affirms the notion. Jacob replied, "They are the children God has graciously given your servant" (Gen 33:5). (6) Joseph also believed his children are gifts from God (Gen 41:51–52). He introduced his children Ephraim and Manasseh to his father Jacob by saying, "these are the sons God has given me here" (Gen 48:9).

The rest of the Old Testament continues to portray children as gifts of God. Joshua reminded Israel that Isaac, Esau, and Jacob are gifts from God (Josh 24:3–4). Israel continued to believe this truth that the Lord gives children to them. The elders and Israelite women in the book of Ruth (Ruth 4:12, 13) and Hannah (1 Sam 1:11, 20) are few examples. The psalmists also saw children as a reward from God (Pss 113:9; 127:3–5; 128:3–4).

Children and the covenant

God related to human beings, his creation, through covenants. In the Old Testament, covenants were extended to their descendants: Noahic covenant (Gen 9:8–17), Abrahamic covenant (Gen 15:9–21; Gen 17), Sinatic Covenant (Exod 19–24), Davidic Covenant (2 Sam 7:5–16) and the New

Covenant (Jer 31:31–37).[81] The "covenant of peace" with priests (Num 25:10–13) was also extended to the descendants of Phinehas.

There are several covenant renewals in the Old Testament. Only Deuteronomy 29 mentions children as those who witnessed the renewal (Deut 29:10). The other renewals are during the time of Joshua (Josh 24), Hezekiah (2 Chr 29, 30), Josiah (2 Kgs 23), and Nehemiah (Neh 8–9). Children may be present in these renewals but they are not mentioned in these passages. However, the covenant one generation made with God included their descendants. The following section discusses the Abrahamic covenant and the Sinatic covenant in association with children.

The Abrahamic covenant. Four aspects of the Abrahamic covenant was in relation to children: (1) the covenant was between God and Abraham and his descendants (Gen 17:7, 9, 10, 19; 22:17–18), (2) children were given circumcision which is the sign of the covenant (Gen 17:11), (3) the promise of many descendants was repeatedly affirmed (Gen 12:1–3), and (4) the promise of the land was declared in association with children.

Although God made the covenant with Abraham, it was repeatedly extended to his descendants. After the death of Abraham, God confirmed the covenant with Isaac (Gen 26:3) and later reaffirmed it to Jacob (Gen 28:13–15). In both of these incidents, the covenant was extended to their descendants.

Circumcision was to be administered to every eight-day old male child (Gen 17:12). This further affirms that children were part of the covenant. When Abraham and his household were circumcised, his thirteen-year old son Ishmael was also circumcised on the same day (Gen 17:23, 26). Later Isaac was circumcised on the eighth day (Gen 21:4).

The promise relating to Abraham's descendants has a "foundational" aspect.[82] The birth of the child Isaac was key in fulfilling the covenant with Abraham. God's plan to perpetuate his covenant with Abraham was through Isaac (Gen 17:19–21) whose birth was repeatedly foretold to Abraham (Gen 15:4; 17:15–16, 19, 21; 18:10, 14). The new names for

---

81. W. A. Grudem, *Systematic Theology: An Introduction to Biblical Literature* (Secunderabad, India: OM Books, 1964), 515–522.

82. P. R. Williamson, "Covenant." In *Dictionary of the Old Testament: Pentateuch*, eds. T. D. Alexander and D. W. Baker (Downers Grove, IL: InterVarsity, 2003), 148.

Abram and Sara were Abraham and Sarai which denoted "father of many nations" (Gen 15:5) and "mother of nations" (Gen 17:15) respectively. The terms "father" and "mother" are in relation to their descendants which can be seen as an indication of the promise of many descendants through Isaac. The promise of descendants was later on assured to Abraham's descendants, Isaac (Gen 26:4, 24) and Jacob (Gen 28:13–14).

The promise of land, which was another part of the Abrahamic covenant, was also pronounced in relation to his children (Gen 15:12–21). Later when it was affirmed to Isaac and Jacob, the promise of the land was also given in relation to their descendants (Gen 26:3; 28:13; 35:12). The promise was also transmitted to their generations. Joseph reminded his brothers about the promise (Gen 50:24). The exodus event was a step towards the fulfillment of this promise (Exod 3:17; Deut 6:23). Moses repeatedly reminded Israel the truth of the land promised to Abraham and his descendants (Deut 1:8, 21; 6:4).

The Sinaitic covenant. This national covenant was subordinate to the Abrahamic covenant.[83] This subordination and "Sabbath rests" which are a "sign" of this covenant[84] show the significance of children in this covenant. The implications of Abrahamic covenant with respect to children are thus applicable to this covenant. Another fact is that the sons and daughters of Israel were obligated to practice the Sabbath rest (Exod 20:8–11; Deut 5:12–14) along with the adults in the community. This shows that children were part of the covenant and were obligated to observe the covenant requirements.

The above discussion shows that when God made a covenant with one generation, their children were part of the covenant. The promises of God to one generation were extended to their children and they were obligated to fulfill the covenant requirements. The birth of the children to the families was important in fulfilling the God's promise to them.

---

83. Ibid., 149.
84. Ibid. 151.

Children and spiritual formation

Wenham notes that Genesis 18:19 states the fuller purpose of God's election of Abraham: "to create a God-fearing community."[85] Reading Genesis 17:11 might imply that the only obligation on Abraham's descendants was circumcision. In Genesis 18:19 the obligation is to "direct," "charge," or "command" his children and his household to keep the way of the Lord. "So that the LORD will bring about for Abraham what he has promised him" (Gen 18:19b), "makes the fulfillment of the promise contingent on Abraham's obedience" of teaching the ways of the Lord to his generation. This is the first reference in the Bible that directly speaks of parent's obligation of instructing children to follow God.

The law continuously states this obligation of teaching children (Exod 12:25–27; Deut 6:1–3, 6–7, 20–25). The Exodus, Deuteronomy, and Joshua passages discussed in a previous section assume children's capability of understanding and appropriating stories which occur in a different time and context. In these passages God commanded the parents to tell their children about the exodus event. Thus God wanted himself made known to the next generation and desired children to be a part of God's action among Israelites. As discussed in the section, "The Use of Stories in the Old Testament," Exodus 12:26; 13:8, 14; and Deuteronomy 6:20–25 show how God used the family unit as a means for children to ask questions about the history of Israel and to receive the necessary information to be followers of the Lord. Central to these passages (Exod 12:26; 13:8, 14; Deut 6:20–25; Josh 4:4–7, 21–24) is the inquiry of the children about their practices which affirms that children are curious and are active searchers to know the religious practices of their parents. "The religious and social practices of the community" were "teaching moments" for children to learn why they are a "treasured possession" to God (Deut 7:6).[86] Children are "invited to share in a secret already trusted and relied upon."[87]

---

85. G. J. Wenham, *Genesis 16–50*, Word Biblical Commentary, eds. D. A. Hubbard and G. W. Barker, vol. 2 (Waco, TX: Word, 1994), 50.

86. Miller, "Children May Know," 51.

87. Brueggemann, *Creative Word*, 16.

Deuteronomy from beginning to end gives a special attention to children with respect to what and how to teach them.[88] Reading Deuteronomy in its entirety reveals that children had to know not only the Ten Commandments, but also the "Book of the Law," which were to guide their lives (Deut 4:9–10; 31:12–13, 26). Those who were teaching children had seen the works of God: "Your own eyes that saw all these great things the LORD has done" (Deut 11:7). But the children haven't seen or experienced it: "your children were not the ones who saw and experienced the discipline of the Lord your God: his majesty, his mighty hand, his outstretched arm" (Deut 11:1). So it was the responsibility of parents to deliberately and consistently teach children in the context of the family (Deut 11:18–20).

Not only in the family setting, but also in the congregational setting, God brought an emphasis that children were to hear the Torah. The children had a place in the reading of the Torah at the Sanctuary (Deut 31:9–12). At the end of every seven years, priests were to read the law to all Israelites including children.

Even though spirituality of children is not the thrust of the passages from the Torah, the fact that God wanted children to hear these events implies that God recognized children's capacity to ponder spiritually significant matters and their capacity to relate to God's revelation. God's repeated instructions to tell the story of deliverance show that he wanted the truth about him to be transmitted to new generations. The curiosity of children was used in innovative ways to preserve the memory of the exodus down the generation.[89] Family life and the congregation were the settings to nurture faith in children.

In the wisdom literature, the duty of parents is twofold: teach and discipline (Prov 1:8; 13:1; 23:12–15). Corporal punishment for unruly children, a practice in ancient Israel and Egypt, is mentioned in Proverbs (Prov 13:24; 22:15). However, it is a sign of love and towards expectation of a life approved by God (Prov 13:24; 19:18; 22:14; 23:13ff; 29:17).[90] Parents

---

88. Miller, "Children May Know," 45.

89. McGinnis, "Text of Terror," 44.

90. R. E. Murphy, *Proverbs*, Word Biblical Commentary, eds. D. A. Hubbard and G. W. Barker, vol. 22 (Dallas, TX: Word, 1998), 99.

were to assure that the child would develop properly as a productive member of the society (Prov 19:18; 29:17). If a father withholds discipline from his son, he neglects his covenant obligation to the child.[91] The father thus instructs his children regarding a proper conduct of life which is necessary for gaining wisdom, prudence, judgment, discernment (Prov 1:3, 4; 4:4, 13). The Old Testament approves the role of discipline along with teaching in the spiritual upbringing of children.

Samuel: the child protégé
Special attention needs to be given to the unique story of Samuel, the child protégé who is compared with Eli, the high priest and his sons who were "wicked men" (1 Sam 2:12). His parents, especially his mother, dedicated Samuel to the Lord for his whole life (1 Sam 1:28). Apart from his parents' dedication of the child to the Lord, he is depicted in the pages of 1 Samuel as a child who was devoted to the Lord of Israel. Because of the wickedness of Eli's sons and his neglect of God, the priesthood, which was promised to his household, was removed forever (1 Sam 2:29–36). Yet Samuel was recognized as a prophet in Israel.

The first three chapters of 1 Samuel portray certain characteristics of the young boy's life:

1) He was a gift from Yahweh (1 Sam 1:27).
2) "He worshipped the Lord" at Shiloh (1 Sam 1:28).
3) He ministered before the Lord under Eli (1 Sam 2:11, 18; 3:1).
4) He grew up in the presence of the Lord (1 Sam 2:21).
5) He grew in favor with the Lord and with men (1 Sam 2:26).
6) He listened to God's word (1 Sam 3:11–14).
7) "The Lord was with Samuel" and "he let none of his words fall to the ground" (1 Sam 3:19).
8) Everyone from Dan to Beersheba recognized him as a prophet of the Lord (1 Sam 3:19).
9) God continued to appear at Shiloh, probably to Samuel (1 Sam 3:21).

---

91. R. D. Branson, "Musar," in *Theological Dictionary of the Old Testament*, vol. 4, eds. G. J. Botterweck and H. Ringgren, trans. D. E. Green (Grand Rapids, MI: Eerdmans, 1990), 132.

10) "God revealed himself to Samuel through his word" (1 Sam 3:21).

Klein comments that the term used to denote Samuel's service before the Lord (1 Sam 2:11, 18; 3:1) was also used to describe the activities of Aaron and his sons (Exod 28:35, 43; 29:30; Num 1:50, etc.).[92] Thus his service before God was recognized as a priestly activity. Samuel grew in the approval of God and people in contrast with Eli's wicked sons. "The word of the LORD was rare; there were not many visions," yet God continued to appear to Samuel and revealed God's word to him. God's appearance to Samuel and God's revelation of his word made him a prophet who was approved by the whole of Israel.

The question is whether the story of a boy's life can be generalized to every child in Israel. Eli's sons grew up in Shiloh and became wicked men. The lives of David's children Absalom (2 Sam 14, 15) and Amnon (2 Sam 13) reveal that children of pious parents can become wicked people. Thus it is acknowledged that Samuel's story is a unique story of a child. Yet it shows the possibility that children can serve the Lord in a priestly role, they can worship God, and listen to God's word. God may be pleased to appear to them and reveal his words to them. People can recognize children as God's prophets. Thus the story of Samuel gives a glimpse of what can be the spiritual life of a child.

The New Testament

In the New Testament, Jesus affirmed the place of children in the kingdom of God through his radical teachings and reception of them. The epistles establish the validity of parental discipline and instruction in nurturing children by establishing the discipline of God in instructing his people. The following discussion sheds light on these two aspects.

Jesus and children

The teachings of Jesus about children and kingdom of God are to be understood against the low status of children in the cultural context of the New Testament. Gundry-Volf notes that in the Greco-Roman world, parents

---

92. R. W. Klein, *1 Samuel,* Word Biblical Commentary, eds. D. A. Hubbard and G. W. Barker, vol. 10 (Waco, TX: Word, 1983), 24.

valued children. However, children were at a low rung of the social ladder.[93] She observes that the Roman fathers had the power of life and death over their children.[94] The low status of children in the Greco-Roman world[95] implied children are unimportant.[96] Jews valued children as a gift from God, yet believed that "a sage should not bother with children."[97] By receiving even lowly children in his arms (Mark 9:36, Luke 9:46–48), Jesus portrays himself as "an example of being the last of all, servant of all."[98]

With respect to children's spirituality, the following teachings of Jesus are significant:

1) The kingdom belongs to such as these: Mark 10:13–16; Matthew 19:13–16; Luke 18:15–17

The Synoptic Gospels portray the unwelcoming attitude of the disciples even though they are silent about the reason. There can be various reasons for disciples' objection: they saw it as a distraction and as a disruption,[99] as an interruption to their journey, or as a bother to Jesus.[100] Jesus wanted children to come to him, and unlike Jewish rabbis he embraced them and blessed them (Mark 10:16). Jesus explains the reasons why children should be allowed to come to him: it belongs to the insignificant ones like children who are important to Jesus.[101] However, the use of "such as these" does not imply children's exclusive ownership of the kingdom, yet their share in it.[102]

---

93. Gundry-Volf, "Least and the Greatest," 32.

94. Ibid., 33.

95. C. L. Blomberg, *Matthew*, The New American Commentary, vol. 22 (Nashville, TN: Broadman, 1992), 294.

96. W. Lane, *The Gospel according to Mark*, NICNT (Grand Rapids, MI: Eerdmans, 1974), 359.

97. D. E. Garland, *Mark*, The NIV Application Commentary (Grand Rapids, MI: Zondervan, 1996), 385–386.

98. R. H. Gundry, *Mark: A Commentary on His Apology for the Cross, Chapters 9–16* (Grand Rapids, MI: Eerdmans, 2000), 519.

99. C. A. Evans, *Mark 8:27–16:20*, Word Biblical Commentary, eds. D. A. Hubbard and G. W. Barker, vol. 34B (Nashville, TN: Thomas Nelson, 2001), 93.

100. R. T. France, *Mark: A Commentary on the Greek Text* (Grand Rapids, MI: Eerdmans, 2002), 396.

101. Ibid., 397.

102. Ibid., 396; Evans, *Mark 8:27–16:20*, 94; W. D. Davis and D. C. Allison, *The Gospel according to St. Matthew*, The International Critical Commentary, vol. 3 (Edinburgh: T & T Clark, 1997), 35.

Brooks notes "children" in Mark 10:13–14, 16 refers to literal children yet in verses 15 and 16 "such as these" and "like a little child" denote children or adults who have childlikeness in them.[103]

Nowhere in Jewish literature are children compared with adults, and in the Hellenistic setting comparison with children was highly insulting.[104] Jews regard children as too young to take the yoke of the kingdom,[105] yet Jesus compared them with those who receive the kingdom. Gundry further notes that their coming to him shows that they are part of the class of little ones who believe in Jesus (Mark 9:32) to whom the kingdom belongs.[106]

2) Children can know divine secrets: Matthew 21:14–16

The context of this passage is the visit of Jesus to the temple after the triumphal entry. The priestly authorities became indignant because Jesus healed the blind and the lame and children shouted, "Hosanna to the Son of David" (Matt 21:15). The question raised by the chief priests and scribes indicates that they were disturbed by the shout of children: "Do you hear what these children are saying?" (Matt 21:16). They wanted Jesus to deny this proclamation[107] yet with an affirmative "yes" and quoting Psalm 8:3, Jesus defended children's enthusiasm by acknowledging that these children are uttering the truth of God.[108] Children either have identified Jesus as the Messiah when they witnessed the miracles Jesus had performed in the temple[109] or have mimicked the chant they previously had heard.[110] Even if children chanted without understanding the meaning, Jesus accepted the

---

103. J. A. Brooks, *Mark,* The New American Commentary, vol. 23 (Nashville, TN: Broadman, 1991), 160.

104. Gundry-Volf, "Least and the Greatest," 39.

105. R. H. Gundry, *Mark: A Commentary on His Apology for the Cross* (Grand Rapids, MI: Eerdmans, 1993), 550.

106. Ibid., 554.

107. J. Nolland, *The Gospel of Matthew: A Commentary on the Greek Text,* The New International Greek Testament Commentary, eds. D. A. Hagner and I. H. Marshall (Grand Rapids, MI: Eerdmans, 2005), 847.

108. D. A. Hagner, *Matthew 14–28,* Word Biblical Commentary, eds. D. A. Hubbard and G. W. Barker, vol. 33B (Dallas, TX: Word, 1998), 602; R. T. France, *Matthew,* The Tyndale New Testament Commentaries, ed. C. L. Morris (Grand Rapids, MI: Eerdmans, 1985), 302.

109. Gundry-Volf, "Least and the Greatest," 46.

110. Hagner, *Matthew 14–28,* 602.

designation they had chanted – "Son of David."[111] The religious leaders could not grasp the spiritual truth which children could identify.[112] Thus the Jewish authorities rejected not only Jesus as "Son of David" but also the children who proclaimed the divine secret.

In Greco-Roman antiquity, children "uttered divinely inspired speech."[113] Here Jesus established that children are not ignorant in spiritual insight but they can receive divine secrets from God.[114]

Epistles and children

The New Testament concept of spiritual formation is through instruction and discipline. It establishes the validity of parental instruction and discipline in nurturing children's faith (Eph 6:4; Col 3:21) by establishing the discipline of God in instructing his people. God's discipline was the evidence of his enduring love and commitment (Heb 12:5f). As in the Old Testament it is equated and compared with parental discipline (Heb 12:5–11). In a family, the status of true sons is recognized by the fact that the father educates and disciplines his children "bring them up in the discipline and instruction of the Lord" (Eph 6:4 RSV). The linguistic distinction between discipline and instruction implies the use of deeds and words in educating children.[115] As in the Greco-Roman world and Judaism, fathers were ultimately responsible for the spiritual upbringing of their children.

The relationship between children and parents is subject to the Lord, which shows that the basis of parental authority to discipline and instruct their children is divinely appointed and transcends biological rights. This also indicates the limit, and meaning of, parental authority and filial obedience.[116] Children are to obey and honor parents (Eph 6:1–3; Col 3:20). Fathers are not to embitter or exasperate their children. This instruction to fathers not only rules out severe discipline and all forms of insensitivity to

---

111. Ibid.; Nolland, *Matthew*, 847–848.
112. France, *Matthew*, 302.
113. Gundry-Volf, "Least and the Greatest," 47.
114. Ibid., 47–48.
115. W. L. Lane, "Discipline," in *The International Standard Bible Encyclopaedia*, ed. G. W. Bromiley, vol. 1: A–D (Grand Rapids, MI: Eerdmans, 1986), 950.
116. W. Werpehowski, "Reading Karl Barth on Children," in *The Child in Christian Thought*, ed. M. J. Bunge (Grand Rapids, MI: Eerdmans, 2001), 394–398.

the needs of children but also presents the purpose of the filial authority to communicate the truth of God through their words, examples, and actions. The care and instruction of children is placed in the filial honor and parent's ambassadorial role.[117]

The New Testament gives limits in parental authority, which is different from Roman practices, where fathers had absolute legal power over their children. Roman fathers had the power of life and death over their children.[118] They often inflicted "cruel and harsh" punishments on children."[119] Even Hellenist Jews saw parents as a superior class to their inferior children. Thus they reemphasized the punishment of death penalty for dishonoring parents as punishment for stubborn disobedience.[120] However, the instruction in the epistles' to not to embitter or exasperate children has played a dominant role in shaping the Christian thought on bringing up children in the fear and knowledge of God.

Summary

Children are gifts of God to the family. Children were an inevitable part of God's promise of blessing to the Patriarchs. They were part of the covenant and were obliged to follow the requirements of the covenant. Questions of children about the meaning and significance of ceremonies, laws and stipulations were an opportunity to recite the mighty acts of God for Israel. The unique child Samuel served God in the temple at Shiloh and was recognized as a prophet of God.

In the New Testament, Jesus is portrayed as one who welcomes children, blesses them and acknowledges their capacity to grasp divine insights. In his approach to children, the Synoptic Gospels present him as the one who exemplifies the paradoxical values of the kingdom to his disciples. The status of children in the Greco-Roman world necessitates such a visual demonstration of Jesus acceptance to confront the perspectives of his disciples and Jewish leaders.

---

117. Ibid., 398.

118. Lane, *Hebrews 9–13*, 399.

119. Ibid.

120. A. T. Lincoln, *Ephesians,* Word Biblical Commentary, eds. D. A. Hubbard and G. W. Barker, vol. 42 (Dallas, TX: Word, 1991), 400.

Both the Old and New Testaments uphold the role of discipline in the spiritual formation of children. Divine discipline gives validity to the discipline of parents. However, the New Testament gives limits of parental authority to discipline as the relationship between parents and children is subject to the Lord.

God's repeated instructions to tell, teach, and instruct children in the things of God implies that the Bible acknowledges the capacity of children to grasp spiritual truth. The following exegetical study of Psalm 78:1–8 will further shed light on this discussion as Israel understood intergenerational transmission of God's mighty acts and wonders as a "testimony" or commandment of God. Transmission of God's truth was to develop children's trust in God, and to enable children to remember God's deeds and follow God's commands.

That the Next Generation Might Know: Psalm 78:1–8

Psalm 78 is a part of the third book of Psalms which is one of the five books containing poems and prayers of Israel as a response to the revelation from God and their covenantal relationship with him.[121] As cited in the introduction of the psalm it is the psalm of Asaph, a seer (2 Chr 29:30) who was associated with David (Neh 12:46). He was the son of Berechiah (1 Chr 6:24) who was one of the chiefs of the Levitical choir (1 Chr 15:17). The following characteristics are noted by scholars: It gives "the longest review of Israel's historical traditions in the Psalter"[122] with practical application for the hearers in mind. It surveys Israelite history from the time of Egypt to the time of David[123] without a chronological framework. The review of history "concentrates on the rejection of the northern tribes and the divine

---

121. P. C. Craigie, *Psalms 1–50*, Word Biblical Commentary, eds. D. A. Hubbard and G. W. Barker, vol. 19 (Waco, TX: Word, 1983), 39–40.

122. R. J. Clifford, "In Zion and David a New Beginning: An Interpretation of Psalms 78," in *Traditions and Transformation: Turning Points in Biblical Faith*, eds. B. Halpern, J. D. Levenson, and F. M. Cross (Winona Lake, IN: Eisenbrauns, 1981), 124.

123. R. N. Whybray, *Reading the Psalms as a Book. Journal for the Study of the Old Testament Supplement Series 222* (Sheffield, UK: Sheffield Academic, 1996), 1996.

blessing on David and his tribe of Judah."[124] The recapitulation of history in the psalm "reviews God's favor and the people's chronic failure."[125]

An Introduction to the Psalm

Gupta notes the significance of Psalm 78 in Jewish and Christian history – this psalm has deep significance for Israel,[126] is quoted many times in the New Testament and in Pseudepigrapha and Philo,[127] and it might have been part of early Christian ethical teaching.[128]

There is no unanimous opinion about the date, genre, setting, and the intention of the psalm. The dating of the psalm varies from mid-tenth century[129] to post-exilic.[130] According to the psalm, it is Asaph's psalm, which clearly puts it during the Davidic monarchy. Regarding the genre of the psalm the various types suggested are as follows: historical psalm;[131] a psalm of praise with historical section,[132] a psalm of remembrance and a wisdom psalm,[133] a liturgical poem[134] and as a didactic poem.[135] Regarding the set-

---

124. L. Boadt, "The Use of 'Panels' in the Structure of Psalms 73–78," *The Catholic Biblical Quarterly* 66, no. 4 (2004): 546.

125. B. Olam, *Psalms: Studies in Hebrew Narrative and Poetry* (Collegeville, MN: Liturgical Press, 2001), 190.

126. N. Gupta, "An Apocalyptic Reading of Psalm 78 in 2 Thessalonians 3," *Journal for the Study of New Testament* 31, no. 2 (2008): 191.

127. Ibid., 181.

128. Ibid., 187.

129. A. Campbell, "Psalm 78: A Contribution to the Theology of Tenth Century Israel," *Catholic Biblical Quarterly* 41, no. 1 (1979): 79; J. M. Leonard, "Identifying Inner-Biblical Allusions," *Journal of Biblical Literature* 127, no. 2 (2008): 259.

130. M. E. Tate, *Psalm 51–100*, Word Biblical Commentary, eds. D. A. Hubbard and G. W. Barker, vol. 20 (Waco, TX: Word, 1990), 285.

131. G. H. Wilson, *Psalms, The New NIV Application Commentary*, vol. 1 (Grand Rapids, MI: Zondervan, 2002), 75; M. C. Pate, S. J. Duvall, and D. Hays, *The Story of Israel: A Biblical Theology* (Downers Grove, IL: InterVarsity, 2004), 72; R. Alter, *The Art of Biblical Poetry* (New York: Basic Books, 1985), 105–106.

132. Westermann, *Praise and Lament*, 141.

133. T. Longman III, *How to Read the Psalms* (Leicester, UK: IVP, 1998), 35.

134. Clifford, "Zion and David," 124.

135. H. J. Kraus, *Psalms 60–150. A Commentary*, trans. H. C. Oswald (Minneapolis, MN: Augsburg, 1989), 122; E. S. Gerstenberger, *Psalms Part 2 and Lamentation, The Forms of the Old Testament Literature*, vol. 15 (Grand Rapids, MI: Eerdmans, 2001), 93; W. A. VanGemeren, *Psalms-Songs of Songs, The Expositor's Bible Commentary*, vol. 5 (Grand Rapids, MI: Zondervan, 1991), 504; H. C. Leupold, *Exposition of Psalms* (Grand Rapids, MI: Baker, 1969), 563.

ting of the psalm, Tate proposes public worship as the setting[136] and Kraus proposes a cultic festival as the setting.[137] Various scholars have suggested different individuals as the speaker of the psalm: king, priests, prophet, teachers or lay person;[138] a Levitical priest;[139] or divine liturgist.[140] Later biblical traditions refer to the psalmist as a prophet (Matt 13:35).

The intention of the psalm also has various interpretations. Westermann presents this psalm as "re-presenting" past events in order to praise God and to preserve the tradition.[141] Clifford presents the intention as a "liturgical celebration of God's merciful choice of Zion and David" and a warning against the worship in the northern sanctuary.[142] The repeated usage of certain terms – "fathers" (NIV) or "ancestors" (RSV) (vv. 3, 5, and 8), "children" (vv. 4–6) and "generations" (vv. 4, 6, and 8) three, four, and four times respectively confirms the didactic purpose.[143] The long introduction with a wisdom or didactic prelude indicates "the demand to instruct new generations confirms that the primary emphasis of the psalm is on the necessity of recognizing and understanding the meaning of the historical acts of God performed for the ancestors."[144] The researcher agrees with the position that this psalm presents the history with a didactic intent.

Exegesis

Psalm 78:1–11 is "a profound interpretation of the ancient traditions revered by the Israelite congregations"[145] which is an introduction to the rest

---

136. Tate, Psalm 51–100, 287.

137. H. J. Kraus, *Psalms 60–150, A Continental Commentary*, trans. H. C. Oswald (Minneapolis, MN: Fortress, 1993), 123.

138. Tate, *Psalm 51–100*, 287.

139. Kraus, *Continental Commentary*, 123.

140. Gerstenberger, *Psalms Part 2*, 94.

141. Westermann, *Praise and Lament*, 238, 245.

142. Clifford, "Zion and David," 137.

143. P. McMillion, "Psalm 78: Teaching the Next Generation," *Restoration Quarterly* 43, no. 4 (2001): 223.

144. Boadt, "Use of Panels," 548.

145. Clifford, "Zion and David," 125.

of the psalm.[146] Westermann sees verses 2–8 as "the most elaborate and beautiful description" of the biblical understanding of tradition.[147]

The language characteristics of verses 1–2 reveal that the psalmist takes the stance of a wisdom teacher: "incline the ear" (v. 1), "the words of my mouth" (v. 1), "proverb" (v. 2), "riddle" (v. 2) occur only in the Psalms and wisdom literature.[148] The use of the word "*torah*" (v. 1) referring to the teaching of a human wisdom teacher is also a feature of Proverbs.[149] This can be distinguished from Torah in verse 5 which refers to "Torah of Yahweh," thus Kraus concludes that Torah in verse 1 signifies "exhortation," "warning," and "directive."[150] The prophet gives instruction which demands a listening, willing, and attentive ear, not from "God" or "an individual person or humanity in general," but from "Israel."[151] "My people" does not mean God is the speaker, but the psalmist is in the name or in the authority of God as his inspired messenger and does so as part of the "divinely constituted duty."[152] Thus, the terms "my people" and "my teaching" indicate an "authoritative" intent from the speaker.[153]

McMillion states that even though the term "parable" (v. 2) has a variety of meanings in the Hebrew Bible – "an allegory" (Ezek 17:1), and wise sayings (1 Kgs 5:12) – yet in this context it is neither of these meaning but "a number of warnings" drawn from the selected events in the history of Israel.[154] The use of the word "parable" (v. 2) and the phrase "be like" (v. 8, NIV, NRSV) or "be as" (ASV, KJV) indicates the desire of the psalmist to exhort the audience to compare themselves with their ancestors so that they can avoid the negative examples of their fathers.[155]

---

146. Ibid., 127; Kraus, *Continental Commentary*, 125.

147. Westermann, *Praise and Lament*, 238.

148. Whybray, *Reading the Psalms*, 48.

149. Ibid.

150. Kraus, *Continental Commentary*, 125.

151. J. Goldingay, *Psalms, Baker Commentary on the Old Testament*, vol. 2 (Grand Rapids, MI: Baker, 2007), 484.

152. J. L. Mays, *Psalms, Interpretation: A Bible Commentary for Teaching and Preaching* (Louisville, KY: John Knox Press, 1994), 255.

153. Goldingay, *Psalms*, 484.

154. McMillion, "Psalm 78," 222.

155. J. C. McCann Jr., "Psalms," in *The New Interpreter's Bible: A Commentary in Twelve Volumes*, vol. 4 (Nashville, TN: Abingdon, 1996), 990; Mays, *Psalms, Interpretation*, 255.

As the speaker proceeds to recount the history of their fathers in relation to the mighty acts of God, he intends to do so in the pattern of a "parable" or "riddle" or "dark sayings" (v. 2). The significance of the term "riddle" is further discussed: Tate sees the significance of the term "riddle" to imply that the story of Israel and Yahweh's relationship with them is a paradox of "Israel's inability to trust God's great act of deliverance."[156] Kraus refers to it as "secret facts"[157] that the speaker wants to convey by the sharing of the history, and Preowne sees the importance of unveiling of the history to apply it in the present situation.[158] Jesus quotes Psalm 78:2 as it found fulfillment in his teaching in parables (Matt 13:35). Hagner notes that by quoting the prologue to the salvation history in Psalm 78, Jesus declared that his message and mission is God's plan of salvation from the beginning. The mysteries of the kingdom, which were "hidden since the creation of the world," are being uttered in the parables.[159]

The call to attention is followed by the content of "my teaching." The content of the instruction is: "praiseworthy deeds," "power," and "wonders of God" (v. 4 NIV). This is not a "new teaching"[160] or "esoteric form of teaching"[161] but rather a part of the tradition that was heard and known to their fathers (v. 3). There are two core elements in the history in the psalm – "Exodus from Egypt, and the Lord's care and guidance across the wilderness." This forms the basis of this psalm with the purpose to "review these well-known events and then to draw a lesson for the present audience."[162] These stories, which are the history of God's action among Israelites, were the source of their knowledge of his relationship to them and theirs to him.[163] These were handed down in the clans and families of Israel and later

---

156. Tate, *Psalm 51–100*, 281.
157. Kraus, *Continental Commentary*, 125.
158. J. J. S. Perowne, *The Book of Psalms, Vol. 1* (Grand Rapids, MI: Zondervan, 1966), 59.
159. Hagner, *Matthew 14–28*, 309.
160. Kraus, *Continental Commentary*, 125.
161. VanGemeren, *Psalms-Song of Songs*, 505.
162. McMillion, "Psalm 78," 226.
163. H. J. Kraus, *Theology of the Psalms,* trans. K. Crim (Minneapolis, MN: Fortress, 1992), 60.

became the content of cultic proclamation, narration, and instruction at the central sanctuary (vv. 3, 4).[164]

This recounting of the stories of Yahweh in worship had its "counterpart" in the storytelling at the family level.[165] It was to Abraham that God first instructs to direct his children and his household in the ways of the Lord (Gen 18:19). Isaac knew God as the God of Abraham and subsequently by the time of Moses, Israel knew God as the God of Abraham, Isaac, and Jacob. There was no formal worship sanctuary or priest until the time of Moses. Thus the transmission of God's revelation was primarily the responsibility of parents. But when priesthood was established, along with the duties in the temple, priests were given the responsibility to teach (Deut 31:9–12; Lev 10:8–11; Ezek 44:23). The responsibility of priests to teach was to complement the teaching at home.

McMillion notes that in the Old Testament the term "fathers" (vv. 3, 5, 8 NIV, ASV, RSV) refers to ancestors regardless of family ties, and here it "suggests a difference in ages or generations."[166] The term, "generations," in verses 4 and 6, is used to denote the coming generation, and in verse 8 it is used to refer to the negative examples of former generations. The term, "children" (vv. 4, 5, and 6), refers to the young or "if they are not young in years, they are certainly young in the faith of the community and in their understanding of the traditions of Israel."[167] So the "ongoing religious life" of Israel depends on "parent's obligations to instruct the next generation so that they may understand and observe the obligations of the covenant in their own lives."[168] This responsibility was stated in the Pentateuch (Exod 10:2; Deut 4:9; 6:1–21) and was practiced among Israelites (Ps 44:1). Repeated use of the terms "children," "fathers," and "generations" denote the significance of the divine "obligation of transmission"[169] of divine truth. The past, present, and future generations have definite roles in transmission

---

164. Ibid., 92.
165. Ibid.
166. McMillion, "Psalm 78," 222.
167. Ibid., 223.
168. McGinnis, "Text of Terror," 43.
169. Kraus, *Continental Commentary*, 126.

– "present generation plays its link between the past generation and the next generation."[170]

Mays notes that remembering and telling the stories are integral for the existence of the people.[171] Through the "lively act of narration" the history of God's people was preserved with an aspect of "forward looking."[172] The repetition of the terms "tell" (vv. 3, 4, 6), and "know" or "teach" (vv. 3, 5, 6), implies that God wanted the law and testimonies to be preserved and established among his people by oral transmission along with the written Law.[173] Intergenerational transmission of God's deeds was a "testimony" and a "law" (v. 5) that God established in Israel. Leupold states that the practical purpose in mentioning the infidelity of the people in the psalms is to show the importance of telling or instructing the younger generation so that they will not be like their fathers.[174] Mays states that verses 5–8 present commandments and that these statues are "inseparably associated" with the mighty acts of God among Israelites, which is the story of Israel.[175]

The expected result of transmission is threefold: each generation is (1) to put their "confidence" (NASV) or "hope" (NRSV) or "trust" (NIV) in God; (2) not forget the deeds of God; and (3) keep the commands (v. 7). The sovereignty of God and his Torah are "not simply as a matter of information but as a matter of life-saving hope."[176] It is not just for "mechanical memorization" because its ultimate purpose is to touch the attitude of the people.[177] As these are the "saving acts" of God to his people, the law of God demands obedience to it.[178]

Christian educator, Groome, gives the three dimensions of Christian faith – cognitive, affective, and behavioral dimensions.[179] Verse 7 can imply these three dimensions – the term "confidence" or "hope" or "trust" can

---

170. Goldingay, *Psalms*, 485.
171. Mays, *Psalms, Interpretation*, 256.
172. Westermann, *Praise and Lament*, 238.
173. Perowne, *Book of Psalms*, 60.
174. Leupold, *Exposition of Psalms*, 564.
175. Mays, *Psalms, Interpretation*, 256.
176. McCann, "Psalms," 991.
177. Leupold, *Exposition of Psalms*, 564.
178. Westermann, *Praise and Lament*, 239.
179. Groome, *Christian Religious Education*, 57–66.

denote the affective dimension. The term "forget" may imply the cognitive dimension, and "keep the commands" may involve action or behavioral dimension which is seen in the obedience of the people.

The psalmist reviews, not only the story of God's history of faithfulness to his people, but also "a history against the people's religious and political self-assertion."[180] The nature of the sins or negative examples of the forefathers (v. 8) is presented in order to warn the present generation from following the footsteps of their fathers.[181] The extent of their rebelliousness was that something was wrong with their "heart" and "spirit" which denotes "the dynamic centre of their being."[182] Their ancestors were "stubborn, rebellious," disloyal and unfaithful (v. 8) whose selected examples are listed in the psalm considering the significance of the audience.[183] Thus as Mays notes there was a gap between the words of the fathers (v. 3) and their deeds (v. 8)[184] which indicates that "knowledge does not guarantee faithfulness."[185]

Summary

Psalm 78 states intergenerational transmission as a command to the parents with the purpose to develop faith in three dimensions: trust, hope, or confidence in God; remembering the works of God; and keeping his commandments (Ps 78:7). Israelites passed on the truths of God to the next generation and encouraged obedience of the law through the use of the story from their history. This transmission was established as a testimony or law among Israelites which indicates the importance of passing on the tradition to the next generation. God's revelation was preserved which also has a forward-looking aspect. That which was perpetuated and thus preserved was to make a difference in the lives of the recipients. Thus stories of God's mighty acts and wonders among previous generations played a crucial role in nurturing faith in the present and future generations.

---

180. Kraus, *Theology of the Psalms*, 61.
181. Leupold, *Exposition of Psalms*, 564.
182. Goldingay, *Psalms*, 487.
183. Gerstenberger, *Psalms Part 2*, 94.
184. Mays, *Psalms, Interpretation*, 257.
185. McCann, "Psalms," 991.

In the process of transmission, three generations have a definite role: father's generation, their children's generations and the next generation (Ps 78:3–5). The present generation is the link between the past generation and the next generation. The intergenerational transmission was a key towards not following the negative examples of their stubborn and rebellious forefathers (Ps 78:8).

This psalm acknowledges the spirituality of children in the sense that they can hear and comprehend the mighty acts of God. They could develop "trust" in God and remember God's works, and follow the commands. How this psalm recognizes the spirituality of children and its affirmation of intergenerational transmission through telling the mighty acts of God in nurturing the spirituality in each generation has significant implications to the current research.

Chapter Summary

This chapter has discussed how the Bible is the story which needs to be told and how it witnesses the long storytelling tradition of Judeo-Christian faith. In the Old Testament, storytelling was the primary way of transmitting and preserving the tradition from one generation to another, and story was an important form of content along with the Law. The telling of sacred stories found its expression in the family setting and then in the common worship of the people. The telling of the mighty acts of God to children was a commandment with the objective of preserving the latter's relationship with God which should touch their heart, mind and action: "put their trust in God and would not forget his deeds but would keep his commands" (Ps 78:7).

The Bible portrays children as active searchers of the things of God. When children asked questions about the religious practices and lifestyle of parents, adults were to use these opportunities to transmit the mighty acts of God – their story to their children. Apart from this, reading and reciting the Torah was also another opportunity for children to know God and fear him. Children in biblical times had opportunities to listen to stories of God's power and might.

The practice of telling the stories of God's action in the past was also true in the New Testament church. The New Testament begins with Jesus who expounded the kingdom truths through his life and parables. The apostles recollected the stories of the Old Testament and Jewish tradition in light of the stories of Jesus of which they were eyewitnesses. The epistles show that even the Gentiles readers knew various episodes and characters of Jewish history. This implies that stories of Jewish history were communicated to first century Christians, both Gentiles and Jews. Thus the role of stories and storytelling in the Bible in preserving and transmitting God's actions of the past to the present generation is unquestionable. The responsibility entrusted on each generation in transmitting the stories implies the value of storytelling in spiritual formation.

Educators, parents, and churches participate in the spiritual formation of children. Storytelling and especially biblical stories are used towards this focus in India. However, how do children see the relationship between biblical narratives and their spiritual formation? The proposed research will investigate children's perceptions of the role of the stories in their spiritual formation. As stories are the primary content of education in churches and storytelling is the primary method of communicating the Bible to children, the current research can have a significant contribution in educating our next generation, which to an extent determines the future of our churches.

CHAPTER 4

Research Methodology

The primary objective of this research is to explore the perceptions of 9- to 11-year-old children about the role of biblical stories in their spiritual formation. As the perceptions of children are subjective, qualitative study is the approach of this research. The researcher hopes to contribute to the existing knowledge of children's spirituality and help educators to improve their proficiency in using biblical stories with children. This chapter deals with the research procedure of this qualitative study. The following pages discuss research design, sample selection process, data collection, and analysis procedure involved in the process.

Statement of the Research Questions

The primary question in this research was as follows: What is the child's perception of the role of biblical narratives in his or her spiritual formation? Five additional questions were used to shed light on the research question.

1) Who tells biblical stories to children? Where do they hear these stories?
2) Why do others tell biblical stories to children?
3) When do children recall biblical stories?
4) Does recalling or listening to biblical stories impact the life situations they face? If so, how?
5) How do these children's perceptions of the role of biblical stories in their spiritual formation compare with the dimensions of relational consciousness in Hay and Nye's study in the United Kingdom: I-Thou, I-self, I-other, and I-world? Are there other

important insights from the proposed study that challenge or go beyond the model developed by Hay and Nye?[1]

Research Design

Researchers continue to ponder ways to learn about spirituality of children. A range of research methods are used with children: questionnaires and standardized tests, semi-structured and informal interviews, focus groups, observation and participant observation, and creative methods.[2] The concern relevant for the current study was to find the appropriate methods for this research. In the regular school system in India, children's capacity to answer the list of structured questions determines what they know and do not know. Even though this practice is undergoing change, structured examinations are given a prominent role to evaluate what a child is able to understand and communicate. Thus a method which requires children to write answers for a certain set of questions may confuse children with academic subjects. Subsequently, questionnaires and standardized tests are not the right tools to grasp children's perceptions of the association between biblical stories and their spirituality.

Four methods of data collection in the current research were as follows: (1) assessing written, oral, and group activities of children during the two-hour gathering each week for six weeks, (2) observing the classroom, (3) focus group interviews, and (4) member checking. Three team members assisted the researcher during the research. The details of the research procedures are discussed below. Classroom activities, focus groups, and member checking were audio and video recorded.

Description of the Schedule for the Two-Hour Gathering per Week

Twenty-nine children were gathered to a common location – the conference hall of Faith Theological Seminary, Manakala, India for the class activities. The seminary was selected as the research site to avoid the fear of "sheep

---

1. Hay and Nye, *Spirit of the Child*.
2. M. Gallagher, "Data Collection and Analysis," in *Researching with Children and Young People: Research Design, Methods, and Analysis*, eds. E. K. M. Tisdall, J. M. Davis and M. Gallagher (Los Angeles, CA: Sage, 2009), 73–80.

stealing" which may be there among pastors. Harney and Harney define sheep stealing as a practice of increasing membership in a congregation by luring people to leave their home church to join another congregation.[3]

Yet, the seminary is an artificial setting since children belong to different churches in the locality. The unfamiliarity to the setting might have been minimized as the seminary is a common site for various inter-church functions. Unfamiliarity with other participants might have been reduced as there are various opportunities for children in the locality to know each other through local schools, VBS, and inter-church activities like seminars and camps. Other means to reduce unfamiliarity were as follows: (1) Selection of a minimum of two children and a maximum of eight children from one congregation, (2) less-structured interaction at the beginning and the end of the classroom session which gave an opportunity to develop rapport between children and team members, and (3) planned group games and group activities to build a climate of friendship and put each child at ease.

For six weeks, children were gathered together once a week on Saturday mornings for two hours in the months of April and May. Arrangements were made for all who needed transportation. Every week, the researcher contacted parents to remind them of the class activities.

As children came to the specified room in the seminary, they were welcomed by the research team members. The first ten minutes was a time for refreshments which was followed by learning a story-based song. For the next twenty-five minutes, children heard six stories from the life of Jesus following the advice of Cavalletti. She recommends focusing on a few themes with six to twelve year olds:

> The older child still needs for the themes to be few, essential and unified in themselves; what he or she especially asks is to be helped to linger over those themes through personal work. Therefore, it is very important that the adult not multiply the themes because this could result in a fragmentation.[4]

---

3. K. Harney and S. Harney, *Finding a Church You Can Love and Loving the Church You've Found* (Grand Rapids, MI: Zondervan, 2003), 99–100.

4. Cavalletti, *6 to 12 Years Old*, x.

The lesson plan for the class activities were six chapters from *Windows to Encounter: Believing is Living Series-I, Book IV*, a publication of India Sunday School Union. The lessons of Book IV entitled *God Our Security* are organized on the basis of the theme "How do we get the security we need?" Six chapters dealt with the story of Jesus: "God with Us," "The First Gift of Christmas," "God Leads God's Children," "God Knows Best," "Jesus Is Alive," and "Believing the Unbelievable."

The designated time of the various activities are given in the following table:

Table 2: The Schedule of the Weekly Class Activities

Activities	Time
Greetings and Refreshments	10 minutes (10–10:10)
Story-based Songs	15 minutes (10:10–10:25)
Storytelling	25 minutes (10:25–10:50)
Games	10 minutes (10:50–11:00)
Story-based Activities	40 minutes (11–11:40)
Discussion and Closure	15 minutes (11:40–11:55)
Departure	5 minutes (11:55–12:00)

The presentation of the story was in the following forms: Week 1: reading the story, Week 2: drama, Week 3: telling the story with puppets, Week 4: telling the story with visual tools, Week 5: telling the story, Week 6: drama. The research team decided the form of presentation during their second meeting on 1 April 2010 based on the plot, number of characters in the story, and the content of the lesson. The primary purpose of the variation is to generate interest in children.

A game followed the presentation of the story. The game was selected based on the story of each day. The next forty minutes was an activity time based on the story. The team members selected the activities for each day from the lesson plan during the weekly training. The last fifteen minutes was a time to review the memory verse, informal discussion, and gear up for the following week.

Assessing the Class Activities

During the twenty-five minute story-based activities, children were divided into three groups based on their age. Three team members facilitated the activities in the groups. The initial plan was to rotate three research assistants among the groups after two weeks. However, after the first week, the team members noted that importance of staying with the same group for six weeks for continuity and to build familiarity with children. The activities involved oral, written, and kinesthetic activities. The activities were selected from the lesson plan for each week. These activities provided an opportunity to listen to the voice of the children regarding how they connect biblical stories to their lives.

Observation

Observation was one of the methods employed in the current research. Graue and Walsh present observation as a continuum from detached to full participant observation.[5] This study followed the participant observation as the research team was present in the classroom during the six weeks. The researcher was available to assist but was also involved in telling the story, teaching the song, or in facilitating story-based activities. This gave the researcher ample opportunities to observe and write field notes.

After the class activities, the research team met together to share what they had observed and noticed. Research assistants recorded their observations and reflections which were collected at the end of May and June. Even with multiple observations, the researcher neither claims to be able to fully "enter the worlds of children" nor "see through their eyes."[6]

A challenge that participant observation brings is the inability to write field notes completely.[7] Video footage helped to compensate for this disadvantage. Graue and Walsh give some advantages and disadvantages of video recording. The advantages are that (1) it records the verbal and nonverbal communication of children, and (2) it can store the data for further

---

5. M. E. Graue and D. J. Walsh, *Studying Children in Context: Theories, Methods, and Ethics* (London: Sage, 1998), 106.

6. Gallagher, "Data Collection," 79.

7. Graue and Walsh, *Studying Children*, 107.

analysis and review.[8] Yet the disadvantages are as follows: (1) it can cause the researcher to be less attentive, (2) it can cause distraction to the researcher if he or she is not familiar with using a camera, and (3) it can distract the attention of children.[9] Instead of holding the camera, the video camera was mounted several feet away from the children. An audio recording was used as a backup device in case the video recording is not clear in any points.

Focus Group Interviews

Another method of data collection for the current research was the focus group interviews. Barbour prefers the term "focus group interview" to "focus group" or "group discussion."[10] This form of data collection has been used increasingly among children.[11] Darybyshire, MacDougall, and Schiller used focus group interviews to enable children "to discuss and articulate 'in their own words' their perceptions, understandings and experiences in relation to play, exercise, sport and physical activity."[12] Morgan, Gibbs, Maxwell, and Britten used focus group interviews with 7- to 11-year-old children to disclose their experience of living with asthma.[13] In the present research, focus group interviews are selected as a data collection method to complement the observation and the assessment of the classroom activities.

Morgan, Gibbs, Maxwell, and Britten have suggested four or five participants as an ideal group size for focus group interviews with younger children of 7- to 8-year-olds. They noted that larger focus group interviews with children will be noisy and transcription will be difficult. In smaller groups, discussion among participants will be reduced and the last minute dropout will affect the group size.[14] Even though Darbyshire, MacDougall,

---

8. Ibid., 117.

9. Ibid., 118.

10. R. Barbour, *Doing Focus Groups: The Sage Qualitative Research Kit*, vol. 4 (London: Sage, 2007), 2.

11. M. Morgan et al., "Hearing Children's Voices: Methodological Issues in Conducting Focus Groups with Children Aged 7–11 Years," *Qualitative Research* 2, no. 1 (2002): 5; P. Darbyshire, C. MacDougall and W. Schiller, "Multiple Methods in Qualitative Research with Children: More Insight or Just More?" *Qualitative Research* 5, no. 4 (2005): 420.

12. Darbyshire, MacDougall and Schiller, "Multiple Methods," 491.

13. Morgan et al., "Children's Voices," 5.

14. Ibid., 8.

and Schiller haven't mentioned the group size, they utilized seventeen focus groups with ninety boys and one hundred fourteen girls of 4- to 12-year-olds.[15]

Morgan, Gibbs, Maxwell, and Britten have noted the importance of gender in focus group interviews with children. In their research, 9- to 10-year-old children had mixed groups of boys and girls, and 11-year-old children had same gender focus group interviews.[16] In the current research, six focus group interviews were conducted during the month of June and July. All focus group interviews were same gender groups. Two focus group interviews were for 9-year-old children with four participants each. The other four were for 10- and 11-year-olds with the number of participants ranging from three to seven.

In this research, the class activities provided opportunities to hear from children as they related biblical stories with their lives. Yet, focus group interviews were the first opportunity in the research for children to directly express how biblical stories help in their spiritual formation. As the interview questions were directly related to the research topic, it also enabled the research team to hear directly from children about their opinions about biblical stories.

The initial plan was that the researcher would moderate all focus group interviews. Research assistants noted that their presence could help the children to feel at ease because of the familiarity they had developed with the research assistants. The researcher observed how children had developed a rapport with the research assistant who facilitated their group. For example, after writing her experience of God's care in her life, a girl showed it to her class facilitator and said, "Please do not show this to anyone." This and other incidents led to a change in the research procedure regarding focus group interviews. Subsequently, two researcher team members were the moderators of the focus group interviews and each age group had the assistant who facilitated their class as one of the moderators.

Refreshments were served during the focus group which helped children to feel at ease during the interview process. The research team

---

15. Darbyshire, MacDougall and Schiller, "Multiple Methods," 491.
16. Morgan et al., "Children's Voices," 8.

continually encouraged the children to munch on the refreshments. It was initially planned to have a break after half hour of focus group interviews as Morgan, Gibbs, Maxwell, & Britten have suggested to ensure the quality of response.[17] Yet in this research, the team members felt that a break can cause disruption to the flow of responses.

As the same group of children participated in the weekly two-hour classes for six weeks, they had an opportunity to relate to each other and overcome shyness. So the group will be similar to a "pre-existing group."[18] This group had the three characteristics prescribed by Hennessy and Heary: (1) A group of 20–25 children with the common experience of being together for six consecutive weeks and listening to stories of the Bible, and participating in songs, games, and activities. (2) This is to gather the subjective experience of children – to investigate children's perceptions of the role of biblical stories or to explore children's understanding of how stories help in their spiritual formation or how they explain the function/significance of the stories in their spiritual formation. (3) It was led by the researcher team as the moderators.[19]

Halkier observed the influence of the social interaction in the group dimension as the specific strengths of focus group interviews.[20] There are other advantages and disadvantages of conducting interviews in a group. Graue and Walsh noted the following advantages: (1) Children will feel more relaxed. (2) It enables the researcher to listen to the interaction among children.[21] It helps to gather the "multiple voice" of the participants, thus highlights the various "concerns and assumptions."[22] Group interviews will empower children to speak up as apprehension to voice their opinion to an adult can be less when compared to individual interviews.[23] Some

---

17. Ibid., 10.

18. Gallagher, "Data Collection," 76.

19. E. Hennessy and C. Heary, "Exploring Children's View through Focus Groups," in *Researching Children's Experience*, ed. S. Greene and D. Hogan (London: Sage, 2005), 237.

20. B. Halkier, "Focus Groups as Social Enactments: Integrating Interaction and Content in the Analysis of Focus Group Data," *Qualitative Research* 10, no. 1 (2010): 72.

21. Graue and Walsh, *Studying Children*, 114.

22. Barbour, *Doing Focus Groups*, 33.

23. M. Freeman and S. Mathison, *Researching Children's Experiences* (New York: Guilford, 2009), 88.

disadvantages are also noted: (1) Less attention on the individual child, (2) Some children may dominate the discussion which may silence the quiet children, and (3) The group can easily drift from the topic of discussion.[24] Prior knowledge of these disadvantages helped the research team to plan the focus groups. The team was able to identify the vocal children and the silent children and encouraged the quiet ones to voice their opinion.

One concern about the focus group was whether children would be tense to respond to the interview questions. So the initial plan was to switch to personal interviews if the research team discerned that the focus group interviews were not effective with this group. Yet, the weekly class enabled the team to see how children responded to discussion questions. Children even voiced their doubts and gave comments during the class section, which were evidences that the focus group interviews were an effective method of data collection with this sample.

The following instructions were given to the children at the beginning of the focus group interviews: "When question are being asked, think about the question and what you want to answer. You do not have to give the answer quickly. Everyone will get a chance to respond. Try not to repeat what you hear; rather, think and say what is in your heart. We are here to study, so you are the teachers and we are the students." One child said he was too tense about this activity as he thought it was a review of what they have learned in the past six weeks. The researcher assured that this was not a review session or a question-answer session as they have seen in schools, but rather, it was a time to hear from them what they have in their hearts. Then the boy said that he was not tense anymore. Each focus group interviews began and ended with a prayer. Children prayed at the beginning and a moderator at the end.

Moderators repeated the answers and/or paraphrased responses of children. This not only helped in audio recording but also enabled the moderators to assure that they clearly understood what was being communicated. Also it gave an opportunity to the children to correct the moderators when the latter had misunderstood children's words. Another technique that was used was to ask clarification questions. This helped to clarify various

---

24. Gallagher, "Data Collection," 77.

concepts that were conveyed. Moderators ensured that every child got an opportunity to speak. They were not forced to answer but gently encouraged to respond by rephrasing the question: "So now what does . . . (name of the child) think of . . . (say the question)?" Or "what would you like to say about this?" If a child showed any body movement like movement of lips, moving forward, that child was given an opportunity to respond. Questions were repeated when the chance was given to another child. This helped the children to hear the question many times and helped the researcher to ensure that children comprehended the question clearly. Another technique that was used was to return to a previous question after asking other questions to encourage those who haven't responded to that question and to encourage children to speak, if they wanted to. This helped to ensure that enough time was given to each questions and they could share whatever they wanted to say about an issue.

Member Checking

Member checking is aimed to bring accuracy in research as participants can correct errors and present new facts or perceptions which they might have been missed in the first round of focus group interviews.[25] Recently, member checking has been used in research with children. Bishop used member checking with 9- to 18-year-old children and young people in his study to understand their perspectives about the experience of a pediatric hospital environment and its relationship to their feeling of well-being. He used member checking to discuss the preliminary findings of his research with selected group of six participants. This helped him to draw final conclusions.[26]

Member checking can be done informally and formally. Informal member checking happens during data collection as moderators ask follow-up questions and paraphrased children's responses to accurately comprehend the meanings of their responses. Formal member checking can be done

---

25. M. D. Gall, J. P. Gall and W. R. Borg, *Educational Research: An Introduction*, 7th ed. ([n.p.]: Pearson, 2003), 464.

26. K. G. Bishop, "From Their Perspectives: Children and Young People's Experience of a Pediatric Hospital Environment and Its Relationship to Their Feeling of Well-Being," PhD diss., (The University of Sydney, 2008).

after the complete analysis of data.[27] Formal member checking enables the researcher to see if the interpretations reveal the realities of the participants' perspectives, and thus is an opportunity to minimize distortion of data. It is a means for feedback or correction and for verification of perspectives and interpretation. Thus, member checking can provide comprehensiveness to the research and enhance credibility and validity of the research.[28]

This is another form of triangulation as it helps in developing authenticity or credibility of interpretations and can shed light on analyses.[29] In the current research, member-check was done informally and formally. Informal member checking was done by follow-up questions and paraphrasing and repeating the responses of children during the focus group interviews. In the month of July, there was a second round of focus group interviews with five same gender groups of four children in each group. The research team sensed the need of further clarification after the first focus group interviews. This was an opportunity to hear children's favorite biblical story and the reason why they like the story the most.

After the completion of the analysis of data, there was an opportunity for formal member checking with six participants. However, there are certain issues to consider in member checking which can go against the intention of obtaining credibility: (1) Participants may not express their disagreement with the researcher out of politeness or out of the belief that the researcher knows better than them, (2) Participants may have a common understanding or have the intention to cover up.[30] To overcome this limitation the researcher paraphrased the research report not only to children but also to the research assistants and to selected students and faculty of Faith Theological Seminary.

Documentation of Data

The research team took field notes to record how children verbally and non-verbally responded to stories they heard. Flick suggested keeping a

---

27. D. F. Polit and C. T. Beck, *Essentials of Nursing Research: Appraising Evidence for Nursing Practice,* 7th ed. (Philadelphia, PA: Lippincott Williams & Wilkins, 2009), 499.

28. Ibid., 545.

29. P. A. Duff, *Case Study Research in Applied Linguistics* (New York: Taylor & Francis, 2008), 171.

30. Polit and Beck, *Essentials,* 499.

research dairy to note the details of the research.[31] In this research, all four research team members kept a personal journal to record their reflection on the research process. It involved the process of approaching the field, challenges and experiences in the research process and in using the research methods. The researcher kept an audit trail which helped to document any change in research procedures. Each week team members shared their experiences with the researcher after the class, and these conversations were audio taped and later transcribed. The partnership among research team members in observing children, keeping research diary, and in facilitating the class sessions provided ample opportunity for triangulation during data collection. Audio and video recording of the class activities and focus group interviews were other means to record the data.

Revisions of the Research Procedures

During the research, the research team made certain changes from the original research plan. Even though these are mentioned in the previous sections, they are listed here as follows for clarity: (1) The number of research participants: the number of children was increased from twenty-five to twenty-nine in order to compensate for possible absentees. All children did not participate in the weekly activities or member checking. The minimum number of participants for class activities was twenty-five and the maximum was twenty-nine. (2) Another change was in terms of the facilitators of the class. The initial plan was that the three research assistants would take turns to facilitate the three classes for 9-, 10-, and 11-year-olds. Yet the team felt the need of the same assistant facilitating the same age group for the six weeks of class activities in order to develop trust, rapport, and familiarity between children and the team. (3) There was a change in the number of moderators for the focus group interviews. It was planned that the researcher would moderate for all focus groups. The team felt that familiarity and trust is necessary for children to share their innermost thoughts. Thus the research assistant who facilitated the class activity of a particular age group of children was one of the two moderators of their focus group. (4) The initial plan was to have a break after the first half hour of the focus group interviews, but the team members felt that

---

31. U. Flick, *An Introduction to Qualitative Research* (London: Sage, 2006), 287.

a break can cause disruption to the flow of responses of the children. So the focus group lasted one hour without any break. Yet, refreshments were served during the focus groups to help children to feel at ease. (5) Another change was to gather further information regarding children's favorite biblical story and the reason why the story is their favorite. After the two weeks of focus group interviews, the research team gathered children in five same gender groups for the purpose. (6) Selected members and students of Faith Theological Seminary were consulted to review the findings of the research. Consultation with research assistants, faculty members, and seminary students were conducted after data analysis. The four faculty members were consulted separately. Seminary students were gathered in two groups to discuss the findings with them. The purposes of the consultation were the following: to review the categories and the descriptions of each of the categories; to hear alternative interpretations for children' responses; to derive implications of the findings for the context; and to shed light on contextual issues that could possibly influence children's perceptions on the topic of research.

Research Hypothesis

Various religious educators have suggested the important role of stories in the spiritual formation of children.[32] A basic hypothesis is being tested in this qualitative research project. In operational terms, it can be stated as follows: Children can know, understand and explain the role of various biblical stories to develop their faith and to deepen their relationship with Jesus Christ, through which they become more like Jesus in their daily lives. A maturing faith will be evident in their relationship with God, self, and others.

---

32. See for example, Westerhoff, *Will Our Children*; Fowler, *Stages of Faith*, *Becoming Adult*, and "Faith Development"; Miller-McLemore, *In the Midst of Chaos*; Yust, *Real Kids*, Sasso, "When Your Children Ask," "Tell me a Story," "Role of Narratives."

Operational Definitions

Even though definitions of key terms are included in the first chapter, the following section deals with the meaning of certain terms in the context of the proposed research.

Children

The UN considers every human being under the age of eighteen as children, unless defined otherwise by a country. In India, boys and girls below age 14 are considered to be children even though social scientists consider girls up to the age of 18 to19 as children. In this research, children denote 9- to 11-year-old boys and girls.

Narratives/Stories

Narratives/Stories can be biblical and real, or fictional. For this research, the stories used were only stories in the Bible. This is not to neglect the historicity the Bible. The term "narratives" and "stories" are used interchangeably. The term "stories" in this research mean stories in the Bible unless otherwise stated.

Spiritual Formation

Spiritual formation is the process of growing in maturing faith and a deepening relationship with Jesus which will be reflected in their beliefs, values, and life style. I-Thou will be evident in I-self, I-other, and I-world. The Holy Spirit and the faith community have a role in how children understand and respond to this relationship.

Christian

The term "Christian" means a follower of Christ. Even though they belong to many denominations which vary in their beliefs and practices, they believe in the Bible and the use of the Bible in teaching children. For the purpose of this research, out of various Christian denominations in the locality, the sample was selected from Pentecostal churches. These denominations are selected because they use the stories of the Bible in Sunday schools and emphasize a relationship with Christ through the born-again experience. As the focus of the research is children's perceptions about the role of biblical stories in their spiritual formation, knowing the stories is an important factor. The term Pentecostal in this article does not only imply classical Pentecostals but also those churches which believe in the born-again experience, baptism of water and Spirit, and the importance of living by the Word, but differ in certain practices from the former like wearing jewellery, empowering lay leaders for ministry, small group gathering, etc. Here five churches were part of various classical Pentecostal churches and the other two are from the second category.

Perception

Perception means being aware of something. In the current research, investigating children's "perceptions" of the role of stories is to explore children's understanding of how biblical narratives help in their spiritual formation. How do they explain the function of the stories in their spiritual formation, or according to children what is the significance of stories in their spiritual formation?ABus it is an attempt to listen and hear what children have to express through verbal, written and non-verbal clues about the relation between the stories and their spiritual formation.

Informed Consent

Gaining access is an important ethical principle while working with children. First, gatekeepers are to give permission to enter into the field. Then informed consent is to be collected from parents and children. Barker and Weller observed that researchers need to be prepared to address any issues that gatekeepers may raise in negotiating access to research with children.[33] In the current research, the Biola University's Protection of Human Rights in Research Committee (PHRRC) guidelines were followed in gaining access and obtaining informed consent. This is to protect the researcher and the participants from various risks involved in research.

The PHRRC committee of Biola University reviewed the proposal for this research to ensure that possible risks were appropriately addressed in this research. Social position of children is that they are minors which implies that they are often required to comply and do what adults ask them

---

33. J. Barker and S. Weller, "Never Work with Children?: The Geography of Methodological Issues in Research with Children," *Qualitative Research* 3, no. 2 (2003): 212.

to do. They are also more open to exploitation than adults[34] and there is a power imbalance in the adult-child relationship.[35] Thus, children are a vulnerable population and they cannot freely give informed consent. Thus, there were various concerns that needed attention in this research: the protection of rights to privacy, the need for informed consent, protection of confidentiality of data, and protection against physical, psychological, spiritual, social, or legal risks.

Children were recruited for the research from various churches. Thus the primary gatekeepers in this research were pastors of churches. The researcher approached pastors in and around Adoor, Kerala, India with a handout explaining the purpose and procedures of the research and requirements for the potential participants. Out of nine pastors approached, seven cordially gave their consent. In many churches, pastors announced some details of the research during the Sunday worship. The researcher then approached parents with a handout. Except for two churches, the researcher did home visits to meet parents and children. In the two churches, the researcher met the parents and children in the respective churches. This gave an opportunity to get to know the participants, and the parents seemed to relax as they raise their queries and concerns. Parents warmly welcomed the research, as they were extremely happy to send their children to any spiritual activities.

After obtaining the informed consent from parents, the researcher approached children with another handout. Children heartily expressed their desire to be part of the research. Since the child's participation was voluntary, signed informed consents were obtained from these parents and children. Appendix A contains the handout for pastors and parents and Appendix B includes the handout for children. The informed consent is in Appendix D.

The question arises whether children are capable to give an informed consent. Hill unveiled the misconception that young children are incompetent to assent. Younger children need a more careful explanation about

---

34. M. Gallagher, "Ethics," in *Researching with Children and Young People: Research Design, Methods, and Analysis*, eds. E. K. M. Tisdall, J. M. Davis, and M. Gallagher (Los Angeles, CA: Sage, 2009), 14.

35. Barker and Weller, "Never Work," 210.

the research and research procedure.[36] Hill noted the importance of obtaining informed consent from children as it allows children to deny or give consent. Also it provides a sense of control for them which can contribute to their well-being.[37]

In the current research, informed consent gave children the freedom to refuse to discuss any matters that would cause discomfort or something that they felt was an invasion of privacy. The following matters were made clear to parents and children: (1) Children could choose not to answer any question if they find it embarrassing or offensive. (2) They could refuse to participate or express their displeasure in continuing participation in the research. (3) They could quit their participation at any time during the research, even though they were requested to participate in all three forms of data collection. (4) The contact information of the researcher was provided to pastors and parents to express their concerns and queries with respect to any aspect of the research. (5) The promised gift was to be given to children even if they could not participate in various research activities.

Sample Selection Procedures

The population was 9- to 11-year-old children who attend Pentecostal/Charismatic churches along with their parents and who have the opportunity to know biblical stories either in home or in church in any town in Kerala, India. The original plan was to limit the sample to twenty-five children. Yet, twenty-nine children were enrolled to cover for the possible absentees in various data collection activities. The minimum number that participated in various data collection except for member checking was twenty-five and the maximum was twenty-nine.

Criteria for the selection of a congregation were not only their denominational background but also proximity to the town of Adoor, Kerala, India. The selection of the purposeful sample of twenty-nine 9- to11-year-old children had the following criteria:

---

36. M. Hill, "Ethical Considerations in Researching Children's Experience," in *Researching Children's Experience*, eds. S. Greene and D. Hogan (London: Sage, 2005), 68.

37. Ibid.

1) Those who have been part of Pentecostal churches for at least the last two years
2) Those who regularly attend worship and other weekly meetings along with at least one of their parents
3) Those who regularly (at least three times a month) attend Sunday schools
4) Those who have the opportunity to listen to the stories at home and church

Seven out of nine pastors gave consent to include children from their churches. With their verbal consent, the researcher approached 9- to11-year-old children and their parents with handouts. The sample represented both genders in equal proportion of 9-, 10-, and 11-year old children. A minimum of two children and a maximum of eight children were recruited from each congregation. The sample represented a semi-urban neighborhood and children from different socio-economic backgrounds.

All participants received a Good News Bible, even if they could not come for all the research activities. This gift was mentioned in handouts circulated among pastors, parents and children.

Seeking Permission from the Seminary Authorities

The researcher contacted the concerned authorities of the seminary for using the conference room in the seminary for the class activities, focus group interviews, and member checking. Permission was granted to use the conference room for research activities and the adjacent room for refreshments.

Recruiting and Training the Research Assistants

The research team consisted of four members including the researcher: two male and two female. The basic criteria for the team members are as follows: (1) Residing in or around the town of Adoor, Kerala, India; (2) prior experience in working with children; and (3) either pursuing seminary education or having a seminary degree.

Three prospective team members were contacted on 18 March 2010. The following topics were discussed: (1) the significance of the topic, (2) the biblical significance of stories and spiritual formation, (3) ethical considerations in researching with children, (4) expectations and requirements, (5) research procedures, and lastly, (6) lesson plans and the teacher's handbook *God Our Security* were presented to them. Subsequently, responsibilities of the team members and a schedule for training were determined. The research procedures, requirements, and expectations are explained the handout for research assistants in Appendix C.

Beginning with 1 April 2010 there was a series of training for research assistants. One day of the week, team members gathered to evaluate the preceding class activity and to plan for the following class activity. The training on these days focused on following topics: research procedures, research questions, key terms, assumptions and delimitation of the research, keeping a research diary, data analysis, and ethics and challenges of researching with children.

Team members helped in organizing and administering the data collection, facilitating class activities, focus group interviews and member checking, and in analyzing verbal and non-verbal data. They helped in selecting participating churches for the research. Their activities during April and May were counted as part of their summer internship requirement at the seminary.

Pilot Study

The pilot study was conducted on 24 April 2010. The purpose of the pilot study was twofold: to gain expertise in facilitating class activity with children and observation, and to see how children view the relationship between biblical stories and their spiritual formation. The class activities were videotaped and transcribed. The following section discusses the pilot study which was communicated to the dissertation committee on the day of proposal defense.

Table 3 shows the demographic details of the students with respect to age and gender. Twenty-eight children from seven churches in and around the town of Adoor, Kerala, India participated in the pilot study.

Table 3: The Demographic Details of Children in the Pilot Study

Age	Male	Female	Total
9	4	5	9
10	6	6	12
11	4	3	7
Total	14	14	28

As it was the first day, the initial twenty minutes were used to get to know each other. This was important to develop trust among children and between children and the research team. Children were enthusiastic in learning the new song. Even before they were asked to write the song, 11-year-old children wrote the song in their notebooks. During the storytime, 10- and 11-year-old children leaned forward with hands on their chin and kept eye contact with the research assistant who shared the story. They answered all the review questions which show that either they had listened to the story or they already knew the story. This was evident when children answered the review questions. The next activity was the game which was to tell a word or a phrase of the memory verse by passing a piece of yarn. They enthusiastically learned the memory verse in less than ten minutes. They giggled and laughed as they passed the yarn and also helped each other to tell their phrase of the verse.

The 9- and 10-year-old boys and girls actively participated in verbal and written activities. The 11-year-old girls were more vocal than boys. But boys actively participated in the writing activity. The group activities were audio taped with an individual audio recorder for each table. Video recording was focused to each table for ten minutes.

The research team gathered in the afternoon to discuss the data. The researcher transcribed these observations and compared them with what she observed and heard. The recording was transcribed giving priority to those conversions in relation to the research questions and class activities.

The first group activity was group discussion.[38] The questions discussed were not review questions, but application level questions. Research assistants did not notice rapid responses or speedy answers from some children. This shows children's engagement with the story in the conceptual level of thinking. Research assistants noted that some children repeated the ideas expressed by other children.

One question discussed was, "How was the Son of God's coming into the world different from the way important visitors come into your town?" Children's responses were as follows: "When politicians come, the roads are cleaned, and there are flowers, yet when Jesus came there was none of this." "Jesus came alone, cabinet ministers come with other people, ministers come in cars, but when Jesus came trumpet was blown." "Ministers cannot remove sin or sickness; we can only tell them about our sickness. They cannot do anything for it." "There will be a lot of people to see ministers with flags, yet there were only a few people to see Jesus." And, "Jesus came to save us from sin, but ministers come only to preach."

Some children are happy that Jesus was born as a baby. Others would like for Jesus to be born as a king, or come into the world as an older person so that others could see and recognize him. Of note is one 9-year-old boy's conversation with the research assistant which shows children think beyond mere literal understanding of the text to connect the story to other biblical stories. Also he may be connecting the story of Jesus with the reality of how parents bring up their children:

Boy:	As a baby can Jesus know that we commit sins?
Research assistant:	As a baby he did not know.
Boy:	But then how did he die for our sins?
Research assistant:	When he grew up.
Boy:	So did he grow up in this earth?
Research assistant:	Yes, he grew up in this earth.

---

38. See India Sunday School Union, *God Our Security: How Do We Get the Security We Need?*, Windows to Encounter: Believing Is Living Series, 4 (Konnor, India: India Sunday School Union, 1998), 77.

Boy:	So did Joseph and Mary live with Jesus?
Research assistant:	Yes, they were with Jesus when he grew up.

The concept of sin was discussed by all the age groups. This may be because the churches that these children attend emphasize the born-again experience by asking forgiveness for their sins and asking Jesus to be Lord of their lives.

The second activity, activity F[39] was to write a story imagining that they were one of the animals in the stable on the night of Jesus' birth. The stories of 10- and 11-year-old children revealed their familiarity with the infant narrative. The 10- and 11-year-olds included the visit of the wise men in their stories. The visit of the wise men was not part of the story of the day. The group of 9- and 10-year-old children discussed their story with children sitting next to them. But 11-year-old children completed their story without any help from others.

Children's stories showed awareness-sensing, mystery-sensing, and value-sensing.[40] An 11-year-old girl wrote: "The baby was beautiful." "Mary and Joseph were happy as they sat near the baby." Three 11-year-old boys wrote as follows: "His parents were very happy after the shepherds' visit and the parents kissed Jesus." "Shepherds returned with joy and Mary and Joseph were very happy after the shepherds' visit and the parents kissed Jesus." "Shepherds returned with joy and Mary and Joseph were filled with joy."

A 10-year-old boy wrote "I overheard the conversation between the parents that let us place the baby on some hay. I saw an angel. It was the first time that I have seen such things." Two other 10-year-old girls wrote, "Then all the animals in the stable were quiet as the baby slept." "There was brightness on his face." "He was so beautiful."

The 9-year-old boys included these lines in the story: "I woke up when I heard the cry of the baby." Two other boys wrote, "I was eating grass, Jesus looked at me, I stop eating grass, he is a great man, I went to Jesus." Others penned as follows: "I was asleep. I saw Jesus, he is a great man, I went to him, he is a sweet baby." "I was drinking water, I heard Jesus crying, I

---

39. Ibid., 78.
40. Hay and Nye, *Spirit of the Child*.

stopped drinking water because Jesus came. I saw Jesus, he is a great man." Stories of this age group did not have any mention of wise men's visit or any other part of the infant narrative.

Summary

The pilot study was in fact an opportunity to listen and hear what children have to express through verbal, written and non-verbal clues about the story of the birth of Jesus. Their prior knowledge of the infant narrative was evident in the stories they wrote. The comparison they made between the coming of Jesus and a politician's arrival shows that they observe their surroundings and can connect the Bible stories with their life situations. They have some understanding of the concept of sin and they know Jesus can remove sins. The 9-year-old boy's conversation shows that he can connect this story with other biblical stories and realties of life. What the pilot study revealed is just the beginning of the exploration into children's perceptions.

Developing an Interview Protocol

Semi-structured interview was the pattern followed in the focus group. Freeman and Mathison encourage researchers to take note of the differences in children while conducting group interviews.[41] The differences in children due to age, inexperience, language ability, and attention span may result in diverse interactive styles during an interview.[42]

Gender was a factor that determines the response of children in the Indian context. The societal expectation of a girl child in rural and suburban India is quite different compared to a boy child. In India, patriarchal elements are still evident, even though it is changing in cities. The social condition of a girl child is that she has lower status in India and "enjoys fewer rights, opportunities and benefits of childhood as compared to the boy-child."[43] A boy child is preferred to a girl child as the notion is that the male child is to take care of his aged parents. Girls are thought of as the person who will leave their parent's home and join their husband's home

---

41. Freeman and Mathison, *Researching Children's Experiences*, 92.
42. Ibid.
43. Thukral, Ali and Mathur, "Background & Perspective."

after marriage. They are expected to be quiet, submissive, and patient "like mother earth." In rural India, many parents are eager to find a suitable bridegroom for their daughters after basic education while the male child is expected to study and get a job and then marry. Such expectations can make girls shy compared to boys. Being aware of this societal expectation, girls were encouraged to share their insights during focus group interviews and member checking. The focus groups for 10- and 11-year-old children and member checking were same gender groups so that girls could share their thoughts with less inhibition.

A variety of concerns and suggestions have been noted in interviewing children about spirituality. (1) Ask children what are the words they use to represent God, (2) repeat or paraphrase children's responses in interviews to enable children to raise deeper issues, (3) children's difficulty to verbally share their spiritual experiences, (4) rapid response and speedy answers of children is "antithetical to the nature of spirituality," (5) there is a possibility of giving memorized answers.[44] The researcher addressed these concerns using adapting the techniques suggested by Boyatzis and Newman: (1) Children were given some time to think and reflect on the question before they responded. (2) The research team repeated and paraphrased children's responses to help children reflect on their responses and invite deeper ideas from children. (3) Multiple responses were invited from children to enable evaluation of children's thinking on various issues.[45] (4) All children were given an opportunity to respond.

Freeman and Mathison propose the use of hypothetical questions in interviews.[46] This is to take children's attention from being concerned about giving the right answer. Thus the interview can be turned into a "pretend play" which they are familiar with and may be more competent than

---

44. C. J. Boyatzis and B. T. Newman, "How Shall We Study Children's Spirituality?" in *Children's Spirituality: Christian Perspectives, Research, and Applications*, ed. D. Ratcliff (Eugene, OR: Cascade, 2004), 169–171.

45. Ibid., 170.

46. Freeman and Mathison, *Researching Children's Experiences*, 115.

participating in an interview.[47] Allen used fewer personal questions at the beginning of the interview and then asked more personal questions later.[48]

The focus group interviews with children were centered on the following topics: Sources of stories, storytellers, others to whom they share stories, situations in which they remember stories, the reasons for enjoying stories, issues they remember from stories, reasons why others tell stories to them, and their interest in sharing stories.

The interview protocol had the following questions:
1) Where do children hear stories? What are the types of stories they hear? Why do others tell stories to children?
2) Where have you heard stories? What are the kinds of stories you have heard? Who has shared stories with you?
3) What are the kinds of stories you like? Why do you like those stories?
4) Why do you think others tell the stories of the Bible to you?
5) Tell some of the biblical stories you remember.
6) Suppose there are some children who have never heard stories about Jesus or God or any biblical stories. What will they do when they feel like doing bad things? When they feel sad? When they feel afraid? How will they treat other boys and girls, or teachers?
7) What makes you remember biblical stories? What are some situations that make you remember these stories? Or when do you remember these stories?
8) What are the things that you know about God because you know these stories?
9) What are some things that you know about yourself because you know these stories?
10) When you recall biblical stories, what happens in you? Does knowing these stories influence your life? If so how?
11) Do you have any questions to ask me?

---

47. Ibid.

48. C. A. Allen, "A Qualitative Study Exploring the Similarities and Differences of the Spirituality of Children in Intergenerational and Non-Intergenerational Christian Contexts," unpublished PhD diss., (Biola University, 2002), 229.

Data Analysis Procedure

The two phases in qualitative research is to collect the data and to analyze the data to discover trends and patterns.[49] Unlike quantitative research, data analysis happens simultaneously with the data collection and the researcher repeats this cycle of data collection and data analysis.[50] In contrast to quantitative research, words are the data in qualitative research. The following discussion considers certain phases involved in data analysis: review of the data, transcription, coding and developing categories, and connecting categories to identify themes.

Review the Data

The first step towards analysis of the data was to review the data soon after the data was collected.[51] This was an opportunity to keep research diaries which noted challenges and prospects of the research process of each day. This was generated with the help of the team's field notes. The researcher read the field notes of observation of the class activities and reviewed the written activities of the children's story-based activities with the research questions primarily in mind. Research assistants' journals were reviewed during this process. The video recording was watched within 24 hours of the recording. The research team members together reviewed the data on the afternoon of the day of class activities. Team members documented the experiences of focus group interviews and these were also used during data analysis.

The data was directly analyzed after transcription. This helped to note key quotations or video segments for later use. Flick presents the collection of data and interpretation as an interwoven procedure rather than a linear process where data is first collected and then interpreted.[52] Review of data helped the researcher to locate possible trends and patterns in the data and to carefully observe this in the following weeks.

---

49. D. Ratcliff, "Qualitative Data Analysis and the Transforming Moment," *Transformation: An International Journal of Holistic Mission Studies* 25, no. 2 & 3 (2008): 120.

50. Ibid.

51. Ibid., 122.

52. Flick, *Qualitative Research*, 296.

Transcription

The researcher transcribed the data obtained from observation, classroom activities, focus groups and member checking. Flick presents transcription as a "necessary step" towards data interpretation.[53] Halkier noted that the transcription of focus group data can miss out on the interaction among the participants. Thus it is significant to include not only verbal data but also other sounds, gestures, and body language in the written text.[54] He has noted non-verbal expression in the following ways: [ ]: overlaps in speech; ( ): incomprehensible speech; . . . : pauses less than five seconds; and [pause]: pauses more than five seconds.[55]

While transcribing audio recording, exact transcription was a priority, but importance was given only for items that were directly related to the research question. Other peripheral issues were not transcribed exactly word for word. Thus time which was consumed in attaining precision in transcribing every spoken word could be better invested in the interpretation of the data.[56]

Coding Data and Developing Categories

An important step towards interpretation of the data is to generate the unit of analysis and determine the categories.[57] Flick presents two opposite goals in interpretation: Placing texts in context which leads to elaboration of written text and paraphrasing, summarizing, or categorizing which reduces the length of the text.[58] This research followed line-by-line open coding as suggested by Flick.[59] This helped the researcher to have deeper understanding of the text and avoid placing any bias and prejudice to the text.

The next step was to categorize the code by grouping relevant themes with research questions in mind.[60] Flick presents certain basic questions to readdress the text in order to develop categories: "What is the issue here?"

---

53. Ibid., 288.
54. Halkier, "Focus Groups," 75.
55. Ibid., 76.
56. Flick, *Qualitative Research*, 290.
57. Ratcliff, "Qualitative Data Analysis," 122.
58. Flick, *Qualitative Research*, 296.
59. Ibid., 298.
60. Ibid., 299.

"Which aspects of the phenomenon are mentioned or not mentioned?" Which persons are involved?" and "What are their roles?" "Which reasons are given or reconstructed?" "What is the intention in mentioning the reason?"[61] This was the pattern followed in the data analysis of the proposed research.

Ratcliff noted the importance of defining the categories in a mutually exclusive and exhaustive manner so that other categories can be identified.[62] He also recommended keeping a detailed record of revisions made in categories and in the definitions of categories.[63] In the current research, answers of each question in the interview protocol were analyzed in order to develop categories. Referring to the previous research studies and journals was a crucial step in this process. This process helped in bracketing out the researcher's experience and expectations from influencing the development of categories. After the categories were defined, consultation with research assistants, selected faculty and students of Faith Theological Seminary was another opportunity to verify the soundness of the categories.

Darbyshire, MacDougall, and Schiller noted that playing the role of "devil's advocate and qualitative-research skeptic" is necessary to avoid premature closure during interpretation of data. The following questions can challenge the thought patterns while analyzing data: "So what?" "Where's the evidence for that?" "What do you mean by 'interesting?'" "What else could this mean?" and "How exactly do these ideas relate?"[64] The researcher considered these questions during data analysis. This enabled the researcher to attend to biases and expectations from infiltrating the interpretation.

Connecting Categories to Identifying Themes

Once subcategories were identified, through inductive and deductive thinking the relationship between categories and subcategories was identified.[65] Data was checked again for new categories until theoretical saturation was

---

61. Ibid., 300.
62. Ratcliff, "Qualitative Data Analysis," 124.
63. Ibid.
64. Darbyshire, MacDougall and Schiller, "Multiple Methods," 428.
65. Flick, *Qualitative Research*, 302.

obtained. This helped in generating themes which represent some causation or relationships.[66]

Identified categories and themes were compared with the dimensions of relational consciousness in Hay and Nye's research with children: I-Thou, I-self, I-other, and I-world. Further attempt was made to discover other significant insights that challenge or go beyond the model of Hay and Nye.[67]

Children as Research Participants: Challenges and Response

The social position of children as minors implies that they are often required to comply and do what adults ask them to do. They are also more open to exploitation than adults.[68] Attending to certain ethical issues creates a children-centered approach, which is vital in developing a highly sensitive and unique research encounter with children.[69] This is because of the increasing awareness among researchers that children are not "simply passive objects" yet "competent social actors that make sense of and actively contribute to their environment."[70]

In the current research, children are considered to be vulnerable not only because of their social position but also as they are observed during the class activities in an artificial setting – the seminary. This requires considering various issues related to ethics of research: children's stand about the topic, data collection, unfamiliarity with the research team, analysis and dissemination, participation and the balance of power, spaces of research, listening to children, children's inability to verbalize the experience of transcendence, and objectivity. Informed consent is part of ethics in research with children, which was discussed in a previous section.

Children's Stand about the Topic

Here the issue considered was that whether children will view this topic of research positively. One of the criteria of sample selection was to select

---

66. Ratcliff, "Qualitative Data Analysis," 126.
67. Hay and Nye, *Spirit of the Child*.
68. Gallagher, *Researching with Children*, 14.
69. Barker and Weller, "Never Work," 222.
70. Ibid., 207.

children who have the opportunity to listen to biblical stories at church and home. This was to ensure that they are exposed to discussing spiritual issues based on the Bible at home and church and such topics are not novel topics for them. Then there is a greater possibility for children to view this topic positively. Further consent was not only collected from pastors and parents but also from children. This is to ensue that only those children who view this topic positively participated in the research.

Data Collection

There needs to be flexibility and creativity not only in the relationship between researcher and children but also in the data collection process.[71] In the interview process, suggested characteristics of the relationship between the researcher and children are as follows: rapport, candor, trust, and authenticity.[72] Familiarity with the researcher also helps children to reveal intimate spiritual matters. In this research, all four research team members participated in at least five weeks of class activities in order to generate familiarity, rapport, and trust with the children.

Besides, all children may not enjoy all activities of the data collection. The following measures enabled the researcher to ensure voluntary participation of children in the current research: (1) The gatekeepers such as pastors and parents had an opportunity to evaluate the research procedures before they allowed children to participate in the research. (2) Obtaining written informed consent from children was used as an opportunity to openly share the purpose of the research and activities involved in the data collection. (3) The consent was sought from children after discussing the details of the research with the children, using a handout. (4) Thus participation of children was voluntary even if parents had given the consent. (5) Any child had the freedom to discontinue or refuse to participate in any activity. They could choose not to answer any questions that they found embarrassing or offensive.

In this research, no children were discontinued from data collection even though some were absent on some of the days of data collection. Their enthusiasm to participate in data collection was noticed by the research

---

71. Darbyshire, MacDougall and Schiller, "Multiple Methods," 428.
72. Boyatzis and Newman, "Children's Spirituality," 170.

team. On the last day of class activities and on the last day of focus groups many children asked, "When should we come again?" and "Will you have similar research next year?" Parents were willing to send children during the next summer vacation for similar activities.

Unfamiliarity with the Research Team and Other Participants

The setting of the research was unfamiliar to some children. As they are part of different churches they may be unfamiliar to other research participants and the research team. This can be overcome to an extent as there are other opportunities for children in the locality to know each other through local schools, VBS, and inter-church activities like seminars and camps. As the seminary has been the venue for VBS since 1985 and a one-week convention site since 1970, some children were familiar with the setting.

To overcome the unfamiliarity to other research participants, a minimum of two and a maximum of eight children were recruited from each participating congregation. During the two-hour classroom activity, a less-structured interaction was planned at the beginning and the end of the classroom session to develop rapport among children and team members. Also group games and group activities were organized to build a climate of rapport and put each child at ease.

Participation and the Balance of Power

Focus group interviews have the challenge of power imbalance in terms of directing and controlling the group and creating a conducive environment where the participants openly share their insights.[73] The power imbalance in the adult-child relationship is also noted by Barker and Weller.[74] When children are the participants, there is an added challenge to overcome the notion that adults are the authority figures and respond accordingly.[75] Boyatzis and Newman noted that perceiving children as teachers and researchers as learners can create a collaborative climate.[76] This requires a

---

73. Morgan et al., "Children's Voices," 9.
74. Barker and Weller, "Never Work," 210.
75. Morgan et al., "Children's Voices," 9.
76. Boyatzis and Newman, "Children's Spirituality," 170.

redefinition of relationships and an atmosphere that encourages spontaneous discussion.

The researcher was not involved in any of the following class activities: teaching songs, storytelling, and story-based activities. The researcher's role during the six weeks of class activities was to assist the three research assistants. This was to avoid creating an identity of authority figure.

Compared to individual interviews, focus group interviews can increase children's comfort level as they are in the company of their friends. This may also develop "interactive synergy" thus generating deep insights.[77] The researcher purposely reminded herself about the need of creating a collaborative climate during the research process. Familiarity with the research team members generated spontaneity from the children. The researcher was aware of the fact that even familiarity may not completely negate the power imbalance that is between any adult and child, even though it can minimize it.

Spaces of Research

Barker and Weller noted that researchers are to "reflexively analyze how the spaces of research" can possibly impact the research processes and the data.[78] With respect to the classroom activity of this research, the six weeks of classes were planned to bring familiarity in children to the research site. The same room that was used for the classroom activities was used for the focus groups to create familiarity. This familiarity of the space can also reduce the power imbalance between the researcher and children. The seating arrangement for the various methods of data collection addressed this challenge by portraying that the research team was not in charge of the discussion. To promote equality, the same age children sat in a circle around a table with the research assistant for the classroom. Children sat in a semicircle for focus group interviews and member checking.

Listening to Children

Barker and Weller noted the non-homogeneity of children and how gender, age, ethnicity, class and other socio-spatial factors influence the response of

---

77. Ibid.
78. Barker and Weller, "Never Work," 211.

children.[79] Coles further observed that regardless of the approach of the researcher some children are reluctant in opening up to a researcher, but some children are a kind of "storyteller" who prolifically expresses their ideas.[80] Coles suggested some techniques to keep in mind to resolve this challenge of not opening up: (1) Researchers can spend time with children to enable children to reveal that which cannot be "easily tapped even by good schoolteachers."[81] (2) Let children know what the researchers are trying to learn from them and their role in the process.[82] (3) The researchers can note the non-verbal clues like silence, smile, and laugh by which children express innermost thoughts on issues.[83] (4) Work with a number of children long enough to earn their trust in order to learn from them.[84] (5) Researchers can pay attention to their moods and work habits.[85]

Besides the difficulty in entering into someone else's thought pattern, there is an added challenge of understanding another generation due to the generation gap that exists between the researcher and children. In the current research, six weeks of research activities was an opportunity to spend time with children. As focus groups and member checking were after the six weeks of two hours per week, children may trust the researcher to share their innermost thoughts. Observation of classroom activity with the help of video helped to note the non-verbal as well as verbal symbols.

Inability of Children to Verbalize Their Experience of Transcendence

Boyatzis and Newman noted some challenges when researching children's spirituality.[86] Children's inability to verbally share their spiritual experiences is a challenge while conducting interviews with children. However,

---

79. Ibid., 209.
80. Coles, *Spiritual Life*, 26.
81. Ibid., 27.
82. Ibid.
83. Ibid., 32.
84. Ibid., 37.
85. Ibid., 26.
86. Boyatzis and Newman, "Children's Spirituality," 171.

Sasso noted that listening to sacred stories can help children to overcome the absence of sacred language.[87]

In this research, the following procedures helped to address this challenge: (1) Focus group interviews were only one of the methods of data collection. Six weeks of observation of class activities gave ample opportunities to further shed light on how children verbally and non-verbally express their spiritual experiences. (2) The sample represented children who have been attending church and Sunday school for at least two years and who are exposed to the stories at home and church. Thus they already have some opportunities to develop their understanding of sacred language to a certain extent. (3) The six weeks of class activities in the current research were further opportunities to hear and discuss biblical stories and learn songs based on the story. These experiences were opportunities to equip the children to overcome the inability to verbalize their experience of transcendence.

Objectivity

Hay and Nye bring in the concepts of the "myth of the outsider" and the "myth of the insider" when studying people's beliefs.[88] According to the myth of the outsider, only an outsider can maintain objectivity in research. On the other hand, the myth of the insider suggests that only an insider can sensitively understand the belief and motivations of the believer.[89] They stress the challenge in maintaining objectivity as the beliefs and values of the sample may color the understanding in one way or another.

The researcher understands that embracing superficial neutrality can question the integrity of the researcher. Yet as the primary goal of research is knowledge, it is the ethical responsibility of the researcher to reduce the personal bias that can distort the data. Thus, others' point of view can be recorded accurately as possible. On the other hand, the pre-understanding and experiences of the researcher can be used constructively to enrich the understanding of the topic of research. As Hay and Nye noted pre-understanding can help researchers to frame the topic with clarity, determine the

---

87. Sasso, "Role of Narratives," 25.
88. Hay and Nye, *Spirit of the Child*, 82.
89. Ibid.

stand on the topic and be sensitive to the aspects of reality which otherwise may be missed or ignored. This can alert the researcher to the limitations and contradictions in assumptions which need change.[90]

The journals of the four members of the research team, various methods of data collection, and formal member checking with selected participants were opportunities for triangulation to guard against possible bias. Discussion with the research assistants and selected faculty and students of the seminary were another technique to check the accuracy of the findings.

Dissemination

Usually children are not involved in data analysis and dissemination. The inclusion of children's voice in data analysis and dissemination is often tinted by adult's preconceptions and prejudices.[91] The member checking involved in the data collection process of the current research was a means to assure that children have a voice in reporting the data. Not using the names of children to represent them was another way to deal with the challenge of providing adequate confidentiality in representing the view of children.

Chapter Summary

The primary research question of the proposed research is as follows: What are the perceptions of 9- to 11-year-old children about the role of biblical stories in their spiritual formation? This is qualitative research with twenty-nine children of Pentecostal churches who have the opportunity to listen to stories at home and church. This was an attempt to listen and hear their perceptions through verbal, written, and non-verbal expressions. Findings of this research may enable educators to improve their skills of delivering stories, modifying their approach to children, confidently arranging the materials and activities for children, and equipping parents and the faith community in better using stories with children for their spiritual formation. Thus this is not only research with them but also for them.

---

90. Ibid., 85.
91. Barker and Weller, "Never Work," 221.

The methods of data collection were as follows: (1) Observing the classroom activities – two-hour per week for six weeks, (2) assessing their story-based activities, (3) focus group interviews, and (4) member checking. The research team of four members was present in the classroom but the researcher was not involved in teaching songs, sharing stories, or facilitating the story-based activities. Thus the researcher had ample opportunity to observe children and to build rapport with them. This was to avoid creating an authority image as the research team conducted the focus group interviews and member checking. The pilot study was conducted on 24 April 2010 to fine-tune the class activities and to gain an understanding of the perceptions of children about stories and spiritual formation.

There are some unique challenges in doing research with children. The social position of children is that they are minors. They are a vulnerable population and they are observed during class activities in an unnatural setting. These point to certain pertinent issues that were considered in this research: children's stand about the topic, recruitment, data collection, inability to verbally express their spiritual experience, analysis and dissemination, participation and the balance of power, spaces of research, listening to children, and objectivity. Various precautions were made and techniques were used to address these challenges.

CHAPTER 5

Results

The purpose of this research is to hear from 9- to 11-year-old children in Kerala, India about their perceptions of the role of biblical stories in their spiritual formation. The stories of the Bible are the major content of teaching children in Sunday schools in Kerala, India. The purpose of telling biblical stories is towards the spiritual formation of children. Sunday school is the only program that happens every week focused exclusively on children, even though children participate in other meetings of the church. Moreover in high-context cultures like India, stories are not seen merely as illustrations yet as vehicles that carry the truth. This shows the significance of the study in the India. This chapter outlines the context of the study and discusses the analysis of data collected from twenty-nine children during the months of April to July 2010.

Context of Study

From the seven participating churches, twenty-nine children participated in the research. These children represented families from different socio-economic backgrounds. The participating churches are selected from the Pentecostal tradition located in and around the town of Adoor, Kerala, India. These churches give a strong emphasis on the teaching of the Bible and weekly gathering together for worship and prayer. All these churches except one have the pastor as the only paid staff. Sunday school, youth meetings and other activities of these churches are organized through volunteers from the church. In the other church, the pastoral team consists of five members – senior pastor, assistant pastor, and three interns. The assistant pastor assists the pastor in every area of the church with a special focus on the training events and Sunday celebration. Three interns take care of worship, pastoral care, and assimilation of new believers.

Pastors of participating churches and parents of the children warmly welcomed the research. The children showed even more enthusiasm than their parents. Even when some children were sick, they insisted to come for the research. Some children would take the initiative to call the researcher regarding the date and time of the activities.

With the help of a questionnaire the following information of the participating churches were collected from pastors. The researcher visited six pastors to collect the data, and information from one church was collected through a phone call. A brief description of the participating churches is given below using pseudonyms. Appendix F contains two tables: (1) demographic data of the churches and (2) distributions of children with respect to churches, gender, and age.

Antioch

The Antioch church is located in a rural area. The purpose of this church is to prepare the members of the church for the kingdom of God and to proclaim the gospel to unbelievers. Other than Sunday worship and Sunday school, the church organizes the following programs: cottage (house) meeting, youth meeting, ladies meeting, fasting prayer, street meeting, and house visiting. Children participate in almost all these programs and also in leading worship, playing musical instruments, setting up the church, collecting offering, and in outreach programs. Various programs just for children are Sunday school, vacation Bible school, talent competition, outreach to the poor and outcast, and one day Sunday school tour. Other opportunities for children are Sunday school camps, seminar, and youth camps, which are organized by the denomination. Twelve classes in Sunday school are organized to mold the young generation and help them to be thorough in the word of God. There is a denominational standardized test each year, which tests the knowledge of the lessons of each class. Sunday school is prior to Sunday worship and Sunday worship is intergenerational. The church emphasizes the need of being born again, adult baptism, baptism of the Holy Spirit, and living according to the word of God.

Colosse

Situated at the heart of the town, this church exists with the purpose of evangelism, deliverance, and healing of souls. The church teaches the Bible with an emphasis on Pentecostal doctrine. Other than worship and Sunday school, the programs of this church include cottage (house) meeting, youth meeting, fasting prayer, Bible class, ladies meeting, and house visiting. Children participate in all of these and express themselves by being part of the worship team, playing musical instruments, setting up the church, helping with the sound system, collecting the offering, and involvement in outreach programs. There are other programs just for children: Sunday school, talent competition, Sunday school tour, and Bible class. Children participate in denominational youth camps and Sunday school camps. Sunday school is prior to Sunday worship and worship is intergenerational. On Sundays, in addition to a Sunday sermon, a short sermon is presented to children based on their issues and struggles. With the vision of Christian growth in children, the Sunday school is organized into five classes. Each year there is a denominational standardized test for each class, which evaluates the knowledge of what the children have learned each year.

Ephesus

Established with the mission of bringing people to the Lord Jesus, this church is located in a rural area. Teaching the Bible, this church highlights the need of the born-again experience, adult baptism, filling of the Holy Spirit, and the second coming of Christ. Besides Sunday worship and Sunday school, this church functions through fasting prayer, women's meeting, youth meeting, intercessory prayer, cottage (house) meeting. Children attend all these meetings and are also involved in denominational Sunday school camps, youth camps, and seminars. With the vision of spiritual development in children and equipping them to be evangelists, the Sunday school is organized into five classes. At the end of each academic year, children take a content-oriented standardized test set up by the denomination.

Jerusalem

The Jerusalem church is situated in the outskirts of the town with the mission of proclaiming the gospel and sending and supporting missionaries.

Other than Sunday worship and Sunday school, it organizes itself through cottage (house) meeting, fasting prayer, ladies meeting, and youth meeting. Children participate in all of these meetings and in denominational Sunday school camps, youth camps, and one-day seminars. The church organizes vacation Bible schools and a Sunday school tour. Children are involved in the worship team, playing musical instruments, helping with the sound system, collecting offering, and outreach programs. With the goal of inviting children to accept Jesus as their personal Savior and to a life dedicated to Jesus, Sunday school is organized in six classes. There is a denominational standardized test at the end of each academic year, which tests the content that children have learned that year. The church teaches the Bible with an emphasis on the Pentecostal doctrine knowing that the world is not worthy for a Christian and that they have to lead a holy life in this crooked world.

Philippi

Located in the vicinity of the town with the mission of evangelizing the community, this church teaches the Bible with an emphasis on the Pentecostal doctrine. Other than Sunday worship and Sunday school, the church functions through youth meeting, chain prayer, ladies meeting, and fasting prayer. Children participate in all these meetings and minister through their involvement in the worship team, playing musical instruments, setting up the church, helping with the sound system, and collecting the offering. On Sundays, along with the regular Sunday school sermon, a special sermon is presented to children during Sunday worship. Children attend denominational Sunday school camps, youth camps, and seminars. With the purpose of equipping children for evangelism the church has eleven Sunday school classes.

Rome

This small-group based church is situated at the heart of the town with the mission of "transforming the community – one person at a time." Sunday worship, Sunday school, cell groups (small groups), fasting prayer, inner healing and deliverance, and community outreach are the programs of the church. Except for inner healing and deliverance, children actively participate in all these programs. Children attend the Sunday service only during the worship session and then they are released to Sunday school. Children's Church functions through nine classes with the vision of "developing a generation that will love and serve God and his creation by focusing on the whole child." There is an examination at the end of each academic year for children who are six years and older. The content-based examination is only a part of the evaluation of the spiritual growth of children. Reciting memory verses, behavior, and attendance of children are further points of evaluation. The church also organizes one-day seminars and vacation Bible school for children and encourages children to attend inter-church conferences. Children are involved in the worship team, ministry team, playing musical instruments, setting up the church, helping with the sound, and leading small groups.

Thessalonica

Located at the heart of Adoor, Thessalonica church exists with a vision to gather people who are disciplined missionaries who do God's work and prepare themselves for his coming. Children participate in various programs of the church: Sunday worship, youth meeting, and Wednesday prayer. Even though youth camps, or VBS, are not organized by the church, children have opportunity to participate in such activities conducted elsewhere. Children below 13 years of age take part in kids' church. Two parts of kids' church are telling biblical stories and story-based activities. They have special programs during Easter, Christmas, and on other special occasions. The church encourages children in their education by giving a packet of school supplies before every school year. Children are involved in the worship team, playing musical instruments, helping with sound, collecting offering, and outreach programs. The church teaches the Bible with an emphasis on building faith and awareness of God in practical life.

Brief Summary of the Research Activities

This research with twenty-nine children during the months of April–September 2010 had three parts: six weeks of two-hour class activities, observation, focus group interviews, and member checking. Faith Theological Seminary, Kerala, India was the location for the class activities and focus group interviews. Apart from the researcher, there were three research assistants to facilitate research activities. A typical two-hour class was as follows: welcome and refreshments, learning story-based songs, story-based games, story-based class activities, discussion, and departure. The lesson plans for class activity were the last six lessons from India Sunday School Union's textbook *God Our Security*. Three research assistants facilitated all the class activities except the games, which were the responsibility of the researcher. The first class activity was the pilot study. This was an opportunity to gain expertise in facilitating class activities and conducting observation.

After six weeks of class activities, children were gathered in six groups for focus group interviews. The research assistants facilitated the focus interviews along with the researcher. The six focus group interviews were same gender groups, which followed the pre-approved interview protocol. The member checking with research participants and research assistants were held in July and September. The findings of this research were also discussed with selected faculty and students of Faith Theological Seminary who are involved in children's ministry.

Data Analysis

Data was collected from the class activities and focus group interviews. The research team noted challenges and prospects of the research process in the research diary. The first part of the analysis of the data was to review it before transcription. The researcher read the field notes of observation of the class activities and reviewed the written activities of children's story-based activities with the research questions primarily in mind. Data obtained from classroom activities and focus groups interviews was transcribed for analysis. While transcribing, the data was translated from Malayalam, the mother tongue of these children, to English. The transcribed data was coded and categories of responses were developed. The aim was to develop mutually exclusive categories. Themes were identified from these categories. This was a time consuming and challenging part of data analysis. This led to review more literature, which shed light on previous research studies with children in terms of their concept of God and self-concepts.

The analysis of children's responses are categorized as follows: settings where children hear biblical stories, storytellers, reasons for communicating biblical stories, recalling biblical stories, awareness of God, awareness of self, awareness of others, linking stories to life, and listening to biblical stories. The categories and subcategories are tabulated in table 4.

Table 4: Categories Derived from Analysis of Children's Responses

Categories	Subcategories
Settings where children hear biblical stories	(1) church (2) home (3) school
Storytellers	(1) at church: pastors, Sunday school teachers (2) at home: parents, siblings, grandparents, aunts, guests (3) at school: teachers and friends (4) children participated in the research
Reasons for communicating biblical stories	(1) to develop the intellectual dimension of faith (2) to develop the internal dimension of faith (3) to develop the volitional dimension of faith (4) to develop an awareness of others or I-others practiced in the transmission of stories (5) to develop an awareness of Satan or I-Evil expressed in the aversion towards sin.
Recalling biblical stories	Intellectual dimension of faith
Awareness of God gained from listening to biblical stories	(1) potency of God (2) punishing God (3) positive God (4) relational God (5) God-like parents

Awareness of self gained from listening to biblical stories	(1) ideological self
	(2) psychic self
	(3) existential individuating
	(4) sense of self-determination
	(5) interpersonal style
	   (i) behavior oriented
	   (ii) being a change agent

Awareness of others gained from listening to biblical stories	(1) others – God: view of others with reference to God

Linking stories to life	(1) emotion-oriented recollection
	(2) situation-oriented recollection
Listening to biblical stories	(1) stimulates religious emotions
	(2) stimulates transformation

Stories and Settings

One of the aims of this research was to identify the settings where children hear biblical stories. Children hear a variety of stories from diverse avenues. They identified three settings where they hear a variety of stories. Church, home, and school provide opportunities to hear different stories: biblical stories, funny stories, folk stories, traditional stories and cultural heroes, cartoons, animal stories, stories of martyrs, and personal stories of other Christians. Television and CDs are the two other means to hear stories. Written media is another avenue for children to come know stories as they read library books, storybooks, and children's magazines.

Storytellers of Biblical Stories

Children see their churches as the primary carrier of biblical stories. It was the first response in all six focus groups regarding where they hear biblical stories. Sunday school teachers and pastors are the two types of storytellers in the church. The variety of activities in churches and opportunities for children to participate in almost all of the programs of the church may be the two reasons why children identified church as the primary setting for hearing biblical stories. As preaching of the Bible is given importance in all the programs, children have ample opportunity to hear biblical stories. They referred to diverse activities in the church as opportunities for hearing biblical stories: Sunday school, Sunday worship, vacation Bible school, cottage (house) meetings, small groups, camps, conventions, youth meeting, fasting prayer, and special programs.

The next setting for biblical stories, namely the home, has a variety of storytellers. The diversity of biblical storytellers portrays the richness of this setting: father, mother, brother, sister, grandmother, grandfather, aunts, and guests. School, which is the third setting for biblical stories, has two types of storytellers: teachers and friends. Children also have access to biblical stories through personal reading of the Bible and through electronic media like television, CDs and DVDs.

During the first focus group interview, the researcher discovered how children are also storytellers to their friends. The children in the other focus group also repeated the practice of telling biblical stories to their friends. They share biblical stories with children in their class, to children of other faiths, and to younger children in their neighborhood.

While sharing stories with their friends, children receive a variety of responses. For some children, their friends repeatedly ask them for more stories, but for others, their responses may not be so positive: "When I share the story they move away but there is one who listens to the stories," "Only one child wants to listen to the story of Jesus as they say their gods are also great."

The following conversations with five children reveal the value they place on sharing the word of God even when the responses are not always pleasant.

First conversation with a 10-year-old boy:

Researcher:	Do you share stories of the Bible with your friends?
Boy:	(*With tears.*) Yes. I wonder why they do not know God. What happened to them? Don't they know that God created them?
Boy:	One day pastor uncle gave me some tracts. He told me to go and give to different houses. I went with someone else to my friends' house. One boy got hold of all the tracts and tore it and told me "never bring this any more, if you bring it I will beat up your pastor." I felt very sad.
Researcher:	So did you feel sad?
Boy:	I went home and prayed.
Researcher:	What did you pray? Did you pray for them to know God?
Boy:	That God won't punish them for doing this and that they may know God.

Second conversation with a 9-year-old boy:

> Researcher: Have you shared Bible stories with others?
>
> Boy: Yeah, but no one accepts that (*in a low voice expressing sadness*).

Third conversation with a 10-year-old boy:

> Researcher: Why do you tell them these stories?
>
> Boy: To comfort them when they are sad.
>
> Researcher: What kind of stories are those?
>
> Boy: That brings comfort.
>
> Researcher: Why do these stories bring comfort?
>
> Boy: When they hear stories of God and stories of miracles, they may think if God has done it, then he will give me comfort.
>
> Researcher: Do you have friends that are sad?
>
> Boy: Yeah, Ben.
>
> Researcher: What happened?
>
> Boy: He had less marks for an exam.
>
> Researcher: Which story did you say?
>
> Boy: Jesus calming the storm.
>
> Researcher: Then what did you tell?
>
> Boy: God will do the same for you.
>
> Researcher: What did he say?
>
> Boy: Nothing.

Fourth conversation with a 10-year-old boy:

> Boy: I wonder why God is not returning to this world. I want to live for him, I want to trust in him even if everyone isolates me, I believe he will make me great (*with a contemplative, sad look*).
>
> Researcher: Do you feel isolated?
>
> Boy: Yeah.

Researcher:	Where?
Boy:	In school
Researcher:	Why?
Boy:	They (referring to his friends) do not like me telling about God.

Fifth conversation is with a 10-year-old girl:

Girl:	There is a girl in my class. She does not go to the temple. She wants to believe in our God. Yet, her parents do not send her.
Researcher:	So does she go to the church without the knowledge of her parents?
Girl:	Yes.
Researcher:	How did she come to the Lord?
Girl:	I had a couple of Bibles, so I gave her one Bible. She came to know about this.
Researcher:	So does she read the Bible?
Girl:	Yes. One day her father threw the Bible out. And she took the Bible and again prayed for some time that God won't punish her father for this.
Researcher:	Anyone else in your class like this?
Girl:	No.
Researcher:	When did you give the Bible to her?
Girl:	When I was in 5th grade.
Researcher:	So it is now one year.
Girl:	Yeah.
Researcher:	So do you tell her about God?
Girl:	Yes, always.
Researcher:	What do you say?
Girl:	God's message. God died for us on the cross, he took the cross for our healing, then about Zacchaeus.

Researcher:	So what does she say?	
Girl:	She cries.	
Researcher:	What does she cry?	
Girl:	She remembers the problems in her home.	
Researcher:	Do you pray for her?	
Girl:	I have told my mom also to pray and we pray.	

In summary, children hear biblical stories in a variety of settings: church, home, and school. Various settings, opportunities, and a variety of storytellers with respect to age, gender, and relationships imply that children have an abundant environment to hear biblical stories. Even when various occasions are available to hear biblical stories, children's willingness to take part in them and parents' dedication to make use of these opportunities by bringing them to these activities are commendable. Children are also storytellers to their friends who do not always tolerantly respond to these attempts.

Discussion with the faculty and students at Faith Theological Seminary shed light on some possible reasons why children are storytellers: (1) the focus on evangelism among Pentecostal churches in the area, (2) children have internalized this emphasis and become storytellers to others, or (3) children imitate adults in sharing stories with their friends.

Types of Stories

Children hear a variety of stories in various setting: biblical stories, funny stories, folk stories, traditional stories, stories of cultural heroes, cartoons, animal stories, stories of martyrs, and personal stories of other Christians. Children cited stories of God or biblical stories as their favorite stories. The reasons for this choice are as follows: "It helps us to walk in the ways of God," "I can learn a lot about God," "I can know more about how God delivers people," and "Know about the miracles of God," "My faith increases," "When God gives a miracle and when God does a miracle in our lives, the faith in God increases that God will save us." The next most common choice was moral stories as "they give us some lessons about life." They also like funny stories because of the fun they provide. These children were with the research team for two hours per week for six weeks. These sessions focused on biblical stories. This may be one of reason why majority of children said that they like biblical stories more than other kind of stories.

Children's Perceptions: Reasons for Communicating Biblical Stories

In this research, children have expressed their perspectives of the intention of their storytellers in communicating biblical stories with them. They clearly see the intentions are beyond just knowing certain facts about God. Their responses portray their awareness of spiritually maturing faith. Spirituality and faith are related: spirituality is "about life of faith – what drives and motivates it, and what people find helpful in sustaining and developing it."[1] The three elements of Christianity are "a set of beliefs," "a set of values," and "a way of life."[2] "A set of beliefs" refers to doctrinal matters, "a set of values" denotes the Christian values, and "a way of life" indicates an everyday life that reflects the beliefs and values.[3] The third element, the way in which one lives out one's faith is spirituality according to McGrath.[4] Yet comprehending the content of faith and to value an authentic life in relationship with Jesus are crucial in living out one's faith. The first element, which he refers to as "intellectual side,"[5] impacts the way in which a Christian lives. Intellectual comprehension provides norms and stability to live out one's faith. This is significant in countries like India where Christians live among many other world religions. The second element, the internalization of the Christian faith,[6] provides a quest to live out one's faith. Spirituality is living out one's faith which is intellectually comprehended and internalized.

McGrath's categories are congruent with Downs' dimensions of a spiritually maturing faith. Downs describes three dimensions of spiritually maturing faith as intellectual (*notitia*), affective and emotional (*assensus*), or

---

1. A. E. McGrath, *Christian Spirituality: An Introduction* (Malden, MA: Wiley-Blackwell, 1999), 2.
2. Ibid., 3.
3. Ibid.
4. Ibid., 2–4.
5. McGrath, *Studies in Doctrine*, 257.
6. McGrath, *Christian Spirituality*, 99.

relational and volitional (*fiducia*).⁷ Intellectual dimension refers to belief in the content of faith. This shows the importance of knowing what God has spoken. Affective dimension moves beyond the intellectual dimension to "an emotional commitment to the object of one's faith." Volitional dimension denotes the desire to be "increasingly obedient" to God.⁸ McGrath's set of beliefs is identical with Downs' intellectual dimension; set of values identical with affective dimension, and way of life corresponds to volitional dimension.

The categories of intentions of telling biblical stories are classified as follows: (1) to develop the intellectual dimension of faith, (2) to develop the internal dimension of faith, (3) to develop the volitional dimension of faith, (4) to develop the awareness of others or I-others practiced in the transmission of stories, and (5) to develop an antagonism against Satan or I-Evil expressed in the aversion towards sin. The last category, which was unique to these children's experiences, has to do with how they view Satan, sin, and other religious beliefs and practices. Children clearly perceive that adults intend to develop these dimensions in them and children as storytellers expect these dimensions of faith in others. The following discussion, which reflects these five aspects, shows how children have grasped the essence of Christian spirituality as living out an authentic life in relationship with God. They described each of these categories with reference to God, thus they are reflections of their I-Thou relationship.

Intellectual dimension of faith

Children clearly perceive that their storytellers intend to develop in them an intellectual dimension of faith. The following responses portray this factor: "to know God," "to know that Jesus is good," "to know that God is good," "for the next generation (referring to themselves) to know God," "so that we may know God," "to know that God is our Savior," "to learn a lot of moral lessons," "to know more about the Bible," "to help us to know this (biblical stories)," "understand and comprehend the story," "to learn moral lessons and obey," and "to do the activities in the lesson." Their responses

---

7. P. G. Downs, *Teaching for Spiritual Growth: An Introduction to Christian Education* (Grand Rapids, MI: Zondervan, 1994), 17–18.

8. Ibid., 19.

range from learning the lesson in order to do the activities in the lesson plan to knowing God as their Savior. They are clearly aware that adults share the stories so that their generation may know God. Knowledge of the content is necessary to believe the content. Thus this intention identified by children is a crucial aspect of the first dimension of Christian spirituality "set of beliefs" in McGrath's categories of spirituality[9] and "intellectual dimension" in Downs' dimension of spiritually maturing faith.[10]

Internal dimension of faith

Children's responses reveal that I-Thou has gone beyond the knowledge level or head level of faith to their hearts. They see that their storytellers intend to touch their feelings, attitudes, and their choices through storytelling. McGrath quotes Jeremiah 4:4 and Deuteronomy 10:16 as he refers to this element of faith as the internalization of spiritually maturing faith.[11] Children see that their storytellers' intention is not just an intellectual comprehension but also an internal appreciation that is to be reflected in trusting the God whom these stories declare. They understood that biblical stories are to affect their values, attitudes, and feelings.

Children perceive that adults communicate biblical stories so that they will internalize the stories which are to be reflected in their values, feelings, and attitudes: "to believe in God," "to have an attitude to confess our sins," "not to grow weary when there are troubles and struggles," "when we have troubles, we can remember the Bible stories and find comfort," "sometimes we may be sad that is when we hear a story then the story touches us and gives comfort," "to remember when we are sad and to find comfort in them," "to be happy," and "we may love Jesus when we remember the stories." Their responses show their perception of adults' intention in telling biblical stories: to find comfort and joy in the midst of troubles and struggles as well as love Jesus and confess their sins before God. Thus they view that the knowledge of who God is needs to be reflected in their values and attitudes.

---

9. McGrath, *Christian Spirituality*.
10. Downs, *Teaching for Spiritual Growth*.
11. McGrath, *Christian Spirituality*, 99.

Children's responses have another aspect of internal appreciation of Christian spirituality – a reality which is growing and vibrant. Children are aware that adults intend to see sanctification in their lives. This is evident in the following responses: "to be born again and to be baptized," "filled with anointing," "to be close to Jesus," "to stand close to Jesus," "to stand close to Jesus regardless whatever problems we face," "to grow in love with Jesus," "to come close to God," "to be children of God," "to be like God," "to strengthen our relationship with God," "to come closer to him," "to come closer to God," "to increase faith in God," "to increase our faith." Children have grasped the essence of Christianity: "to be like God, to come close to God, to grow in love with Jesus." These words seem to portray their desire for what McGrath called "the quest for a fulfilled and authentic Christian existence."[12]

Meanwhile, the terminologies and phrases children used to describe this aspect reflect the traditions and theology of the Pentecostal churches. The terms they hear in their churches are the tools with which they could explain their experiences with God. Fowler notes this as an important aspect of faith among children during the mythic-literal stage – 6–12 years of age.[13] Westerhoff notes that stories of the faith community provide a sense of meaning and identity to children in the stage of "affiliative faith."[14] The question that emerges here is the extent to which children understand the meaning of the terms they have used. Later sections show that there is an attempt to connect these stories to their various personal experiences. Their understanding of God will change as they grow older.[15] In this research, the team confirmed the accuracy of the comprehension of children's responses, by asking follow-up questions and paraphrasing the responses.

Volitional dimension of faith

Downs describes the third dimension of a maturing spirituality, the volitional faith as the "crowning element of faith" as faith moves beyond being

---

12. Ibid., 2.
13. Fowler, *Becoming Adult*, 149.
14. Westerhoff, *Will Our Children*, 70.
15. J. Bellous, "The Educational Significances of Spirituality in the Formation of Faith," in *International Handbook of the Religious, Moral, and Spiritual Dimension in Education*, eds. M. De Souza et al. (Dordrecht, Netherlands: Springer, 2006), 178.

an activity of heart and mind to be reflected in our lifestyle.[16] In McGrath's term it is the way of life that reflects our beliefs.[17] The Apostle James stresses the importance of deeds of faith when he said, "faith without deeds is useless" (Jas 2:20 NIV).

Children's perceptions about sharing biblical stories with them reveal that biblical stories have helped them to understand spirituality as a way of life: "not to fight and be a good child," "when we go to college and school to live as a child of God," "to know God and live," "to live a good life," "to live for God," "to live as children of God," "go in straight path," "to live a good life in the future," "to understand the stories and there will be a change in life and comfort in the times of sorrow," and "to have a new life different from old life." They are aware of them being role models to their friends: "they would behave as they see us doing it."

Antagonism against Satan reflected in the aversion towards sin

When children perceived that I-Thou is expected in them, they are also aware of the intention of storytellers in relation to I-Evil. Children have perceived the intention in terms of the works of Satan: "to expel Satan from our homes," "not to go with Satan," "in this wicked world we may not be slaves to Satan." The words children used in relation to I-Evil, "expel," "not to go with," and "not be slaves," have the sense of antagonism in them. I-Evil relationship is defined as antagonism as the Bible teaches about actively opposing devil by resisting him (Jas 4:7) and through the struggle against the spiritual forces of evil in the heavenly realms (Eph 6: 12).

The antagonism with reference to I-Evil is also expressed in their aversion to sin not only in the present but also in the future. The understanding of sin is essential in Protestant understanding of spirituality. This is not to negate the potential of children's relationship with God. Children's responses show their awareness of sin in the context of forgiveness in Christ. Children perceive that biblical stories can enable them in their lives to develop aversion towards sin: "not to sin but be good children," "not to be sinners," "not to go in sinful paths," "not to lie," "in the future that we won't become wicked and do sins," "not to use swearing words," "not to do

---

16. Downs, *Teaching for Spiritual Growth*, 19.
17. McGrath, *Christian Spirituality*, 2.

wrong things," "not to do sin or wrong but be good children," "to save us from sin," "not to go into sin," "for the salvation of the sinners," and "when I talk rudely to others then to ask forgiveness to God." The antagonism towards Satan and sin further supports children understanding of spirituality as the way of life in relationship with God. The awareness in these children about sin, need of confession and receiving forgiveness, and turning away from sin shows their awareness of sanctification, which is a significant in spiritual growth in children.[18]

Awareness of others practiced in the transmission of stories

Proclamation of the good news is a key practice of Christianity that is an obligation for any disciple of Christ who obeys the greatest commandment of loving God and loving your neighbor. Children clearly perceive that their storytellers intend to develop an awareness of others or I-other in them in terms of transmission of biblical stories. This awareness is expressed in their perceptions of reasons for sharing stories with them: "to share the stories with others," "when we grow up tell others," "when we get older tell other children," "tell biblical stories to people of other faiths and then they will come in this path," "to share God's word with others," and "to help others."

Children as storytellers to their friends have already portrayed this I-other aspect. The conversation with a 10-year-old girl reveals this:

Researcher:	You have heard biblical stories; do you think there are any children who haven't heard such stories?
Girl:	These homeless children who sleep in street, they may like to hear stories, but they have no opportunity to hear stories.
Researcher:	Yeah.
Girl:	Those people who sit in front of churches and beg. They may also have the desire but they may not have heard them.

---

18. Ratcliff and Ratcliff, *Childfaith*, 11.

Children deliberately share biblical stories with their friends. Their intentions in sharing biblical stories with their friends are as follows:

1) These children share stories with the intention of developing I-Thou relationship in their friends. They have a clear understanding of the need of the cognitive dimension in I-Thou relationship in their friends. This is reflected in their intention: "they may believe the stories," "so that others can know God," "to let them know God," and "to know God."

2) Children hope to touch the feelings and emotions of their friends which is the outcome of internalization of faith: "they may receive comfort and find joy in it," "for my comfort and to rejoice with friends," "to comfort them when they are sad," "when they hear stories of God and stories of miracles they may think if God has done it, then he will give me comfort and then they can become happy," "when they hear stories of God and stories of miracles, they may think if God has done it, then he will give me comfort," and "they wonder that if there is such a God like this and then they come to this God thinking that he will do many miracles for them." They desire to see their friends have a growing and vibrant relationship with I-Thou in their friends: "so that others can have faith," "so that my friends may come closer to God." Thus children are aware of I-self as an outcome of I-Thou, which is what adults desire to develop through sharing of biblical stories.

3) The internalized faith that children desire in their friends has an aspect of making a conscious choice in their relationship with God which is also reflected in the way of life-volitional dimension: "to live as children of God," "so that my friends can have a relationship with God," "to live for God," "to love God," "to live their life for Jesus," "to be saved to worship the true God," and "when they hear about miracles they may go and see in churches and have miracles and they will go in the way of the Lord." Beyond intellectually grasping stories or knowing God, children intend biblical stories to affect their friends' attitudes,

and feelings. This is the awareness of I-self with reference of God reflected in the sense of self-determination.

4) Children share stories with their friends to develop I-other in them in terms of transmission of biblical stories. So they expressed: "when we tell our friends, they will go and tell them to their parents" and "they may in turn tell this to others now and when they get big."

5) Children as storytellers expressed their intention with respect to I-Evil in their friends' lives: "they won't become slaves to Satan but believers of God," "not to sin, and be good children," "to live without sinning," "not to sin and not to walk in the path of sinners." Thus children believe that biblical stories can develop the antagonism to I-Evil and sin in the hearers.

In essence, children have perceived the intentions of their storytellers and have internalized the intentions and are developing a lifestyle which mirrors those purposes. This is evident in their aims in telling stories to their friends.

Even when these children share stories with others, they are aware of their need to focus their attention on God. The conversation with a nine-year old girl reveals this:

Girl:	There . . . when I shared about this God to the girl who sat next to me last year, then she told me many things about her god.
Researcher:	So when you tell, then she tells to you?
Girl:	Yeah, when I share something, whatever I am telling, the thoughts are deviated to their thoughts as if thoughts of the devil kind of get hold of me.
Researcher:	So when you share about God, their thoughts are deviated?
Girl:	No, as I am telling the story, they would say their god is great, then my thoughts are deviated from God.
Researcher:	Oh, your thoughts are deviated.

Girl:	Yeah, and my focus changes from Jesus to her god. Then we began to like those stories. Then I forget our God.

The faculty and students of the seminary expressed their surprise as they heard that children are storytellers. This led the researcher to approach children to further ask about their primary reason for sharing stories with others. The researcher reported the five reasons derived from the data analysis with selected children. Children affirmed that the primary reason for sharing biblical stories with others is for their friends to know God. They explained the word "know" as follows: "to comprehend God" so that "they may have a relationship with him."

Data analysis reveals that children have certain understanding of the intentions of their storytellers. By becoming storytellers to others they have internalized the intentions of their storytellers. Their reasons for sharing biblical stories with their friends reflect this phenomenon. However, the reasons for sharing stories with children are their perceptions of the storytelling activity. It would have been interesting to ask those who share biblical stories with children to see whether their reasons are congruent with children's reasons.

Recalling Biblical Stories – Intellectual Dimension of Faith

During six days of class activities, children answered review questions based on the story that was told on that day. They recalled stories by describing events, names, and plots in stories. During focus group interviews, children were asked to tell stories they remember to see if they could remember biblical stories. Children recalled specific events from the lives of various characters in the Bible. These events and characters were mainly from the first six books of the Old Testament and from the Gospels. Many of the same stories were repeated in the focus group interviews.

Discussion with the students of Faith Theological Seminary shed light on probable reasons for recalling stories from certain books of the Bible. (1) In India, preaching is more commonly narrative based rather than propositional. (2) Recently, a variety of stories from the Pentateuch and the Gospels are available in electronic forms. (3) There is a cartoon presentation of the gospel stories on Christian TV Channels in the area. There can be other possible reasons for telling stories from some books in the Bible: maybe these stories are often shared at home, they may find these stories to be more attractive than other stories, these stories may be easy to remember, the narrative style of these books that children find interesting to read or adults find easy to recite to children, or the plots or events in these stories help them to remember these stories. It would be interesting to see if this phenomenon is repeated in other parts of Kerala, India with a similar sample.

Recalling biblical stories is an important aspect of what McGrath and Downs referred to as the intellectual component of spiritually maturing faith. Recalling biblical stories portray remembering and understanding according to Anderson's revised taxonomy of learning.[19] These children retrieved and paraphrased the stories, events and characters. They could name a certain event among the many events from various biblical stories. So they portray the first two levels of learning: remembering and understanding.[20] Recalling the characters and events of the Bible is thus referred to as the intellectual/cognitive dimensions of the maturing faith or I-Thou relationship. The knowledge of the content is crucial for believing the content of faith. Children recalled many of the Old Testament stories which are included in tables 5 and 6. The New Testament stories that children recited are in tables 7 and 8.

---

19. L. V. Anderson, *Classroom Assessment: Enhancing the Quality of Teacher Decision Making* (London: Lawrence Erlbaum, 2003), 32.

20. Ibid.

Table 5: Stories from the Old Testament Part A

The Book of Genesis	The Book of Exodus
The creation story	Moses taken from the Nile
Creation of Adam and Eve	Israel delivered from Pharaoh
Satan tempting Adam and Eve	Ten plagues
Cain and Abel	Crossing of the Red Sea
Enoch walked with God	Israel's journey through desert
Noah's ark	Manna
Birth of Isaac	Dislike of manna
Abraham sacrificing Isaac	Water from the rock
Jacob became Israel	
Joseph's dream	
Joseph's brother betraying him	
Joseph in jail	

Table 6: Stories from the Old Testament Part B

Books from Numbers to Joshua	The rest of the Old Testament
Caleb and Joshua spying the land	Ruth and Boaz
Crossing of the Jordan	Hannah's prayer for Samuel
Twelve stones as memorial stones	Samuel's vision regarding Eli
Joshua capturing Jericho	David and Goliath
	Saul chasing to kill David
	Saul asking forgiveness from David
	David delivering his sheep
	David counting the people
	Solomon and the two women
	Elijah fed by ravens
	Elijah on Carmel
	Elijah under the broom tree
	Naaman's healing
	Elisha purifying the water
	Struggles of Job
	Daniel in the lion's den
	Jonah in fish
	The fall of Satan

Table 7: Stories from the New Testament Part A

Miracles of Jesus	Teachings of Jesus
Jesus at the wedding of Cana Jesus healing the leper Jesus healing the blind Raising Lazarus Raising Jairus' daughter Calming the storm Jesus feeding five thousand Jesus feeding seven thousand Disciples catching the fish Jesus walking on water	The parable of lost sheep The parable of lost son The parable of ten virgins The parable of the vineyard

Table 8: Stories from the New Testament Part B

Other events in Jesus' life	Events during Passion Week	The rest of the New Testament
Visiting Zacchaeus The lady with alabaster jar of oil Jesus cleansing the temple Jesus visiting Martha's and Mary's house	The Last Supper Judas betraying Jesus Peter denying Jesus Crucifixion of Jesus Resurrection of Jesus Women at the empty tomb Thomas' unbelief	Peter delivered from prison

Favorite Biblical Story: Evidences of Maturing Spirituality

These children identified their favorite biblical stories and explained reasons for their choice. Some children did not explain why they liked the story. Such stories were as follows: the lost sheep, lost son, Daniel delivered from the lion's den, Noah's ark, and Jacob becoming Israel. In all the other instances, children described why they liked a particular story which shows the impact of stories in their lives. In the various focus group interviews, different children had a same story as their favorite story but they gave different interpretations and applications. This shows that they are not only recalling the events, but also interpreting them with respect to various situations in life. The reasons why a particular story is a favorite story give a clear indication of a maturing spirituality in terms of understanding of God, self, others and Satan.

Remembering various biblical stories is crucial in developing the intellectual component of a spiritually maturing faith. Deriving interpretations from stories and appropriating them to life situations show that they value stories as important for their lives. Thus there is an internalized element of Christian faith which is the outcome of believing the content of faith.

Based on Anderson's taxonomy of learning, children have understood the story and connected stories into their own day-to-day lives.[21] They have moved beyond simply retelling the stories and can organize and synthesize their understanding of stories. They have taken the stories from mere intellectual dialogue to a deeper appreciation and possession of the reality they represent.

Analysis of children's responses in this research with respect to why they like a story shows that the stories have helped them in their awareness of God, awareness of self, awareness of others, and the awareness of sin. Biblical stories have helped them to have a relationship with God which is reflected in their awareness and desire to live a life of continual trust and sanctification. To expound further on these themes, various research studies that shed light on children's God-concepts and self-concepts were utilized in the following section to categorize the responses of these children.

Awareness of God

Children's explanation of the reason why a particular story is their favorite reveals their awareness of their relationship with God – I-Thou. The relationship with God is the key element of spirituality.[22] The use of the pronouns "I," "us," and "our," in children's responses emphasizes the I-Thou element in their relational consciousness.[23] Few examples of the use of "I" are as follows: "That is why I am a Christian," "I have faith in God that he can heal me when I am sick," and "I got eternal life and new life for me." This researcher was quite fascinated by children's frequent use of "we" "us"

---

21. Anderson, *Classroom Assessment*, 33.
22. Issler, *Wasting Time with God*, 252.
23. Hay and Nye, *Spirit of the Child*, 109.

and "our" even when they were referring to their relationship with God or others. This is because of the "collective dimension" in countries like India compared to individualistic aspect found in western countries.[24]

Various categories are used to explain children's God-concepts in previous research studies. Hood, Hill, and Spilka present Deconchy's stages of development to God-concepts: attributive themes, personalization themes, and interiorization themes.[25] Table 9 displays the three stages and characteristics.

Table 9: Deconchy's Three Stages of the Idea of God

Age	Stages	Description
7–11	Attributive Themes	God is described in a set of attributes. Concepts are independent of other religious constructs like the historical events in the life of Jesus.
11–14	Personalization Themes	God is understood in terms of parental characteristics and in more anthropomorphic terms like just, good, strong.
14 on up	Interiorization Themes	Concepts of God become more abstract and reflect relationship with God-like trust. This is emerged from within the person not just certain descriptive characteristics.

Deconchy's categories are well defined but Roos' study[26] indicates that children younger than the age prescribed by Deconchy display all three themes. Roos listed the five scales to explain God-concepts among kindergarten children: (1) Potency of God, (2) Punishing God, (3) Positive God, (4) Relational God, and (5) God-like Parents.

---

24. J. L. Gibbons and D. A. Stiles, *The Thoughts of Youth: An International Perspective on Adolescents' Ideal Persons* (Charlotte, NC: Information Age, 2004), 86; R. Reddy and J. L. Gibbons, "School Socioeconomic Context and Adolescent Self-Descriptions in India," *Journal of Youth and Adolescence* 28, no. 5 (1999): 620.

25. R. W. Hood, P. C. Hill, and B. Spilka, *The Psychology of Religion: An Empirical Approach* 4th ed. (New York: Guilford, 2009), 97.

26. S. A. de Roos, "Young Children's God Concepts: Influences of Attachment and Religious Socialization in a Family and School Context," *Religious Education* 10, no. 1 (2006): 84–103.

Roos described each of the characteristics as follows:

> The scale Potency of God has items like: "God sees everything you do," "God is the boss," "God is very strong." Punishing God is composed of the following three items: "God punishes often," "God punishes when you are naughty," and "God is angry when you do something bad." Positive God alludes to items like: "God helps people," "God cares for people and animals," and "God can comfort you when you're sad." The scale Relational God contains four items, namely: "God loves me," "God makes me happy," "God is a friend," and "God is nice." Finally, God-like parents has two items, that is, "God looks like daddy" and "God looks like mummy."[27]

Analysis of children's responses in this research with respect to relationship with God is found in the following tables 10, 11, 12, and 13. These tables quote children's words using Roos' classification of God-concepts.

Table 10: Awareness of God: The Relational God

The Favorite Story	Reasons Why the Story Is Favorite
Birth of Jesus	"Jesus was born to remove the sin and he was crucified for our sins. So our sins are forgiven." "Jesus was able to die because he was born. It shows the love of God towards the world. That is why I am a Christian."
Crucifixion of Christ	"Jesus died to take us to heaven when he returns. He died for our sins." "Jesus was nailed on the cross, so I see his love for me and I think of my love for him. My sins are forgiven, I got eternal life, and new life for me."
Joseph's dream that he will become a minster	"God will fulfill the vision that he gives. God is everywhere. If we are God's children, we may be among friends who do not know God. They may cause trouble for us by saying falsehood to teachers. Then when they come to know the truth, teachers realize that I am a good child."

---

27. Ibid., 95.

Table 11: Awareness of God: The Positive God

The Favorite Story	Reasons Why the Story Is Favorite
Woman with the issue of blood	"Jesus healed the lady with the issue of blood. I have faith in God that he can heal me when I am sick."
Saul healed of his blindness:	"God will heal the sick."
Crucifixion of Jesus	"Jesus healed others, he took the big punishment and took the cross and went on the mountain to die. Because of that I have healing. So I know that God will sustain me through all my problems. And he will lift me up. He took the big punishment for the sin and deception of others. When I think of that I am happy but sad. This was the story that my mother first told me."
David counting the Israelites	"God punished the people, but David asked for guidance from God. And God restored everything to them."
Job's sickness	"Job had sickness, he lost his wealth, but he got everything back. Even when we are in any danger, he will not forsake us. I have a faith." "Even in the midst of great sufferings, he was delivered from that. His wife asked him to betray God, he did not betray God, he loved God and God delivered him."
Saul following David into the cave	"Jesus will save us when we face dangers. We should not kill even our enemies, but Jesus will save us."

Table 12: Awareness of God: The Potent God

The Favorite Story	Reasons Why the Story Is the Favorite
The Second Coming of Jesus	"The event that will happen during the time God will take us to heaven and his enemies will be defeated."

Table 13: Awareness of God: The Punishing God

The Favorite Story	Reasons Why the Story Is the Favorite
Jonah's disobedience	"But Jonah did not obey God. And God punished him. God will punish those who disobey."

They are aware of God as their Savior whose birth and death were crucial for their salvation and the cleansing of their sins. Their responses further reveal that biblical stories help them to see God as their healer and sustainer. They are able to derive meanings from various biblical stories that give them hope in the faithfulness of God. They see him as the one who delivers them from all dangers – even from their enemies. Children's favorite stories helped them to be aware of God as the relational God, and positive God. Their favorite stories have helped them to see God as their Savior, who forgives their sin, and who loves them. Children are aware of God as the Punishing God but they know that God restored his people when David asked for guidance (see Table 12). These comments show their trust in God, which according to Deconchy,[28] is interiorization. Personalization themes and attributive themes are only implied here.

Awareness of self

Shavelson, Huber, and Stanton defined self-concept as the way people perceive themselves with respect to their experiences and interpretation of their environment.[29] It has to do with our "attitudes, feelings and knowledge about our abilities, skills, appearance, and social acceptability."[30] People not only develop a perception of themselves in a particular situation, but

---

28. J. P Deconchy, "The Idea of God: Its Emergence between 7 and 16 Years," in *From Religious Experience to a Religious Attitude*, ed. A. Godin (Chicago, IL: Loyola University, 1965).

29. R. J. Shavelson, J. J. Huber, and G. C. Stanton, "Self-Concept: Validation of Construct Interpretations," *Review of Educational Research* 46, no. 4 (1976): 411; K. Littleton, C. Wood, and J. K. Staarman, *International Handbook of Psychology in Education* (Wagon Lane, UK: Emerald Group, 2010), 502.

30. B. M. Byrne, "The General/Academic Self-Concept Nomological Network: A Review of Construct Validation Research," *Review of Educational Research* 54, no. 3 (1984): 429.

also form an evaluation of their actions against a standard.[31] Thus there is a cognitive, perceptual, affective, and evaluative facet to self-concepts.[32]

Beginning with William James there were several studies that explained self-concept. James proposed three aspects of self: material self, social self, and spiritual self – the pure ego.[33] Material self refers to one's body, abilities, family, and possessions. Social self involves people's perceptions of other's view of themselves. Spiritual self comprise of experiences related to emotions and motivation. One's inner thinking and feeling self.[34] James sees spiritual self as the central nucleus of life. He describes this as the "intimate part of self" and the "sanctuary" of life.[35]

Shavelson et. al. explain self-concept as multidimensional and hierarchical: general self-concept is at the apex, followed by non-academic self-concept and academic self-concept. Non-academic self-concept is subdivided into social, emotional, and physical self-concept. Social self-concept is further divided into relationship with peers and with significant others. Physical self-concept is divided into physical ability and physical appearance.[36]

Montemayor and Eisen categorized self-conceptions as follows: occupational role – describing oneself in terms of future occupation; existential, individuating – self-reflection, "I," "me"; ideological and belief references – with reference to what one believes; the sense of self-determination – sense of volition; the sense of unity; interpersonal style – social and personal characteristics; and psychic style – how they think of themselves.[37]

In this research, these children's favorite stories reveal that they are not only aware of their relationship with God whom they see as their Savior,

---

31. Ibid., 429.

32. Robert D. Hoge, and Joseph S. Renzulli, "Exploring the Link between Giftedness and Self Concept," *Review of Educational Research* 63, no. 4 (1993): 449.

33. William James, *The Principles of Psychology*, vol. 1 (New York: H. Holt & Company, 1980), 292.

34. B. J. Poll, and T. B. Smith, "The Spiritual Self: Toward a Conceptualization of Spiritual Identity Development," *Journal of Psychology and Theology* 31, no. 2 (2003): 130.

35. James, *Principles of Psycholoy*, 297.

36. Shavelson et al., "Self-Concept," 412; Littleton, Wood, & Staarman, *Handbook of Psychology*, 502.

37. R. Montemayor, and M. Eisen, "The Development of Self-Conceptions from Childhood to Adolescence," *Developmental Psychology* 13, no. 4 (1977): 314.

healer, and sustainer but they are also aware of their part in the relationship with God. Their responses reveal that stories remind these children of the values of their actions and the need for obedience. The use of pronouns "I," "us," and "we" responses show internalized faith, which is reflected in I-self. This is with reference to their favorite stories and the reasons for their selection as the favorite stories. This is categorized as "existential individuating" as they are reflecting on their action with respect to the need of obedience to God's words. Table 14 shows this element using their own words.

Table 14: Awareness of Self: Existential Individuating

The Favorite Story	Reasons Why the Story Is Favorite
Noah and the ark	"Noah immediately obeyed God. Because he obeyed, God protected him from all dangers. If I obey God, he will protect me from dangers." "Noah's family stood alone for God. Only he did good things. If we do good things, God will be with us, he will save us from dangers. God told to Noah to build an ark. God can speak to us in the midst of our problems."
David's fight with Amalekites	"David asked for God's guidance before he fought with Amalekites. If we obey God he will help us to accomplish things."

Awareness of sin

The children's list of favorite stories not only included those which show a positive and relational God but also those which show the importance of obeying God. They are aware of their responsibility in strengthening the I-Thou relationship or to keep it as a vibrant and maturing relationship. Another component of their responses was in relation to I-Evil. This category was unique to the responses of these children. They have understood how giving in to sinful ways has led others away from God. So they perceive these stories as warning signs to heed so that they won't tumble in their I-Thou relationship. Table 15 depicts this awareness.

Table 15: Awareness of Sin: Something to Avoid

The Favorite Story	Reasons Why the Story Is the Favorite
Judas betraying Jesus	"When we grow up we should not betray God or be greedy for money. This will lead to danger. We should not steal when we are small. When we grow up we will be big thief."
Samson	"We need to take care of the grace of God that we have received without losing it. When we sin, we may lose our grace. We need to obey God's commands and lead a life without losing it. When I sin or when I disobey God's commands, I remember the story of Samson."

Awareness of others

While describing their favorite stories, instead of giving any personal applications, some children appreciated certain extraordinary actions in some biblical characters. Children felt an awe, wonder, and appreciation towards these individuals and their actions. Awareness of others in this context has to do with how they valued others' relationship with God. They have understood and valued these unusual opportunities in the lives of these individuals. Table 16 shows this expression of them.

Table 16: Awareness of Others: Appreciating Others' Action

The Favorite Story	Reasons Why the Story Is the Favorite
John the Baptist	"John was not even fit to carry the sandals of Jesus, yet Jesus was baptized by John. John said that the one who is coming after me will baptize you with the Holy Spirit. A dove came upon Jesus when he was baptized."
Zacchaeus	"Because he liked Jesus very much and he climbed on the tree to see Jesus."
Noah	"God allowed Noah to bring everyone to a new world by letting them enter the ark and they all got a new life."

The explanation of their favorite stories gave a glimpse of children's awareness of God, self, others and sin. Their awareness of self, awareness of others and awareness sin are with reference to their awareness of God. Children in this research had derived meanings from biblical stories with respect to the realities in life. This finding supports Stonehouse and May's research.[38] Children's responses depict their relationship with God and their attempt to live a sanctified life in continual relationship with God. Living in relationship with God and a life in continual sanctification are the two sides of spirituality.[39]

Recollecting Biblical Stories: Linking Stories to Life

Children have a variety of storytellers. However, do they remember biblical stories? If so when do children remember biblical stories? These were some of the research questions for this study. Their responses show that they remember stories during different situations in life. They attempt to link stories with various life situations, which further support internal and volitional dimensions of spirituality. Their responses demonstrated that there were opportunities for appropriation and interpretation of stories as they try to link stories with their lives.

Why is it important to know when they remember stories? The Bible is an adult book written by adults, yet according to Sasso, children meet God in the story. The Jewish tradition affirmed that the children could participate in the process of ongoing interpretation of the story.[40] Groome stressed the importance of providing an opportunity to personally appropriate the Story and its vision to the lives of the participants.[41] Yust presents story-linking, "becoming the story," as a means to engage in a way of life that links spiritual awareness to daily life.[42] Here children are enabled to see the connection between their lives and the lives of the biblical characters.

---

38. Stonehouse and May, *Listening to Children*, 76–78.
39. Issler, *Wasting Time with God*, 252.
40. Sasso, "Role of Narratives," 16.
41. Groome, *Christian Religious Education*, 207.
42. Yust, *Real Kids*, 67.

In this research, children's responses show that remembering biblical stories is a part of their day-to-day life. They have a relationship with God – they believe in God's word is true and see God as the one in whom they trust in their various situations in life. Thus their lives are being re-oriented based on their awareness of God. Children are aware that their way of life needs to be in alignment with the message the biblical stories proclaim. This reveals their understanding of the process of sanctification in Christian life.

Children identified certain circumstances in which they remember biblical stories: while reading the Bible, while listening to a sermon, when they pray, during Sunday school, during their leisure, and when they are getting ready to sleep. The conversation of a 10-year-old boy shows how children embrace the challenge from various biblical stories in their lives:

Boy:	I usually think of David.
Researcher:	Why is that?
Boy:	I study that always.
Researcher:	Why do you think of him?
Boy:	David lived a righteous life and I want to be like that.

Children's responses show that they connect different characters of the Bible to particular events in their lives. These references were categorized into two: emotion oriented and situation oriented.

Emotion-oriented recollection

Children remember biblical stories when they feel certain emotions: happiness, sadness, fear, isolation and loneliness. Children not only recognize their emotions but they identify themselves with certain characters and try to link a particular story with their situations. This supports Tamminen's observation that children aged 7–11 sense closeness to God when they are in situation of loneliness, fear, and emergencies like danger and illness.[43] These stories have helped them to be aware of God who cares for them.

---

43. K. Tamminen, "Religious Experiences in Childhood and Adolescence: A Viewpoint of Religious Development between the Ages of 7 and 20," *International Journal of Psychology of Religion* 4, no. 2 (1994): 81.

Emotion Oriented: When I Am Sad. Children shared how they remember stories when they are sad. The 10-year-old boys shared, "When I am sad I only remember the story of Job," "When I am sad, I think of how Jesus calms the storm," "When I am sad, I think of Noah, because no one listened to him and entered the ark," "I remember the stories of those who faced struggles in the Bible." The following conversations show that different children find their solace in remembering different stories:

Conversation with a 10-year-old girl:

Girl:	When I am sad, I think about the crucifixion of Christ.
Researcher:	Why?
Girl:	Because he bore my sins and went on the cross.

Conversation with a 9-year old boy:

Researcher:	When do you remember biblical stories?
Boy:	When I am sad.
Researcher:	Like when?
Boy:	When my mother goes to other places and when I wonder where my mother is. My mother may not be home when I return from school. I ask my neighbors where she is, they say some lies, and I feel a struggle inside.
Researcher:	What kind of stories you remember then?
Boy:	When I sit on the steps and cry out to the Lord for my mother to return.
Researcher:	What story do you remember then?
Boy:	The lost sheep.
Researcher:	Why do you remember that?
Boy:	That one? (*He recites the story of the lost sheep.*)
Researcher:	What happens in you when you remember that story?
Boy:	I know that my mother will return.

A 10-year old boy also remembers the stories when he is sad:

Researcher:	Which story do you remember?
Boy:	(*After a few seconds of silence*) Stories from the Bible.
Researcher:	Which story from the Bible?
Boy:	A hope that God will never leave me.
Researcher:	A hope that God is with you and will never leave you.
Boy:	Yeah, that God is with me.

A conversation with a 9-year-old boy shows how he evaluates himself to see if his sadness is due to his disobedience. Then he thinks of the story of the lost son.

Boy:	When I become sad I wonder if it is because I have done any disobedience to God.
Researcher:	What do you mean by disobedience?
Boy:	Disobeying mom and dad.
Researcher:	Do you remember any stories then?
Boy:	My friends say that we cry and ask God for forgiveness.
Researcher:	Do you remember any stories then?
Boy:	Yes, the story of the lost son.
Researcher:	Why do you remember that story?
Boy:	A son did not listen to his father. Father gave half of his property to his two sons. Second son did not listen to his father and mother and went his way.
Researcher:	Why do you remember this story?
Boy:	When I did not obey my parents.

Emotion Oriented: When I Am Afraid. Fear is another common emotion in children. Different children remember different stories, but through the stories they find hope in God who can save them. A 10-year-old girl described how she remembers biblical stories when she is afraid. "When we are in a bus, the bus goes very fast and we get afraid. Then I think of how God saved Noah in the ark, even when we fall, God will save us." Another 10-year-old girl described her experience:

Girl:	When I am afraid, I think of David and Goliath.
Researcher:	Why?
Girl:	David was a small man, Goliath was a giant, but God was with David and helped him.

Emotion Oriented: When I Feel Isolated and Lonely. When children face isolation and loneliness, they find comfort by remembering biblical stories. A 10-year-old girl said the reason why she remembers biblical stories when her friends leave her "because then I am sitting by myself." An 11-year-old girl shared her experience when she does not have anyone to talk to: "When Moses was a shepherd, he was not eloquent in speech. But God spoke to him even when he had no one to talk to. When we do not have anyone to talk to, God will speak to us." Another 11-year-old said, "In my class I am the only believer, so they (friends) isolate me. Then I remember the story of Saul going after David – how God was with David." A 10-year-old girl shared her experience, "When I am alone I think of how Saul came to kill David but God helped David." Another 10-year-old girl said "When I went to the school for the first time, I did not have friends. Then when children would find faults in me, I remembered the stories of Jesus, how he was and how he forgives our sins." A 9-year-old girl shared the following incident:

Girl:	In my class there is a girl name Akshaya, she stopped talking to me, and I had no one, I became alone, then I remembered some stories of God and found joy.
Researcher:	What are the stories you remembered?
Girl:	Stories of God, when he died on the cross, the time he was born.

Biblical stories have helped them to cope with certain negative feelings. This shows the trust these children have in God, which is internalization of Christian faith.

Situation-oriented recollection

Children's responses reveal that they remember biblical stories not only when they have certain emotions but also when they are in different life situations. Various situation-oriented responses focused on their actions and others' action with reference to biblical stories. They have identified troubling situations in their lives and situations when sin confronts them. Biblical stories have helped children to see biblical standards as the norm for their behavior, thus attributing authority to the Bible.

An 11-year-old boy shared that when he receives an answer to his prayer, he thinks of the story of Hannah "about how Hannah received a child through prayer." When trouble and suffering come, children remember various biblical characters who faced challenges in their lives. They identify with the problems in the lives of these characters. Remembrance of stories generates hope in the power of God to deliver them. An 11-year-old girl shared her experience when she is hungry: "When I am hungry, and parents are not home to give food to us, especially when I return from school, I think of Elijah and how God fed him with bread and meat." A 9-year-old girl shared her experience of remembering stories during times of trouble:

Girl:	When we are in trouble.
Researcher:	What kind of trouble?
Girl:	Suppose someone takes our inheritance, (*she was in tears by this point*) then we remember the sufferings of Christ and that God will deliver us and comfort us (*later on she said that one of her relatives took her fathers inheritance.*)

How children are able to identify with the troubles and pain of these characters are clear in the following discourse. A 10-year-old boy shared his experience: "When I am in suffering, I think of the mother of John. She got John and her people made fun of her when God did a good thing." An 11-year-old boy said, "When I am in suffering, I think of Job and his suffering." A 10-year-old girl whose classmate passed away recently said she remembered how Jesus raised the dead. She wished for her friend to come back to life.

Children could not only identify with the pain of the characters but also with the need for trusting in God that a story portrays. Biblical stories help children to surrender their lives even in the midst of uncertainty and discouragement. An 11-year-old girl describes how biblical stories helped her in finding faith in God's sustenance:

Girl:	One time when my dad's motorcycle had an accident and I had a twisted ankle. I had a cast. Then I remembered Daniel's story.
Researcher:	Which story of Daniel?
Girl:	Daniel in lion's den.
Researcher:	What did you experience when you remembered that story?
Girl:	This will go away. I will be healed.
Researcher:	So did God heal you?
Girl:	Yeah, in two days the cast was taken off.

A 10-year-old girl said she remembers stories during her examinations:

Girl:	When we do not remember the answers during the examination, at that moment I remember biblical stories.
Researcher:	What stories?
Girl:	I do not remember which one now, but I remember then.

What happens when you deal with those who are in authority and/or those who are stronger than you? A 10-year-old girl said, "When teachers punish us, I think of Joseph in the jail. Friends laugh at us, when teacher punish us." She continued describing her experience when participating in a talent competition: "When there is someone who can sing better than us in a song competition, I think of the story of David and Goliath."

Children are aware of I-Evil and sin. They remember biblical stories not only in their trouble, sickness, and sorrow but also when they sin. Comparatively, older boys have such experiences more than girls and younger boys. They not only grasp the importance of repentance and the need of forgiveness of sin in Christ but also interpret biblical stories when they face sin in their lives. Three 11-year-old boys shared their experiences when they sin: "When I sin, I remember the story of Saul. Saul did not repent when he sinned and his end was in big struggle. If we repent, God will forgive"; "I remember Isaiah about how he was convicted of sin, his surrender, and his guilt"; "When I sin, I remember the story of Judas, who betrayed Jesus"; and "He (Judas) went to the priests and they said they cannot help and he hung himself. If he had gone to the cross, he could have asked forgiveness to Jesus."

A 9-year-old girl shared that when she sins, she thinks of Jesus' death on the cross, and how much she has sinned, then she cries. The following conversation with a 9-year-old girl reveals that they are aware of Satan and the need of resistance. This particular conversation has similarity with Stonehouse and May's findings. In their research children expressed how they hear God's voice in their heart and mind in terms of moral guidance.[44] Ratcliff and Ratcliff refer to this experience of hearing a "still small voice" as a form of spiritual experience.[45] This girl recognizes the still small voice which helps her in resisting Satan.

Girl:	When Satan comes to us.
Researcher:	(*quite surprised*) Oh! When does the Satan come to us?
Girl:	Sometimes we. One day in school. My mother has told me that when Satan comes to you, you need to pray to God and claim the blood of Jesus. In school, he comes saying, "you are like this"; "you are like that"; "to betray Jesus."
Researcher:	Who comes?
Girl:	Satan comes.
Researcher:	How do you know it is Satan?
Girl:	When he comes in me saying like "Jesus is bad."
Researcher:	Does it come in your mind, you mean?

---

44. Stonehouse and May, *Listening to Children*, 47.
45. Ratcliff and Ratcliff, *Childfaith*, 22.

Girl:	Yeah, in my mind, then Jesus would tell me, "no child." And then I claim the blood of Jesus.

An 11-year old boy emphasized the need of repentance when he sins:

Boy:	When I do wrong, I remember how Peter went and said sorry to Jesus.
Researcher:	Why do you remember this? Is it because Peter said sorry or Jesus forgave him?
Boy:	No, when we do wrong, we should say sorry to Jesus.

A 10-year old girl explained her thoughts when her friends do wrong:

Girl:	I remember stories when my friends do wrong things.
Researcher:	So you remember biblical stories when your friends do wrong things? Which story do you remember?
Girl:	God forgave Mary and wiped his feet with her tears and God forgave her.

Growing up in a country like India, children learn stories from non-Christian scriptures in their schools. A 9-year-old girl described her thoughts when she learned a story from such a non-Christian scripture: "One lesson in Malayalam was about . . . (name of the god). Then I thought, this god died without knowing anything, but our God knowingly died for our sins. And when I thought of that I cried in class." Here children can compare and contrast Christian stories and other religious stories and could place their faith and trust in the God they believe.

Children have the opportunity to hear biblical stories at church, home, and school. They remember stories and they have their favorite ones. This discussion portrays how biblical stories help them to deal with their issues in life. As Stonehouse and May reported children derive meanings from the biblical stories in relation to their lives.[46] Embedded in these responses is their belief in God as one who protects, one who cares for them, and

---

46. Stonehouse and May, *Listening to Children*, 76–78.

one who provides. They know God as the faithful one who forgives their sin when they confess. This is the evidence of the internalization of faith and volitional dimension of faith. Biblical stories have developed certain values in them and they have an increasing desire to be obedient to God. This highlights their awareness of God as the positive and relational God.[47] There is a sense of self-determination to follow God and obey God as Montemayor and Eisen described.[48]

Listening to Biblical Stories

Children remember biblical stories in different situations. Other questions follow this discussion: "What happens in children when they recall stories? Does knowing these stories influence their life? If so how does it impact children?" These children have revealed their perception of adult's intention in telling stories with them. Their responses with respect to favorite stories show their awareness of God, self, others and Satan. However, underlying the awareness of self and Satan is the awareness of God. If this is so, how do they express the impact of remembering/listening to stories? The following section shows that listening to stories has enabled them in their relationship with God, which is reflected in their desire for sanctification. The children's responses reveal the listening or remembering stories have stimulated certain emotions and transformation in them.

Listening to stories: stimulates religious emotions

Religious emotions are emotions that are aroused with reference to God.[49] Jarvelainen notes that even though there is an affective feeling component and an evaluative cognitive component in religious emotion, the thought of the divine, the cognitive object condition, is a necessary element.[50] For the person feeling religious emotions, this object is existentially significant.[51]

---

47. Roos, "God Concepts," 95.

48. Montemayor and Eisen, "Development," 314.

49. R. C. Roberts, "Emotions Research and Religious Experience," in *The Oxford Handbook of Religion and Emotion*, ed. J. Corrigan (New York: Oxford University, 2008), 493.

50. P. Jarvelainen, "What Are Religious Emotions?" in *Religious Emotions: Some Philosophical Explorations*, eds. W. Leemens and W. Van Herck (Newcastle, UK: Cambridge Scholars, 2008), 18.

51. Ibid., 20.

Emmons calls this "sacred emotions."[52] In this research, children experience certain emotions when they remember or listen to a biblical story. Children are aware of themselves in relation to the God that the story declares. Thus, it is referred to as religious emotions. The significance of this stimulation is noted by Emmons. He sees a suggestive link between emotions and spiritual transformation. Emotions can be motivation for and consequence of spiritual transformation.[53]

Children are aware that certain emotions arise in them when they listen to or remember stories: happiness, comfort, peace, joy, hope, and sadness. Children explained their reasons for experiencing these feelings. Some of the 9-year-old girls responded: "I feel comfort when I remember stories because I receive grace." "I feel happy when we know that God we serve is great." "I feel happy when I think of stories because God is good." "I like stories so I feel happy." "I feel happy because I know God will save me." A 10-year-old girl shared her experience: "I had chicken pox when I was small, then I thought, oh, God is healing everyone, why is God not healing only me? Papa told me the story of Paul that how Paul prayed for his illness but was not healed. Then I understood, Jesus will help me to go forward even if I am healed or not healed." Listening to biblical stories has helped a 10-year-old boy to have enthusiasm to go forward because God will not leave him alone.

When children think of certain stories they feel sad. An 11-year-old girl said that she becomes sad when she remembers the story of the birth of Jesus. This is because "when we were born we were laid in a bed or cradle, but Jesus was in a manger in Bethlehem." Yet for an 11-year-old boy, his hurt goes away when he remembers biblical stories in the midst of pain, hurt, and troubles: "Then we remember the stories of God about how he saved us, our hurt goes away." For a 10-year-old girl her pain goes away as she thinks of the miracles of God and she feels happy.

Children have expressed the impact of listening to biblical stories in religious terms. Some 9-year-old girls expressed that when they listen to stories they experience "joy in spirit," "a special anointing," "I feel like giving my

---

52. R. A. Emmons, "Emotion and Religion," in *Handbook of the Psychology of Religion and Spirituality*, eds. R. F. Paloutzian and C. L. Park (New York: Guilford, 2005), 238.

53. Ibid., 247.

spirit to God," and "I feel as if I am not the person I know." An 11-year-old girl experiences the following: "I feel like the Holy Spirit is coming into my mind." Ten- and 11-year-old girls and boys have experiences in relation to their faith in God: "my faith increases," "faith in God increases," "I get faith to share the Bible with others." Listening to biblical stories help 10-year-old boys to think of God and to have a hope that God will not leave them in the midst of suffering.

Children have experienced assurance in God's care when they listen to or remember biblical stories: Some 11-year-old boys expressed this in the following words: "God will give us good things in life," "He will deliver us from our sufferings." A 10-year-old girl said, "When I get sick, I know that my sickness will go away." These feelings that children experience are in reference to their awareness of God as a positive God, relational God, and potent God.[54]

Listening to stories: stimulates transformation

Children experience an impetus for change as they remember or listen to biblical stories. Girls described how biblical stories help them as an impetus to practice spiritual disciplines: prayer, fasting, and reading the Bible. Hearing biblical stories has helped an 11-year-old girl to have "a desire to pray more." A 9-year-old girl described her experience: "I fasted during the last three days of the fasting prayer in the church. Then mother asked me, 'Why do you fast?' I told her that I need the grace to study to get full marks for mathematics and science (examination). I cried and prayed. I got full marks. I cried and prayed for a good dress, and God gave me a good dress." Her trust in God, which reflects the internalized faith, led her to fast and pray. Conversation with a 10-year-old girl about her practice of fasting is included in Appendix G. She believes that God expects her to fast and pray. Listening to biblical stories has enabled an 11-year-old girl to have a "desire to read the Bible more as there are many good stories in the Bible." A 10-year-old knows that God wants her "to pray to him and read the Bible and think of God's counsel always."

A 10-year-old girl has the desire to "come closer to God," which she clarified as "to move forward in her spiritual life." A 10-year-old boy has "a

---

54. Roos, "God Concepts," 95.

desire to live for him" and an 11-year-old boy senses that "I need to submit myself to the Lord." Another 11-year-old boy has grasped that because he knows from biblical stories that "we are not serving idols like Gentiles." These responses show the volitional dimension of faith or a desire to live a life of faith.

Listening to biblical stories has helped them develop an aversion towards sin. A 10-year-old girl said that biblical stories remind her that she should not stand in the path of sin because if she stands there can be opportunities to betray her God. An 11-year-old boy noted that listening to biblical stories warns him not to do the things that God does not like. A 10-year-old boy senses the same "I should not do bad things." An 11-year-old boy expressed in terms of the need for forgiveness: "I need to ask forgiveness for my sins."

In summary, listening to stories has awakened certain emotions in them with reference to who God is and based on what God can do for them. These are emotions they feel even in the midst of problems, troubles, and sickness. This shows their developing trust in God, which reflects the internal dimension of faith. They have a strong sense of God as the positive and relational God in Roos' terms.[55] Listening to biblical stories has enabled them to be aware of the need for change as they listen to/remember stories. It has enabled them to practice spiritual disciplines. They do not want to do things that displease God, which is a clear indication of self-determination as Montemayor and Eisen noted.[56] Underlying in these responses is their belief and trust in God as their God and Savior.

Biblical Stories and Awareness of God

Another question for focus group interviews was as follows: "What are the things that you know about God because you know these stories?" This was to hear directly from children about their understanding of God. Their favorite stories, situations when they remember stories, and impact of listening to stories gave a glimpse of their awareness of God. Yet this session gave an opportunity for the research team to hear their voices with respect to this aspect.

---

55. Ibid.
56. Montemayor and Eisen, "Development," 314.

Table 17: Children's Understanding of Characteristics of God from Biblical Stories

Characteristics	What children said about God . . .
Potency of God	"Nothing is impossible for him, almighty God, he knows our mind, he knows what we think, a great God, he is stronger than anyone, he does miracles, he has victory over death, victorious over sin, Satan, and death and there is no other God so big like him in the world."
Punishing God	"If we keep on doing wrong he will not communicate to us, God punishes those who disobey."
Positive God	"God will never change his words, heals the sick, hears our pain, helps us, he helps us to remember answers in examination, removes pain, provider, comforter, he will never leaves us alone, saves us from danger and sufferings, hears our prayers, helps us when we face temptation, heals our sickness, he provides for more than our needs, he will never leave us in our sufferings, righteous God, compassionate God, he gives us wisdom to study, forgives our sins, he will not remember what he has forgiven, he give us good things, he gives us our desires."
Relational God	"My God, my Savior, died on the cross for my sins, faithful, good God, friend, we can tell him anything, we can openly share our pain with him, we have a God to talk when we do not have any one to talk, he gives us joy like no can give, God talks to us, he loves us the most, he knows us closer than a friend, guides us, sustains us, shepherd, he will never change his words, whatever troubles come we can trust in God."
God-like Parents	"Father, we are his children, comfort me like a father."

Bellous notes that God-concepts are essential for human beings. "There is no such thing as a person without an image of God."[57] One will never lose the image of God that has once developed in childhood. Even though images of God "undergo revision, repression, recovery and reconciliation" as one grows up, images of God acquired during childhood resurge in adult

---

57. Bellous, "Educational Significances," 179.

life during difficult times.[58] Thus understanding God-concepts of children will help to see how biblical stories are enabling them in their spiritual formation. Previous discussions have included Hood, Hill, and Spilka's description of Deconchy's three stages of the idea of God and Roos' five scales to explain children's understanding of God. Table 17 indicates children's response based on Roos' classification.

More examples of awareness of God

Conversations during six weeks of class activities revealed these children's awareness of God. On the second day of the class activities, the following conversation happened in the class of 10-year olds. The research assistant did not expect such responses from 10-year-old children. He was quite surprised by the extent to which children have understood God and his work on earth. This shows how children are aware of God as the potent God. G1, G2, and G3 represent three different girls and B1 and B2 denote two different boys.

Assistant:	Why did Herod want to kill Jesus?
G1:	In one kingdom, if another king emerges, the king does not like that.
B1:	You do not need another king in a kingdom.
G2:	The position of the king will go.
Assistant:	What is the position of a king?
G3:	One.
Assistant:	One means one, can two people be number one?
B2:	No, he is number two, the number one is God; God is surely number one.

During class activities, children's conversations show their awareness of who God has led to trust in him above everything in this world. Children's responses showed evidences for internalized faith as they trust in God as the one who saves them from dangers, one who heals them, one who is faithful, and one who is omnipresent. On the third day of class activity, the lesson was about the lady who poured an alabaster jar of perfume on

---

58. Ibid., 178.

Jesus' head and Judas betraying Jesus. The research assistant gave a writing activity to 11-year-old children. G1 and G2 denote two different 11-year-old girls.

Assistant:	Who is the person whom you believe the most, the most in the world? Why? Write your response in your lesson.
G1:	In heaven or in the world?
Assistant:	In the world?
G2:	Can we include Jesus?
Assistant:	It is up to you if you want to include Jesus or not. If it is papa or mummy write why do you make that choice?
G2 and G1:	Can we include Jesus?
Assistant:	If you believe in Jesus you can write his name. Whoever it is it has to be the one who you believe the most in the world.

Children thought for sometime and wrote the following responses. Boys wrote the following responses: "I believe in Jesus, he helps me when I face hindrances," "Jesus because he has done many things for me," "I have trusted Jesus for some things and he had done that for me, so I believe in him," "I believe in Jesus because he removed my sins, when death and dangers come he will save me." Girls wrote the following responses: "He came to the world to save sinners," "Jesus will not change his words, if he says something," "He has the ability to come to wherever place I am," "I love him because he heals my sickness." This shows their trust in God.

These children understand God as powerful and sovereign. They form God-concepts by connecting one biblical story to other stories. On the third class activity, a part of one of the discussion questions was as follows: "Why did not God protect Jesus when he was older like he protected him when he was a baby?"[59] Conversation of girls and boys in 11-, 9-, and 10-year olds in their respective class with a research assistant is worth noting.

---

59. India Sunday School Union, *God Our Security*, 226.

The first conversation happened among 11-year olds. B1, B2, and B3 represent two 11-year-old boys and G1 and G2 11-year-old girls.

Assistant:	Why did God not protect Jesus when he was older like he protected him when he was a baby?
B1:	It was plan of God.
G1:	God may have already decided that he has to die for our sins.
B2:	God gave his son for our sins, for the removal of our sins, so that we may not sin.
G2:	In olden days, sin was removed by sacrifice, instead of sacrifice of animals; Jesus became our sacrifice.
G1:	See God was crucified because of our sins, he was crucified so that no one may sin again.
Assistant:	Did you hear this? In olden days, people offered sacrifices. Why did they offer sacrifices?
G2:	Because we sin.
Assistant:	What was offered as the sacrifices?
G2, G1, and B3:	A lamb.
Assistant:	Then?
B1:	A dove
Assistant:	What was God's purpose in not saving Jesus from the cross?
G2:	God became a sacrifice for our sins.
Assistant:	Then? God could have saved Jesus from death, but God did not do that, why?
B1:	To remove the sins of human beings.
G1:	Only if he dies, Jesus can be king, so that missionaries could learn this and tell others to worship Jesus.

Assistant:	Why was Jesus allowed to die? When every boy who was born during Jesus' time was killed, Jesus was saved as a boy.
B1:	To defeat the plan of Satan.
G1:	To receive born again.
G2:	He rose again, then he resurrected, and then will come to take us to heaven.

However, in the class of 9-year olds, the research assistant expressed her surprise to hear that a girl asked the above question before the research assistant shared this question in the class. She was further surprised when a boy gave the answer before the assistant could say her thoughts about this question. G1 and B1 are a 9-year-old girl and boy respectively.

G1:	If God could protect Jesus when he as a child, how come Jesus was not protected when he became big?
B1:	If God was to protect Jesus, then he cannot be killed. If he was not killed then our sins cannot be removed.

Ten-year olds' responses to the question had more theological content than others: "When Jesus was small, it was God's plan to protect him as a baby, yet it was God's plan to let him die later." Another child said, "God knows everything, even our thoughts, even before we were born, till we die God knows everything."

During class activities, these children drew pictures, wrote poems and their experiences to show how God protects them in life. These show their awareness of God as the positive God, relational God, and potent God. These are included in Appendix G.

Biblical stories have helped them to develop certain God-concepts. Their voices reveal that they are aware of the attributes of God: faithfulness, goodness, and omniscience. They know that God is presently active in their lives through his acts: he helps them, hears their prayers, protects them, hears their pain, and saves them from problems. The previous sections have several examples of how children have experienced God's activities in their lives. They know God intervenes in their lives to help them, protect them, heal them, and save them. This shows that children have understood God in personalization themes as well. Interiorization themes are evident, as they have understood God as the one whom they can trust for their problems and needs. Children see God as one who is concerned with their physical and emotional needs. As Roos has already noted, this research supports that even younger children have grasped God with reference to the three themes proposed by Deconchy.[60]

Based on Roos' description,[61] children's responses show that they know God more in terms of "potency of God," "positive God," and "relational God." They are aware of God as a "punishing God" and "God-like a parent." Their responses show that they have understood him as an omnipotent and omniscient God. The omnipresence of God was not implied in their conversations.

Besides this, children expressed their awareness of God in the following terms: Savior of the world, true God, living God, Son of God, Prince of Peace, Everlasting Father, creator God, and Jesus died so that he can take us to heaven when he returns. Children thought for a second before they said these descriptors, except for a few items like Prince of Peace and Everlasting Father. Previous discussions with respect to situations when they remember biblical stories and how stories impact their lives demonstrate that they were not trying to give a satisfactory answer to researchers. They have experienced the potency of God in their lives. They have tasted God as the positive and relational God. Thus with respect to awareness of God, children have an intellectual comprehension and an emotional and relational appreciation.

Drawing inferences from previous research,[62] God-concepts of children in thisresearch reveal the positive influence of family and church on them. Hood, Hill, and Spilka note the consensus among researchers regarding the influence of parents in the development of God-concepts in children.[63]

---

60. Deconchy, "The Idea of God."
61. See Roos, "God Concepts."
62. J. M. Nelson, *Psychology, Religion, and Spirituality* (New York: Springer, 2009), 257.
63. Hood, Hill and Spilka, *Psychology of Religion*, 96.

The influence of mothers in the formation of God-concepts in children is supported by research by Roos, Iedema, and Miedema.[64] Roos noted that a positive relationship with any one of the caregivers – mother, father, or teacher – can help children in developing concepts of God as kind and loving.[65] Religious socialization at home and school in terms of God-concepts of the adults and goals of religious socialization impact children's God-concepts.[66]

These children's responses about their awareness of God reveal that they have positive and loving concepts of God, which indicate spiritual well-being in them. This can be an indicator of their future understanding of God as adults. Rowatt and Kirkpatrick noted how secure attachment with God promotes physical and mental well-being.[67] Nelson discusses the positive impact of the importance of benevolent and loving God-concepts in life on participation in religious activities, spiritual maturity, and relationship with God.[68] It is also linked to positive interpersonal relationships, higher self-esteem, greater effectiveness, low anxiety level, and stress tolerance and effectiveness in life settings.[69]

Biblical Stories and Awareness of Self

What do children know about themselves as they learn biblical stories? Previous discussions show that this theme has been derived from their responses of favorite stories, intentions for sharing stories, impact of stories in their lives, and situations when they remember stories. This question was a unique opportunity to hear their voices regarding this aspect. Self-awareness impacts their behavior[70] and it is significant in their emotional

---

64. S. A. de Roos, J. Iedema, and S. Miedema, "Influence of Maternal Denomination, God Concepts, and Child-Rearing Practices on Young Children's God Concepts," *Journal for the Scientific Study of Religion* 43, no. 4 (2004): 528–533.

65. Roos, "God Concepts," 100.

66. Ibid., 101.

67. W. C. Rowatt and L. A. Kirkpatrick, "Two Dimensions of Attachment to God and Their Relation to Affect, Religiosity, and Personal Constructs," *Journal for the Scientific Study of Religion* 41, no. 4 (2002): 646–647.

68. Nelson, *Psychology*, 259.

69. Ibid.

70. M. Rosenberg, "The Self-Concept: Social Product and Social Force," rev. ed. in *Social Psychology: Sociological Perspectives*, eds. M. Rosenberg and R. H. Turner (Piscataway, NJ: Transaction, 1990), 593.

and social development.[71] Thus it is important to hear children's voices in this aspect.

Hay and Nye have described I-self as one of the dimensions of relational consciousness,[72] and related to one's self-identity. Self-concept begins to develop in childhood yet grows as children get older.[73] Research among boys and girls from 4th to 12th grade noted that children's self-understanding becomes more abstract and less concrete as they grow older.[74]

Children's responses in this research can shed light on how stories help in their self-awareness. It has to do with how they see themselves before God, their self-reflection of their actions when they sin, their self-determination to follow God, and how they see themselves in relation to God and others. All these responses are in relation to God, which indicates what James referred to as the spiritual self, which is the inner core of a person.[75] This understanding of children can be one aspect of their non-academic self-concept in the definition of Shavelson, Huber, and Stanton.[76] An adapted form of Montemayor and Eisen[77] categories are used to classify children's self-awareness as portrayed in table 18.

---

71. Littleton, Wood, and Staarman, *Handbook of Psychology*, 505.
72. Hay and Nye, *Spirit of the Child*, 109.
73. Shavelson, Huber, and Stanton, "Self-Concept," 428.
74. Montemayor and Eisen, "Development," 318.
75. James, *Principles of Psychology*, 292.
76. Shavelson, Huber, and Stanton, "Self-Concept," 412.
77. Montemayor and Eisen, "Development."

Table 18: Children's Awareness of Self from Biblical Stories

Categories	Children's Responses
Ideological beliefs	"Those who believe in God is a new being. We need to ask forgiveness for our sins. God will save us in the midst of suffering. When we ask, God will give us our needs. When we pray we have relationship with God, and prayer strengthens our relationship with God. God forgives us when we confess."
Psychic style	"We are precious to God. We are God's child. I was a sinner, when I hurt others I know it is wrong to do that. When I lie, I need to confess it to God and he will forgive me."
Existential individuating	"When we become aware that we are not living according to the story we hear, make a decision to live accordingly. If we are not walking in God's path, we are walking in sinful path."
Sense of self-determination	"Never go away from the Bible, never go behind as a failure, but run forward. To have faith in God and stand firm, do not run looking at the people who failed. Think of what we can do for God. We need to walk in the ways of God."

Conversations portraying awareness of self

There were many long conversations with children during the six days of class activities and focus group interviews that showed children's awareness of God. The following discussion gives some evidences about their ideological beliefs, sense of self-determination and interpersonal style.

Ideological beliefs. The following conversation with a 9-year-old girl amazed focus group moderators. Her awareness of God shows self-evaluation but reveals her belief of God –"ideological beliefs" in Montemayor and Eisen's terms. She has understood God as a forgiving God. But she also understood that when she treats God as insignificant, God turns away from her.

Girl:	God will forgive us when we do wrong. God will not remember what he has forgiven, he tells us not to do it again. If we go in that way again, he will not communicate to us. Then we are not walking in God's path we are walking in sinful path.
Researcher:	Why does he not talk to us?
Girl:	We did not obey him, we treat him as insignificant.
Researcher:	So then we treat God as insignificant.
Girl:	Ah ah (*meaning "yes"*).

Examples of Self-Determination. Eating food offered to idols and singing film songs became a topic of discussion in some focus groups. This discussion shows the "sense of self-determination" in children to obey God. This is further evidence of internalized faith and volitional faith as Downs mentioned.[78] These conversations are with 9-year-old girls:

First Conversation:

Girl:	They bring food offered to idols to our classes and give it to us. And we say we do not want it.
Researcher:	So they bring food to you?
Girl:	We do not take it and say we do not want them. Then they say, we take whatever you give us why you do not take what we give you?

Second conversation:

Researcher:	What were you going to say?

---

78. Downs, *Spiritual Growth*.

Girl:	Our teacher is a temple goer. She brings things to the class, temple things to class. Temple goers bring things to class. My friend (her friend goes to her church) almost ate it. I said no do not eat it. I told them do not eat it, we know God, we should not eat it. Then she did not eat it.

Third Conversation:

Researcher:	What were you going to say?
Girl:	In my second grade, there was a boy with thread on his hands. When he went to a pilgrim place, he brought some food. My class teacher was a temple goer. He gave this food to everyone. There was one another girl who was a Christian, she ate, but I did not eat. And the teacher scolded me for not eating it.

Fourth Conversation with an 11-year-old girl:

Researcher:	Have they given such items to you?
Girl:	Yes, but I have never eaten it. I am the only one in my class who is a believer; I am the only one who did not eat it.
Researcher:	Why you do not take it?
Girl:	It is because they are offered to idols.

Fifth Conversation with another 11-year-old girl:

Girl:	When we visited a home, there was a group of older girls. They distributed these kind of food. There was a believer she also ate it. I said I do not want this.

A 10-year-old girl shared the following: "When we were in Bombay, our neighbor brought some sweets during a religious festival, and we did not eat it." An 11-year-old girl shared her conviction: "My mother has told me that whatever others give, we have to pray first and then eat it."

Another topic was about singing songs. Children have a strong conviction about what kind of songs they can sing. This needs to be understood in the context of a form of pietism that prevails among Pentecostal churches in Kerala. Watching movies is taboo for believers. The following conversation of children shows that children have developed a "sense of self-determination"[79] regarding this aspect. A 9-year-old girl described her experience in a song competition where only film songs can be sung. But she sang a Christian devotional song:

> In my school, when I join the music competition, I did not get any prizes (because she sang a Christian song). So they ask me to join for speech competition in English, Malayalam or Hindi. They said that I can join music competition, but I need to sing a film song. If I sing a religious song I will not get a prize. I was very sad. I participated in the competition. I sang a song about God. Judges were from different schools. Judges said that I have good tune and I got first prize.

A 10-year-old boy shared his conviction about singing Christian songs: "In the school bus, children sing film songs, but I do not mind that. I sing our songs." A 9-year-old boy shared his experience when his friends play a game of singing the next song with last letter of the previous song: "When we play the game in school, my friends told me that only film songs are allowed. I said that if I need to play I can only sing Christian songs."

Another conversation with a 9-year-old girl was about learning a lesson from one of her textbooks, which talks about other gods. This shows her self-determination to focus on the things of God and to prevent her mind from indulging in things that distract her attention from God. This researcher opted to use only part of the conversation to protect the child's identity.

Girl:	The first four lines that need to be memorized. I only study that in school not in home. I do not study that well.
Researcher:	Why do you do that?

---

79. See Montemayor and Eisen, "Development."

Girl:	This is because my thinking became focused on their god and I forget our God and love those gods. Then I do not have the thought of drawing close to our God.

On the second day of class activity, a research assistant who worked with 10-year-olds expressed his surprise as he heard the conversation of the children. These children are aware of the need of complete surrender from their part as they offer themselves to Jesus in return to what he had done for them. This is a long conversation with children, which shows children's self-understanding with respect to Jesus' coming in this world. B1, B2, and B3 represent three boys and G1, G2, G3, G4, and G5 represent five girls.

Assistant:	God gives gifts to us because he loves us, what will you give him back?
B1:	Praise.
G1:	Give ourselves.
G2:	Surrender ourselves to him, a complete surrender.
Assistant:	What do mean by complete surrender? (*The research assistant was amazed by this reply from the child.*)
G2:	Confess our sins and give ourselves to him.
Assistant:	What do you give to God as a gift?
G3:	Thank God for all he has done, accept him as my personal Savior.
Assistant:	Then what will you do?
G3:	Absolute surrender to God.
G4, B2 and B3:	Do the things that he likes.
G5:	Tell sorry when I do wrong.
G5:	I will say thanks for saving me.
B2:	Obey the commandments of God.
Assistant:	What do you mean by commandments?
B2, B2, and B3:	Ten Commandments.

B1:	I will do everything that pleases God.
B2 to B1:	Do not tell lie, do you not sin? (*laughing*)
B1:	Thank God for saving me from danger (*without paying much attention to the previous comment*).
Assistant:	When we give gifts to him we give him the greatest gift? Isn't right? What can we give him?
G1 and G3:	Our prayers.
Assistant:	Is prayer a gift to him?
G2:	Our love.
Assistant:	Yeah, our love is the greatest gift. He loved us so he gave Jesus to us. How can we love God?
B1:	Do what pleases God. Pray to him.
Assistant:	Okay, give thanks, say sorry.
Assistant:	Loving him more than anything is the greatest gift to him, isn't it?
Assistant:	Do we give the same gift to everyone? Do we give our brothers and sisters the same gift as we give our friends?
Children:	No (*many children said this together*).
Assistant:	Why is that? When we give gifts we give ...
Children:	Different, different (*many children said this together*).
B1:	Those we love the most we give good gifts.
B2:	Then we offer ourselves in complete surrender to him.
Assistant:	We give gifts depending on how we love them. When God gave the gift to us, did he give like that?
Children:	No (*many children said this together*).
Assistant:	Just think, how did God give the gift?
B1:	He gave everyone the same gift.
B2:	Because he loves everyone the same.

C1:	(*waited for a second*) I will tell God to take me (*in a contemplative tone*).
Assistant:	What is the best gift you have received?
B1:	Spiritually or materially?
Assistant:	Spiritually or materially! (*The assistant did not expect to hear this*).
B2:	Both?
Assistant:	What do we give more priority to?
B1:	Spirituality.
G3:	To Jesus.
B1:	That is spiritual.
Assistant:	Then what is the best gift we have received?
Children:	Jesus, Jesus (*many children said this together*).
B2:	The second best gift is my brother.
B1:	That is because you can play cricket with him (*laughing*).
Assistant:	So the greatest gift we received was Jesus, so when we give to him . . .
Children:	We give the greatest gift to God (*many children said this together*).
Assistant:	If I give you a paper, you won't give me a hero pen.
G2:	See we cannot give anything to him in return.

Interpersonal style. Interpersonal style is one of the categories of Montemayor and Eisen in explaining self-concepts.[80] This refers to the social and personal characteristics of individuals. Children's responses gave an opportunity to hear how biblical stories influence their relationship with others. Analysis of their responses resulted in two categories: behavior oriented, and being a change agent.

Interpersonal Style: Behavior Oriented. Children are aware of their behavior towards others. An 11-year-old girl shared her conviction: "We

---

80. Montemayor and Eisen, "Development," 314.

never speak anything against them. Never say back answers to them. If they had known God they would not say this to us." Another 10-year-old girl shared her thought: "If they are rude to me and if they do not ask for forgiveness, then I think it is because they do not know God." A 10-year-old boy said: "When we hurt others, we need to comfort them, and try not to do this to them again." A 9-year-old boy shared the need of helping others: "We need to help them in the ways that we could." A 10-year-old girl expressed the need to love others: "I need to be loving and gentle. Even when we are angry, we need to be kind to others. Even when others are angry we need to be ten times loving towards them." This shows that these children are aware that they are to control their emotions when they deal with others. They may attempt to behave according to their awareness. Yet how far they are able to succeed in their attempt is worth noting.

Interpersonal Style: Being a Change Agent. Children are not only aware of their friends' need of God but also their role in the lives of their friends in the process. Children see themselves as change agents in the lives of those who do not follow God. Previous discussions about the reasons for sharing biblical stories reveal their awareness of storytellers' intention to introduce God to others. Children have internalized this intention. They share biblical stories with their friends with the following reasons: their friends would intellectually understand God, be aware of themselves with respect to God and develop internal and volitional dimension of faith, develop an antagonism towards Satan, and transmit biblical stories to others. By sharing stories with others, children seek to become change agents. The responses they receive as they share stories are not always pleasant. They are also aware of a lack of freedom to worship God in certain states in India. A 10-year-old boy has a suggestion: "If there is no freedom to worship God, they can come to our state (to worship) and go back to their state." The analysis of children's responses with respect to their role as change agents in the lives of their friends are categorized as follows: Giving advice, be a role model, and share the Word. Table 19 portrays this understanding of children.

Table 19: Awareness of Self: Being a Change Agent

Categories	Children's Words
Giving advice	"If anyone does bad things like stealing we need to advice them and bring them to the ways of God; Those who are going astray from God, need to be brought back to God; I would like to tell them that do not do wickedness, do not punch them, do not make fun of others, not to steal, do not find fault in others, do not do revenge."
Be a role model	"When they see us, people from other faiths may think that, oh their God is a big God, let me follow this God."
Share the Word	"I would like to tell them the stories of the Bible; I would like this people in the world to come to know the Lord and to hear the word of God; We need to give tract and bring them to the ways of the Lord; When we share the stories to children, they will in turn go their parents and they will tell them to their relatives and bring them to the Lord; We need to pray to God for them; We need to try to bring others to the Lord and my relatives are not in the church."

Children's responses reveal that biblical stories help them to be aware of their beliefs and interpersonal relationships. They make self-evaluation and determine what kind of lifestyle they want to live. They are being change agents in the lives of their friends. This shows these stories have influenced their feelings, attitudes and values. They have a desire to live a life in obedience to God. This reveals internalization and volitional dimension of spiritually maturing faith.

Reflecting on the self-concept of these children is important for various reasons. Rosenburg notes that social factors impact the formation of self-concept, yet self-concept influences behavior.[81] Research studies affirm the importance of self-concepts in emotional and social development in

---

81. Rosenberg, "Self-Concept," 593; Shavelson, Huber, and Stanton, "Self-Concept," 411.

children.[82] Self-understanding and self-awareness are crucial for spiritual formation.[83]

Biblical Stories and Awareness of Others

Awareness of others, I-other is one of the dimensions of relational consciousness.[84] They discovered how children bridge I-other relationships to and from I-Thou.[85] McGhee sees another aspect of this association. The "traditional criterion" to measure one's awareness of God in the religious context is one's sympathetic awareness to others and the discernment of the nature of the needs of others.[86] Loving God and one's neighbor is the essence of Christian spirituality.[87] Loving one another is the characteristic of those who love God (1 John 4:7). McGhee stresses that inner awareness of others is the reflection of awareness of God.[88]

Previous sections have gleaned children's understanding of their awareness of others as they talked about their favorite stories and reasons for sharing biblical stories. Children's responses based on their favorite stories reveal that they have developed certain norms about their interpersonal relationships. They appreciate biblical characters' actions in terms of obedience to God and their love for God. They have accepted the disobedience in the lives of certain biblical characters as warnings in their lives. In this session, children directly spoke about their awareness of others. They responded to the following question: what have you understood about others through listening to biblical stories?

---

82. Littleton, Wood, and Staarman, *Handbook of Psychology*, 505.

83. Downs, *Spiritual Growth*, 102; G. Simmonds, "Spiritual Formation," in *The New Westminster Dictionary of Christian Spirituality*, ed. P. Sheldrake (Louisville, KY: Westminster John Knox, 2005), 310.

84. Hay and Nye, *Spirit of the Child*, 109.

85. Ibid., 116.

86. M. McGhee, "Making Spirits Attentive: Moral-and-Spiritual Development," in *Spirituality, Philosophy and Education*, eds. D. Carr and J. Haldane (New York: RoutledgeFalmer, 2003), 30.

87. C. Stonehouse, "After a Child's First Dance with God: Accompanying Children on a Protestant Spiritual Journey," in *Nurturing Child and Adolescent Spirituality: Perspectives from the World's Religious Traditions*, eds. K. M. Yust et al. (New York: Rowman & Littlefield, 2006), 105.

88. McGhee, "Making Spirits Attentive," 30.

Others-God: view of others with reference to God

Children's responses show that biblical stories have helped them to view others with reference to God. They understood the need of God's forgiveness in others' lives, the need of hearing God's word. They make evaluation of the people around them. A 9-year-old girl's conversation shows the need of forgiveness in others: "Those who sin, if they ask for forgiveness, God will forgive." An 11-year-old girl knows that others around her are also a creation of God and thus children of God. Certain emotions arise in them when they see others who do not follow God. A 9-year-boy shared his feelings: "I feel sad that they do not know God." They wish to see others follow God. An 11-year-old boy desires that it would have been good if they had known God.

Some children gave an evaluation of others with reference to their worship and the way of life. A 10-year-old boy commented about people of other faiths: "They worship idols. They think they worship God, they worship Satan, a god who is not living." A 10-year-old girl lamented about Christians who do not believe in God: "In this world there are a lot of Christians, but they do not believe in God."

Children are aware of what is happening in the world. A 10-year-old girl said, "The authorities of the world do not care about God but they think about their position in the world." A 10-year-old boy shared his thoughts about persecution: "Those in the world, kill the people who spreads the Word. That makes me really sad." A 10-year-old boy said: "In this world . . . people in this world have no peace, no love, and no joy. They fight with others." Children know what can make a difference in their friends' lives. A 10-year-old boy said: "Hearing God's word can bring them to God." Children can see the need of God in the lives of others. Here we see the link between their perception of the need of God in their friends and their practice of telling biblical stories with their friends.

Chapter Summary

The research with twenty-nine 9- to 11-year-old children during the months of April to July was to study children's perceptions of the role of biblical narratives in their spiritual formation. This chapter gave the analysis of data collected through class activities and focus group interviews. Certain themes emerged as an outcome of the analysis of the data. These themes were explicitly portrayed in this chapter with specific illustrations using verbal and written data collected from children.

Children hear a variety of stories from various settings. They identified three settings in which they hear biblical stories. At church, home, and school they have various storytellers. These children share biblical stories with their friends at school and in their neighborhood. Children have perceived five reasons why others tell biblical stories to them. These children also tell biblical stories to their friends for the same reasons. The five identified reasons are as follows: (1) to develop the intellectual dimension of faith, (2) to develop the internal dimension of faith, (3) to develop the volitional dimension of faith, (4) to develop an awareness of others or I-others practiced in the transmission of stories, and (5) to develop an awareness of Satan or I-Evil expressed in the aversion towards sin.

These children could recall biblical stories and have their favorite stories. Recalling stories implies intellectual dimension of faith. Times when they remember stories show how they link stories to their day-to-day life. There are emotion-oriented recollections and situation-oriented recollections. When children remember or listen to stories, it stimulates religious emotions and transformation in them.

Biblical stories have helped these children to be aware of God in the following categories: Potency of God, Punishing God, Positive God, Relational God, and God-like Parents. Biblical stories enable them to be aware of self in terms of ideological self, psychic self, existential individuating, sense of self-determination, and interpersonal style. With respect to interpersonal style they are aware of themselves with reference to their behavior and as agents of change. They are aware of others through listening to biblical narratives. This awareness is basically with reference to others' need for God in their lives.

How do children perceive the role of biblical stories in their spiritual formation? The next chapter will answer this by evaluating the themes that emerged in the data analysis in light of the literature review and theological worldview presented in the previous chapters. Further, limitations and recommendations for further research will also be noted.

CHAPTER 6

Conclusions

This research was done to explore children's perceptions of the role of biblical narratives in their spiritual formation. Class activities, focus group interviews, and member checking with twenty-nine 9- to 11-year-old children enabled the researcher to hear the voices of children about the topic. Spiritual formation of children is not a new area of research. Research on children's spirituality has received international attention as a multidisciplinary field of study. The Bible witnesses how the stories of God's mighty acts and wonders among previous generations played a significant role in nurturing faith in subsequent generations. Yet the uniqueness of this research is to listen to children about their perception of the role of biblical stories in their spiritual formation. This research is significant as biblical stories are the major content of teaching children in Sunday schools in Kerala, India and Sunday schools, in general, are seen as a crucial and exclusive ministry with children.

This research is significant because of the high-context culture of India, where stories are communicated as vehicles of truth, not just to illustrate a point. Research done in high-context cultures has different implications than research done in low-context cultures. This research explores children's perceptions of the role of biblical stories in their spiritual formation.

This chapter reflects on the results of this study in relation to the literature review and theological understanding presented in the previous chapters. Implications for practice, limitations of the study, and the recommendations for future research are also discussed in this chapter.

Major Findings

Certain categories emerged out of data analysis. The main research question posed at the beginning of the study was as follows: What are children's perceptions of the role of biblical narratives in their spiritual formation? Five additional questions were used to derive children's perceptions on the research questions. The following section discusses the results of the research using these questions.

1) Who tells biblical stories to children? Where do they hear stories?
2) Why do these storytellers tell biblical stories to children?
3) When do children recall biblical stories?
4) Does recalling or listening to biblical stories impact the life situations they face? If so, how?
5) How do these children's perceptions about biblical stories compare with the four dimensions of relational consciousness in Hay and Nye's study in the United Kingdom: I-Thou, I-self, I-other, and I-world? Are there other important insights from the proposed study that challenge or go beyond the model developed by Hay and Nye?[1]

Research Question One

Who tells biblical stories to children? Where do they hear stories?

This question was designed to identify the extent to which children in churches and Christian families are exposed to biblical stories. Children see church, home, and school as the three settings for hearing biblical stories. They have a variety of storytellers with respect to age, gender, and relationship. However, children perceive church as the primary carrier of biblical stories with pastors and Sunday school teachers as storytellers. The diverse activities in churches are avenues to hear biblical stories. Home also has a variety of storytellers: parents, siblings, grandparents, aunts, and guests. Children hear biblical stories from schools where teachers and friends are the storytellers. The majority of the children said that their favorite stories are biblical stories. There is a methodological concern here as these children

---

1. Hay and Nye, *Spirit of the Child*.

heard biblical stories from the research team members for two hours per week for six weeks.

These children also share biblical stories with their friends at school and in their neighborhood. By sharing biblical stories they seek to be change agents in their friends' lives. The research team members were quite amazed by the passion with which children shared their experiences of sharing stories with their friends. The reasons of the unique phenomenon for children sharing biblical stories can be as follows: (1) The emphasis of the participating churches on evangelism, (2) internalizing of this emphasis, (3) imitating significant adults in their lives. The fact that they share stories with their friends even when the latter do not respond favorably indicates that these children know the importance of sharing biblical stories with others. Also their unanimous response during member checking that they want others to know God, indicates that their practice of storytelling originate from internalizing the teaching of the churches.

Review of previous literature demonstrates the importance adults give in telling biblical stories to children. Goldman recommended the use of very little biblical material to children before the age of twelve.[2] Yet, Fowler, Westerhoff, Cavalletti, Pritchard, Sasso, Yust, and Garland are some of the researchers who recommended the telling biblical stories to children. These recommendations show the value Christian educators give in sharing biblical stories with young children. In the Old Testament, telling stories of the past to children is a commandment of God. This was an opportunity to explain the unique lifestyle of the Israelites to children. God's revelation was transmitted from one generation to another through storytelling and reading of the Law.

Research Question Two

Why do these storytellers tell biblical stories to children?

This question was intended to see what children perceive as the reasons for telling biblical stories to them. It is significant to hear children's voices in this aspect as biblical stories are shared in churches to foster spiritual formation in children. In this research, children clearly see that adults

---

2. Goldman, *Religious Thinking*, 67.

deliberately communicate biblical stories with them. The analysis of their responses identified five reasons: (1) To develop I-Thou in the intellectual dimension (i.e. to know God and to know the content of stories). (2) To develop faith in the internalized dimension, which will affect their values, feelings, and attitudes so that their relationship with God will be a growing and vibrant reality. (3) To develop the volitional dimension of faith. They not only know the content of the story but also value the content to order their lives in obedience to what the content teaches. Even though they see that the evidences of these dimensions are to be reflected in their lives, they see this with reference to their relationship with God. (4) To develop I-other with reference to transmission of biblical stories. They understood that they are to share biblical stories to others not only when they are young but also when they are old. (5) To develop an awareness of I-Evil. This is to develop an antagonism against Satan which is expressed in an aversion towards sin. Children are aware of sin in the lives of biblical characters and they have accepted these examples as warnings in their lives. They are aware of the need of actively resisting the devil. This shows their awareness of sanctification in their lives which is an important phase in spiritual growth.[3] These identified reasons are unique to this research.

Children share biblical stories with other children with the above five intentions. This is another unique finding in this research. During member checking, children affirmed that the primary reason for sharing biblical stories with others is for their friends to know God. They explained the word "know" as follows: "to comprehend God" so that "they may have a relationship with him."

Previous research has neither mentioned children's perceptions of reasons for sharing biblical stories with them nor stated reasons why children share biblical stories with other children. Meanwhile, the terminologies and phrases children used to describe this aspect reflect the traditions and theology of the Pentecostal churches. "To be filled with anointing," "to be born again," "to increase faith in God," "to expel Satan from our homes," are few examples of such terms. The terms and stories that they hear in these churches are the tools with which they could explain their experiences

---

3. Ratcliff and Ratcliff, *Childfaith*, 11.

with God. Fowler notes this as an important aspect of faith among children during the mythic-literal stage: 6 to 12 years of age.[4] Westerhoff notes that stories of the faith community provide a sense of meaning and identity to children in the stage of "affiliative faith."[5] The question that emerges here is the extent to which children understand the meaning of the terms they have used. Their descriptions of reasons why a particular story is their favorite, the times when they recall biblical stories, and how these stories impact their lives are evidences to the fact that to a certain extent they have internalized what they hear in churches and homes. They try to connect these stories to their various personal experiences, which show that they experience God as children. Their personalized and experienced understanding of God will "undergo revision, repression, recovery, and reconciliation" as they grow older.[6] In order to confirm the accuracy of the comprehension of children's responses, the research team asked follow-up questions and paraphrased the responses.

Children's reasons for adults sharing biblical stories with them are congruent with the previous discussion on Psalm 78:1–8. The expected result of the intergenerational transmission of God's deeds was threefold: each generation is to put its trust in God, not forget the deeds of God, and keep the commands (Ps 78:7). Responses of children in this research show that they have understood the need to know biblical stories, trust in the God which biblical stories declare, and order their lives in accordance with the Bible. The psalm states the need of communicating stories to the next generations. Children have identified this aspect as they perceive that their storytellers intend to develop in them the habit of sharing biblical stories with others. The negative examples of those who were stubborn and rebellious (Ps 78:8) portray the lives of those who disobeyed God. This verse was the psalmist's warning so that the new generation won't follow the examples of their forefathers. This is congruent with children's understanding of I-Evil. They are aware of the need of aversion that they need to develop to sin and Satan.

---

4. Fowler, *Becoming Adult*, 149.
5. Westerhoff, *Will Our Children*, 70.
6. Bellous, "Educational Significances," 178.

Research Question Three

When do children recall the stories?

This question was intended to see whether children recall biblical stories they hear and what are the life situations that cause children to remember biblical stories. This can give insight to how children link biblical stories to their lives. This is important as it can shed light on whether they remember stories in their day-to-day life. Analysis of children's responses gave a glimpse of how biblical stories help them to be aware of God, self, others, and sin. During focus groups, they could describe names, events, and plots from forty-three stories from the Old Testament and twenty-nine stories from the New Testament. During class activities they could recite the story of the day and the previous days. Recalling or remembering biblical stories shows their intellectual comprehension of stories. Knowing the story is an important step towards believing the story and living a life in accordance to the story. As these children could retrieve and paraphrase biblical stories they portray the first two levels in the Anderson taxonomy of learning: remembering and understanding.[7]

These children also have their favorite stories. The stated reason why a story is the favorite story has clear indication of their awareness of God, awareness of self, awareness of sin, and awareness of others. Biblical stories have helped them to have a relationship with God. These stories have enabled them to be aware of their part in the relationship with God. Their responses show that these stories remind them of the need of obedience to God. They know the stories of biblical characters who disobeyed God. They have internalized these stories as a warning sign in their lives to develop aversion towards sin and to desire a life of obedience to God.

Children remember stories in their lives during various situations: emotion-oriented and situation-oriented recollections. They not only described life situations but also mentioned a biblical story through which they find meaning in each of the situations. When they confront fear, sadness, isolation, loneliness, and happiness, they identify these emotions and remember biblical stories from which they find comfort. Various situations in which children remember stories show that biblical stories have helped

---

7. Anderson, *Classroom Assessment*, 32.

them to find comfort in various troubling situations in their lives. They also remember stories when sin confronts them. This shows their awareness of right and wrong. Biblical stories have helped them to gain norms for their behavior.

This discussion shows that their intellectual comprehension has helped them to trust God, which is the internalized dimension of faith according to Downs,[8] or internalized faith according to McGrath.[9] They could organize and synthesize their understanding of stories, which is the next level in the Anderson's taxonomy of learning.[10] The fact that they know the stories shows the intellectual dimension of faith or in the psalmist's words they "do not forget the deeds" of God (Ps 78:7). They remember biblical stories at times of need, portraying their trust, which is the internalization of faith or their trust or confidence in God (Ps 78:7). Their intentions to follow God's commandments are implied by the fact that they remember biblical stories when sin confronts them. They want to live a life of holiness, a life of walking in the paths of God. This shows the volitional dimension of faith or according to the psalmist their intention to "keep the commands" (Ps 78:7).

Circumstances in which children remember biblical stories reveal that these stories have helped them to have a relationship with God and to have a growing and vibrant relationship through a life of continual trust and obedience to God. From these stories they derive meaning in relation with their lives. This supports the findings of Stonehouse and May.[11] As Coles proposed, these children are seekers who seek out God and try to integrate their understanding through own conclusions and wonderings.[12] Their responses show an awareness of sin in the following areas: the need of aversion towards sin, the need to confess sin and receive God's forgiveness, and the need to live as children of God. This understanding reveals their grasp of the need of sanctification, which is an important factor in spiritual growth.[13]

---

8. Downs, *Spiritual Growth*, 17–18.
9. McGrath, *Christian Spirituality*, 99.
10. Anderson, *Classroom Assessment*, 33.
11. Stonehouse and May, *Listening to Children*, 76–78.
12. See Coles, *Spiritual Life*.
13. Ratcliff and Ratcliff, *Childfaith*, 11.

Research Question Four

Does recalling or listening to the stories impact the life situations they face? If so, how?

The previous discussion shows that children remember biblical stories, they have favorite biblical stories, and they remember these stories in different situations in life. The intention of this question was to see how children perceive the impact as they listen to, or remember, biblical stories.

Children's responses portray that biblical stories impact them as they remember or listen to the stories. The analysis of their responses denotes that these stories stimulate religious emotions and a desire for transformation. Certain emotions arise in them as they listen to or remember stories: happiness, comfort, peace, joy, hope, and sadness. These emotions are referred to as religious emotions, as they are aroused with reference to God. They used religious terms to explain the impact. They described this with reference to their faith in God, anointing of the Holy Spirit, grace of God, and hope they have in God. There is a suggestive link between religious emotions and spiritual transformation. Emotions can motivate spiritual transformation, and they can be an outcome of spiritual transformation.[14]

Children also described how listening to or remembering biblical stories is an impetus to change in their lives. It has encouraged them to practice spiritual disciplines such as fasting, prayer, and reading the Bible. The research team members were surprised to hear children's stories about their experiences of fasting. Fasting prayer is a weekly phenomenon in the churches in this context. So these children could have internalized fasting as a significant part of spiritual life. Biblical stories have helped them to trust in God who will answer their prayers, provide for their needs, and forgive their sins. It has enabled them to have a desire to submit their lives to walk in the paths of God. This shows that listening to stories have helped them to develop an internalized and volitional dimensions of faith.

Previous research studies portray children's response to stories. Worsley, Burt, Trousdale and Everett, and Trousdale and McMillain are a few examples of such research. These studies show that children could recall stories, comprehend stories, understand author's intended meaning to a

---

14. Emmons, "Emotion and Religion," 247.

certain extent, and relate to characters in the stories. Their understanding of stories changes as they grow older. However, the researcher could not find any research that described children's perspectives of the impact of stories on them.

Children's responses in this research reveal that hearing biblical stories has generated certain religious emotions and an impetus for transformation. Certain emotions – happiness, comfort, peace, joy, hope, and sadness – arise in them when they listen to or remember biblical stories. These emotions can motivate spiritual transformation and/or can be the effect of spiritual transformation.[15] With respect to biblical stories as an impetus to transformation, one aspect is with respect to an increased desire to practice spiritual disciplines like prayer, fasting, and reading the Bible. Another aspect of transformation is reflected in children's awareness of aversion towards sin. Biblical stories remind them about the importance of turning away from sin and the need to confess their sins. These are both key elements in a sanctified life.[16] Thus two important aspects of spirituality identified by Issler[17] namely, relationship with God and sanctification, which results from this relationship, are seen in these children.

The practice of telling biblical stories among the Israelites and in congregations shows that the impact of stories on children is assumed. Biblical references which command reciting of stories to children (Exod 12:26; 13:8, 14; Deut 6:20–21; Josh 4:6, 21; and Ps 78:1–8) reveal the value God placed on the practice of telling biblical stories to children. The purpose of reciting is to develop obedience and fear of God (Deut 6:24). The intention is to trust God, keep his commands and to remember the deeds of God (Ps 78:7). God intends to develop certain emotions and transformation through the recital of stories.

Research Question Five

How do these children's perceptions about biblical stories compare with the four dimensions of relational consciousness in Hay and Nye's study in the United Kingdom: I-Thou, I-self, I-other,

---

15. Ibid.
16. Ratcliff and Ratcliff, *Childfaith*, 11.
17. Issler, *Wasting Time with God*, 252.

> and I-world? Are there other important insights from the proposed study that challenge or go beyond the model developed by Hay and Nye?

The significance of this question is that it compares categories of this research with that of Hay and Nye's groundbreaking research. Hay and Nye's research has become a key reference point for subsequent research in children's spirituality. Children's spirituality is described not only as a mental activity but also as a relational awareness with four dimensions: I-Thou, I-other, I-self, and I-world.[18]

In this research, children's responses show that they are aware of their relationship with God, self, and others. The explanation of I-Thou, I-self, and I-other in this research is identical with Hay and Nye.[19] These children's awareness of I-world is only with reference to the fact that God is the creator of the universe. The new dimension that emerged in this research is I-Evil: the relationship with Satan and sin. Children's awareness of these dimensions of relationship was evident throughout their responses in this research. The following section explains these categories with reference to the present research.

I-Thou

Analysis of children's responses generated certain categories of concepts of God. Previous research with respect to these concepts was consulted to categorize children's responses. Children's awareness of God is categorized using Roos' classification: potency of God, punishing God, positive God, relational God, and God-like parents.[20] Analysis of their responses reveals that they not only know the attributes of God but they also show their trust in God. They shared many experiences that reflect their awareness of God's present activity in their lives as the healer, Savior, and protector.

Based on previous research,[21] God-concepts in this research indicate the positive influence of church and family on children. Children's

---

18. Hay and Nye, *Spirit of the Child*, 109
19. Ibid., 115–117.
20. Roos, "God Concepts," 95.
21. Nelson, *Psychology*, 257; Hood, Hill, & Spilka, *Psychology of Religion*, 96; Roos, "God Concepts," 100.

God-concepts will change when they get older.[22] Yet, previous research studies[23] portray that the positive God-concepts of these children can lead to physical and spiritual well-being, provided that they continue to have an environment which nourishes their spirituality.

I-Self

These children's awareness of self was classified based on Montemayor and Eisen's categories – ideological self, psychic self, existential individuating, sense of self-determination, and interpersonal style.[24] Their conversations show that biblical stories have helped them to develop self-awareness with reference to God. They believe certain truths in the Bible and know their self-identity as children of God. Based on their knowledge they do self-reflection and show evidences of determination to follow God and to walk in the ways of God. When these children face peer pressure in certain issues at school, like eating food devoted to idols and singing secular songs, they decide not to do so. This shows their self-determination to follow God. The responses of children show that biblical stories have influenced their interpersonal style in terms of their behavior and their desire to be change agents in their friends' lives.

I-Other

These children have identified five reasons for sharing biblical stories with their friends. One of the reasons was that they would transmit biblical stories to others. This shows that they have developed the awareness of the need of God in others' lives. The children as storytellers are living out what they have perceived as what is expected of them. By sharing stories, these children also intend to develop I-other in their friends so that their friends would in turn tell biblical stories to others.

Biblical stories have helped them to be aware of their interpersonal relationships, which is another aspect of I-other. Analysis of children's responses generated two themes with respect to interpersonal style: behavior oriented and being a change agent. Behavior-oriented interpersonal style is

---

22. Bellous, "Education Significances," 179.
23. Rowatt and Kirkpatrick, "Two Dimensions," 646–647; Nelson, *Psychology*, 259.
24. Montemayor and Eisen, "Development," 314.

with reference to their awareness of being kind, loving, and gentle to others even when others are angry. Being a change agent, they not only see the need of God in the lives of their friends but also their role in introducing others to God. They see their role as follows: (1) giving advice, (2) being a role model, and (3) sharing biblical stories with others.

I-World

I-world, children's sense of awareness to the natural world as providing "secondary context" for spirituality did not emerge in the sense discussed in Hay and Nye.[25] In the present research, awareness of the world is also an outcome of their awareness of God – they see God as the creator and the sustainer of the whole universe and affirm the creator God's love for the world. Discussion with the faculty and students at Faith Theological Seminary shed light on some possible reasons for this phenomenon: Stories which encourage I-world relationships may not be shared with children, such an application may not be encouraged, children do not derive such application from stories they hear, or the de-emphasis of world with an emphasis on eternal life among Pentecostal churches. Another fact is that textbooks used in Sunday school among Pentecostal churches have less I-world focus compared to other categories. Thus there is an overall deficiency in the way the message of the Bible is being communicated to children. Ministry time with children could also focus on enabling children to grasp not only the special revelation but also the general revelation of God.

I-Evil

I-Evil is a unique category derived from these children's responses. This has to do with how they view Satan, and sin. This theme emerged throughout the conversation. They sense that by sharing biblical stories adults intend to develop an antagonism towards Satan. They are aware of the need of resisting the devil. The antagonism against I-Evil is also expressed in their aversion to sin. Children as storytellers intend to develop antagonism towards Satan in their friends.

These children's favorite stories include events in the lives of biblical characters who have sinned against God. They view sin in the lives of these

---

25. Hay and Nye, *Spirit of the Child*, 116.

characters as a warning sign for them and as an obstacle in their relationship with God. Another aspect of their understanding of sin is their trust in Christ whose death has brought cleansing for those who confess their sins. The understanding of sin and redemption is essential in Protestant understanding of spirituality. Ratcliff and Ratcliff note this understanding as one of the areas of spiritual growth.[26]

The conversation with the pastors of the participating churches reveals that these churches teach about evangelism, the importance of born-again experience, and a life lived in accordance with the experience. Thus their understanding of Satan and sin reflects the environment in which they are nurtured.

Main Research Question

What are children's perceptions of the role of biblical narratives in their spiritual formation?

Children understand the role of community in sharing biblical stories with them. They identified a variety of storytellers in three settings, namely: church, home, and school. Children clearly perceive why storytellers tell biblical stories to them. Their conversations reveal that they have intellectually grasped the content of biblical stories, which is a perceived reason for these stories being told. They mentioned events, plots, and characters from different stories in the Old and New Testaments. Biblical stories helped them to be aware of God, self, other, and world. Their responses reveal their attempt to act upon their knowledge of God, self, others and Satan. This shows that these stories have touched their feelings, values, and attitudes. These are evidences for their internalized faith, which is the next perceived reason. Their internal appreciation has caused them to desire their relationship to be growing and vibrant. The volitional dimension, the third perceived reason, is mirrored in their desire to live a life in complete surrender to God. Thus, children's conversations support their idea that biblical stories have enabled children to develop three dimensions of spiritually maturing faith – intellectual, internalized, and volitional.[27]

---

26. Ratcliff and Ratcliff, *Childfaith*, 11.
27. McGrath, *Christian Spirituality*, 2–3; Downs, *Spiritual Growth*, 17–18.

As children have perceived reasons for communicating stories with them, they share stories with other children with the same reasons. Their reasons for sharing stories with their friends show that they deliberately share biblical stories with their friends. They share biblical stories with their friends so that they may know God and live a life in the ways of God.

Further, they remember stories during various life situations. They remember biblical stories when they feel certain emotions like sadness, fear, isolation, loneliness, and happiness. They not only recognize their emotions but they identify themselves with certain characters. Thus they try to link a particular story with their situations. They feel closeness to God when they feel these emotions and in turn biblical stories help them to be aware of the God who cares for them. Various situations in life also remind them of biblical stories. They remember biblical stories not only when they are in trouble, sorrow, and sickness but also when sin confronts them. When they face uncertainties, and discouragement they remember biblical stories and trust God who can deliver them. Remembering stories when they sin helps them to be aware of God who forgives them. They are also reminded of the need to resist the devil. Embedded in these responses is not only their knowledge about the attributes of God, but also their belief and trust in God as their Savior, protector, provider, and one who cares for them.

Recalling biblical stories stimulates religious emotions and a desire for transformation. As they listen to or remember stories certain emotions are developed in them: happiness, comfort, peace, joy, hope, and sadness. Research shows a suggestive link between religious emotions and spiritual transformation. Listening to stories has stimulated transformation – a desire to participate in spiritual disciplines like prayer, fasting, and reading the Bible. Another aspect of transformation is the antagonism against Satan and aversion towards sin. This shows that children not only have a relationship with God but also their desire and commitment to a life of sanctification. Both of these factors are important aspects of spirituality.[28]

With reference to the operational definitions of spiritual formation given in this research, children's voices indicate that they perceive that biblical stories have a role in their spiritual formation. Biblical stories not

---

28. Issler, *Wasting Time with God*, 252.

only enable them to be aware of God, self, and others but also serve as an impetus to act upon that knowledge. This is congruent with Blair's definition of spirituality in two aspects: awareness and acting upon the awareness.[29] Biblical stories enable them not only to enter into a relationship with Christ but also to stir a desire to develop that relationship to be growing and vibrant, which is the goal of spiritual formation according to Stonehouse.[30] They see the role of community-church, home, and school in sharing biblical stories with them. By sharing the stories, the community of believers has helped them in acquiring the awareness and in acting upon the awareness, which is noted by Allen.[31] These children have become the community that shares biblical stories with their friends. They are aware of the fact that they need to share the stories not only when they are young but also when they are old.

It is worthwhile to note Stonehouse and May's remarks at this juncture. Listening to God's story is one of the factors that facilitate spiritual formation.[32] They have observed the importance of activities in the church, families' involvement in the church, experiences and relationships that children receive in church and family as other factors which enrich spirituality in children.[33]

Children's conversation showed the three dimensions of relational consciousness, namely, I-Thou, I-self, and I-other in Hay and Nye's research.[34] These children's awareness of I-Thou, I-self, and I-other has similarity with Hay and Nye's description of these categories. The I-world dimension in the sense that natural world is a context to develop spirituality is to be further encouraged in these children. I-Evil is a unique dimension in the present research. Biblical stories have enabled them to develop an antagonism against Satan and an aversion towards sin. This is to be understood in light with the process of sanctification, which is significant for the relationship with Christ to be growing and mature.

---

29. Blair, "Women's Spirituality," 534.
30. Stonehouse, *Joining Children*, 21.
31. Allen, "Exploring Children's Spirituality," 11.
32. Stonehouse and May, *Listening to Children*, 81–82.
33. Ibid., 98, 102.
34. Hay and Nye, *Spirit of the Child*, 109.

Implications

The findings of this research affirm that children can recall biblical stories and link biblical stories with various situations in life. Biblical stories have enabled them to develop an awareness of God, self, others, and sin. Children not only perceive the reasons for sharing biblical stories but also attempt to walk in the path of God that the stories declare. God's plan for the church is to bring transformation in individuals and communities. Churches are to see Sunday schools and other ministry opportunities with children as significant opportunities to share biblical stories with children.

This research has implications for the practice of children's ministry in the particular Christian tradition in which the participating churches belong. This research acknowledges biblical storytelling as a primary tool to develop spiritual formation in young children. The church leaders are to focus on helping teachers and parents to be effective storytellers. Adults can be encouraged to discuss the implication in their lives while telling stories. They should be encouraged to connect stories to the life situations of the hearers.

As children identified various storytellers in their lives, the entire congregation can be encouraged to develop the skill of storytelling and to identify teachable moments to share stories. Another implication is that various intergenerational programs and activities of the church can be further developed as avenues in which adults can share biblical stories with children. As children are also storytellers, churches are to equip children to be effective storytellers.

Even though children identified a variety of storytellers at home, they listed more opportunities to hear biblical stories in churches. This implies that families of children could be educated to make wise use of their time at home. Morning and evening family devotions and meal times can be used to share biblical stories. If parents have limited knowledge of biblical stories, churches can provide variety of storybooks for children and adults to use at home.

Children in this research recalled more stories from the first few books of the Old and New Testaments than from the other books. Even though this study did not look into the reason for this phenomenon, it may have an implication on the content of the storytelling that is prevalent in churches.

If more emphasis has been given to these books of the Bible, churches can enable storytellers to share stories from other books of the Bible as well.

A danger that prevails in churches while sharing biblical stories is the tendency to fragment the Bible into bits – "moral bits, systematic-theological bits, devotional bits, historical-critical bits, narrative bits, and homiletical bits."[35] If such a trend is identified in the churches, storytellers should present the whole story so that children can know the thread of the Story that the Bible declares. The antidote to this trend is to constantly refer to the "big picture of salvation history" which may reduce the "risk of breaking down one rich history of God" into bits and pieces.[36]

A concern of many educators is the general trend among Pentecostal youths to leave one's home church in their later adolescence and early adulthood. Another observation is the discontinuity between the spirituality in childhood and adulthood. It would be good to identify the missing link in this phenomenon and attempt to sustain the spirituality of the people.

As this research was an exploratory study with a limited sample, the researcher is cautious in suggesting wider application of the findings. The findings of the study may be generalized to other contexts, as the reader finds relevant similarities. The Judeo-Christian tradition encourages the use of story in communicating the revelation of God. Christians are to continue to encourage telling biblical stories to children to build trust in God, to remember God's deeds, and to keep God's commandments. If the stories of God's deeds can enrich spiritual formation in children, sharing stories of God's deeds in the lives of contemporary Christians can encourage children to see the work of God at the present time.

Limitations

The first limitation of this study was in relation to the sample. A limited sample, twenty-nine children, was selected from seven Pentecostal/Charismatic churches in Kerala, India. These churches give importance to the preaching of the Word and weekly gathering together for worship and prayer. There were certain criteria of selection of sample with respect to the

---

35. Goheen, "Reading the Bible," 5.
36. Cavalletti, *6 to 12 Years Old*, 20–21.

number of years in the church and regular attendance to Sunday school and church meetings. For those children who do not fit these criteria of selection, their perceptions of the role of biblical stories may be different. Moreover, in high-context cultures like India, storytelling has significant implications. A message is often communicated through stories, proverbs, fables, metaphors, similes and analogies.[37] Stories are not understood merely as illustration, but also as vehicles that carry the truth.

This study did not deal with the various methods of storytelling or the use of various types of stories in the spiritual formation of children. Thus this research can neither depict which is the most effective method of storytelling with children nor what is the role of other types of stories in the spiritual formation of children.

Spiritual disciplines like prayer, worship, listening to worship songs, and meditating on the word of God were not the focus of the research. Participation in various activities and programs of the church and spiritual formation was also not the concern of the research. Involvement in such activities and practice of spiritual disciplines may have contributed to children's awareness of God, self, others, world, and Satan. The researcher considers these aspects as important influences for the spiritual formation of children, yet this research does not address these issues.

This research does not discuss postmodern interpretation of meta-narratives. Postmodernism has attempted to reduce Christian meta-narrative as one story among many others, thus negating its universal claims. This research affirms that the Christian story is a meta-narrative, a grand story – a meta-narrative of faith.

The researcher made attempts to be unbiased in deriving themes from data analysis. The researcher reviewed the data collected through class activities, focus group interviews and member checking and carefully read the transcripts and watched the videos. Involving research assistants and member checking with children and those involved in children's ministry were some ways to minimize potential bias. However, as a teacher of young children for over twenty years, the researcher cannot claim absolute objectivity in the research.

---

37. James, *Crisis Intervention*, 28.

Recommendations for Future Research

As this study is only an exploratory investigation into children's perceptions of the role of biblical stories in their spiritual formation, this topic of stories and spiritual formation in children can be further researched in other localities and among other Christian traditions.

Analysis of these children's responses identified five reasons for adults sharing biblical stories with them. Another suggested research focus would be to find the perception of adult storytellers with reference to their reasons for sharing biblical stories with children. The reasons given by children and adults can be compared to see the congruency of their perceptions.

These children recalled more stories from the first five books of the Old Testament and four books of the New Testament than other parts of the Bible. Another research could be done to see if this phenomenon is repeated in other parts of India with a similar sample. A variation of this research would be to include different samples from other Christian traditions.

This research clearly indicates the role of biblical stories in the spiritual formation of children. Another suggested research would be to see how children in various age groups see the role of biblical narratives in their spiritual formation. Also, how do adults see this association in their lives looking back to their childhood? A retrospective research effort with adults with the same focus could be another helpful variation of this research.

Another suggested research effort would be to explore the role of spiritual disciplines like prayer, fasting, and meditation of the Word in the spiritual formation of children. How does listening to worship songs and hymns influence spiritual formation? How does participation in various programs of the church impact spiritual formation among various age groups?

This research focused on the role of biblical narratives in the spiritual formation of children. Beckwith proposes that stories from church history and personal stories of those in the faith community can enable spiritual formation in children.[38] Not only biblical stories but also stories of missionaries are shared with children during vacation Bible school. Sharing personal testimonies is also a practice among Pentecostal churches in the

---

38. I. Beckwith, *Formational Children's Ministry: Shaping Children Using Story, Ritual, and Relationship* (Grand Rapids, MI: Baker, 2010), 41, 48–49.

area. If so, a recommendation for future research would be to study the role of stories of other Christians in the spiritual formation among various age groups. The role of stories from church history in the spiritual formation could be another topic for research.

Concluding Remarks

The last two decades witnessed increasing scholarly attention on the topic of children's spirituality from multidisciplinary fields of study. Subsequently research with children as participants has become a widespread phenomenon. Simultaneously, there has been a recent resurgence in telling stories. This research integrated these two areas of interest by exploring children's perceptions of the role of biblical stories in their spiritual formation.

This research presents the voices of twenty-nine 9- to 11-year-old children from Pentecostal/Charismatic Christian tradition in Adoor, Kerala, India. This qualitative study used class activities, observation focus group interviews, and member checking to hear from children and understand their perspectives. The collected data was analyzed using qualitative data analysis tools to derive themes about the research topic. The researcher was assisted by three assistants who helped in organizing and facilitating class activities and as moderators for focus group interviews.

Children's responses with respect to their awareness of God, self, others, and sin often surprised the research team and often challenged our preconceived ideas of children's spirituality and their grasp of biblical stories. Biblical stories have enabled two important aspects of spirituality, namely, relationship with God and a life of sanctification. The researcher wonders whether adults at home and church have clearly grasped the religious potential of children. The time has come to challenge the view that adults' experiences and perceptions are the norms to evaluate children's spirituality. Those who are involved in children's ministry are to be appreciated for devoting their time with children and further equipped to do their task with excellence.

At this point, the researcher would like to thank the commitment of missionaries and national and international organizations like Compassion International, Operation Mobilization, World Vision, and Viva Network to brighten the lives of children in India. The time has come for Indian

Christians to consider the issues and needs of children if churches are to continue in their efforts to build a better future for Indian children. India has the highest number of children in the world, yet issues of children should be a topic of priority in her theological institutions. The researcher hopes that this study will kindle an interest in theological institutions in India to do further research with children.

APPENDIX A

Information Leaflet for Pastors and Parents

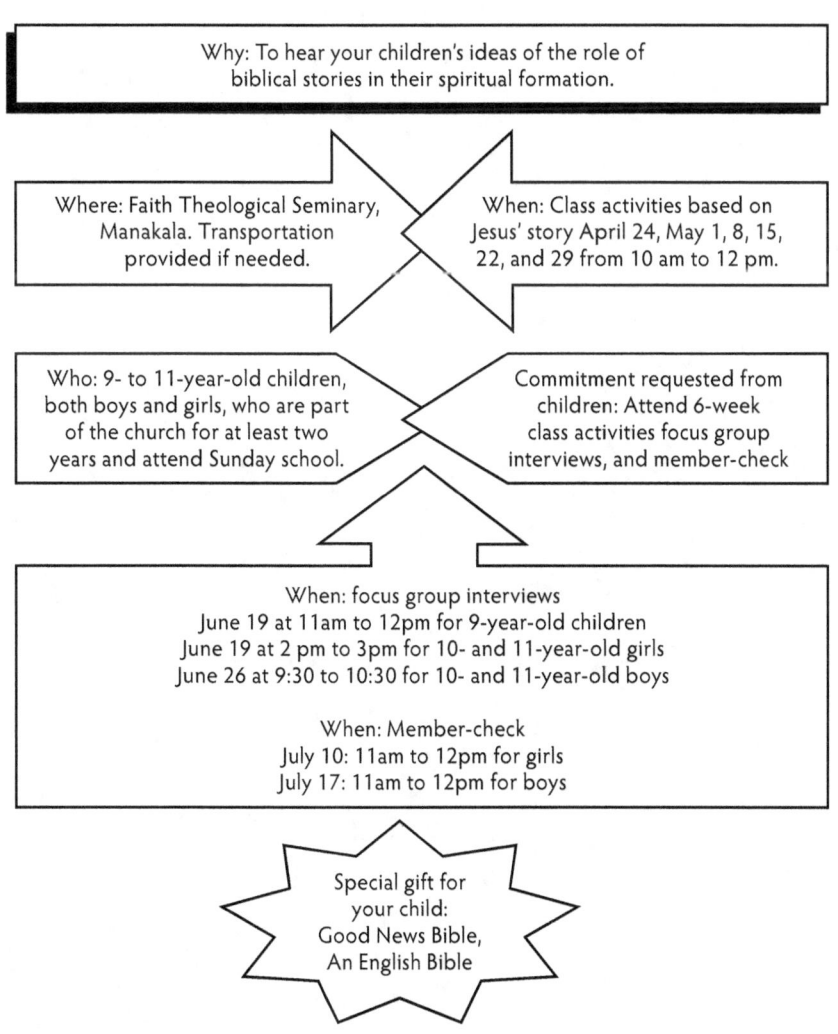

APPENDIX B

Information Leaflet for Children

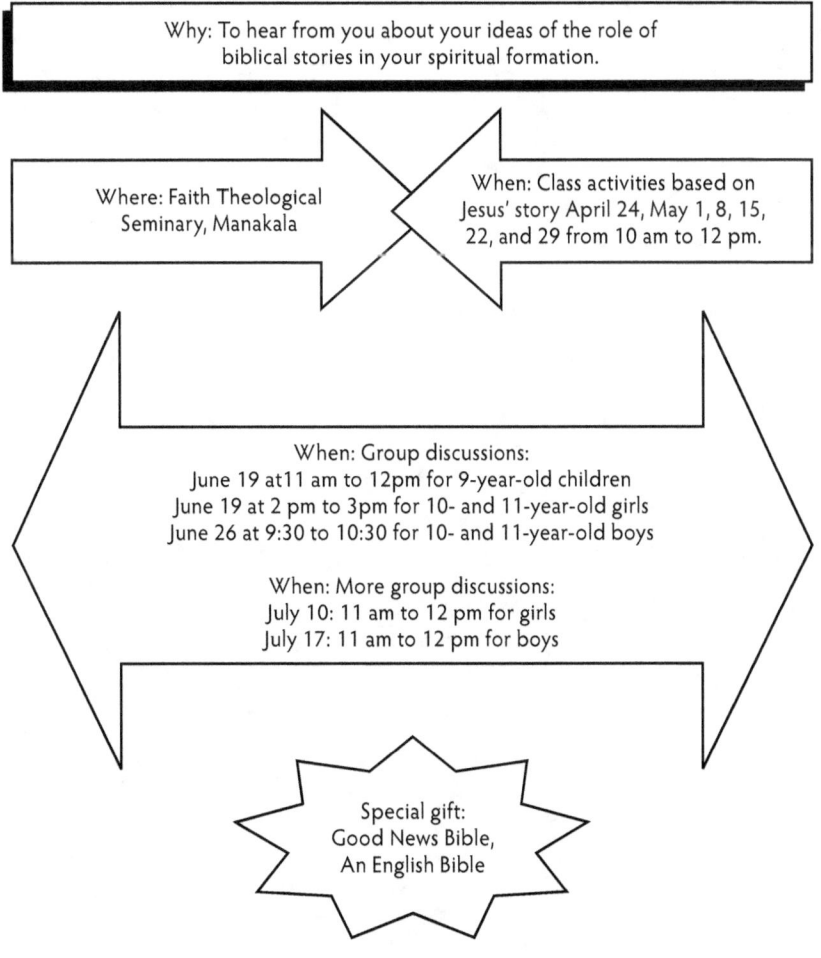

Why: To hear from you about your ideas of the role of biblical stories in your spiritual formation.

Where: Faith Theological Seminary, Manakala

When: Class activities based on Jesus' story April 24, May 1, 8, 15, 22, and 29 from 10 am to 12 pm.

When: Group discussions:
June 19 at 11 am to 12pm for 9-year-old children
June 19 at 2 pm to 3pm for 10- and 11-year-old girls
June 26 at 9:30 to 10:30 for 10- and 11-year-old boys

When: More group discussions:
July 10: 11 am to 12 pm for girls
July 17: 11 am to 12 pm for boys

Special gift:
Good News Bible,
An English Bible

APPENDIX C
Information Leaflet for Research Assistants

Guidelines for team members

Aim: Children's perceptions of the role of stories in their spiritual formation

Preparation required:
(1) Read pages 7–29 from Teacher's handbook of God the Security
(2) Prepare chapters 15–20 from the textbook God the Security with the help of pages 55–63 in teacher's handbook of God the Security
(3) Be thorough with the overview of research

Expectation:
1. Help in the organization and administration of the research
2. Facilitate and lead class activities for 9- to 11-year-old children
3. Help in interpreting and analyzing verbal and non-verbal data

Virtues needed:
Love God and love children
Appreciate children's faith

Minimum time commitment:
- From April 1 to 18 half day per week
- From April 19th May 30st: Two days per week (every Thursday and Saturday 8:30–4 pm)
- On June 12, 19, 26 and July 3, 10, 17, and June 20, 27 and July 11, 18
- Two more days in August and September.

Potential Benefits for you:
- ✓ An experience in doing research with children
- ✓ Gain experience in working with children
- ✓ Influencing the children's lives with Christ
- ✓ Monetary benefits

APPENDIX D

Informed Consent Forms

Informed Consent Form 1

Participant's name: _____

I authorize *Annie George* of Christian Education, Biola University, La Mirada, California, and/or any designated research assistants to gather information from me on the topic of children's perceptions of the role of God-stories in their spiritual formation.

I understand that the general purposes of the research are to hear from children about the following topics:

(1) To what extent children in churches and Christian families are exposed to stories from the Bible? What do they like about these stories?

(2) What are children's perceptions of the influence of biblical narratives in their spiritual formation?

(3) Why and when do children recall the Bible stories?

(4) How does the recalling of the Bible stories impact the life situations they face?

and that I will be asked to attend a two-hour class per week for six weeks in the month of April and May, Focus groups and member-check in the month of June and July, and that the approximate total time of my involvement will be 720 minutes of classes, 60 minutes of focus group interviews and 60 minutes of member-check.

The potential benefits of the study are:

(1) An opportunity to listen to children's voice about biblical stories. Thus this will be research not only with them but for them. (2) Comprehending how children perceive the role of stories in their spiritual formation will benefit teachers and educators who work with children. (3) Educators can sharpen their skills of delivering stories, modify their approach to children, confidently arrange the materials and activities for children, and further equip parents and faith community in using stories with children. (4) This will be a new piece of knowledge which can further enlighten the study of children's spirituality. (5) This study can kindle research and ministry among children in academia and congregations in India. (6) This is towards the partial fulfillment of my educational pursuit.

I am aware that I may choose not to answer any questions that I find embarrassing or offensive. I understand that if, after my participation, I experience any undue anxiety or stress or have questions about the research or my rights as a participant, that may have been provoked by the experience, *Annie George* will be available for consultation, and will also be available to provide direction regarding medical assistance in the unlikely event of physical injury incurred during participation in the research.

I consent that the researcher may release my individual results.

Signature _____   Date _____

There are two copies of this consent form included. Please sign one and return it to the researcher with your responses. The other copy you may keep for your records.

Questions and comments may be address to *Annie George, Christian Education,* Biola University, 13800 Biola Avenue, La Mirada, CA. 90639-0001. Phone: (562) 903-6000.

Locally you can contact me at Annie George, Faith Theological Seminary, Manakala, Adoor, Phone: 9349647571.

Informed Consent Form 2

This consent form should be used when research participants are minors

Child's/Minor's name: _____

Parent's/Guardian's name: _____

I authorize Annie George of Christian Education, Biola University, La Mirada, California, and/or any designated research assistants to gather information from my child on the topic of children's perceptions of the role of God-stories in their spiritual formation.

I understand that the general purposes of the research are to listen from children the following topics:

(1) To what extent children in churches and Christian families are exposed to stories from the Bible? What do they like about these stories?
(2) What are children's perceptions of the influence of biblical narratives in their spiritual formation?
(3) Why and when do children recall the Bible stories?
(4) How does the recalling of the Bible stories impact the life situations they face?

and I understand that my child's participation will involve: class activities, focus group interviews, and member-check. The approximate total time of my child's involvement with be 720 minutes of classes, 60 minutes of focus group interviews and 60 minutes of member-check.

The potential benefits of the study are
(1) An opportunity to listen to children's voice about biblical stories. Thus this will be research not only with them but for them. (2) Comprehending how children perceive the role of stories in their spiritual formation will benefit teachers and educators who work with children. (3) Educators can sharpen their skills of delivering stories, modify their approach to children, confidently arrange the materials and activities for children, and further equip parents and faith community in using stories with children. (4) This will be a new piece of knowledge which can further enlighten the study of children's spirituality. (5) This study can kindle research and ministry

among children in academia and congregations in India. (6) This is towards the partial fulfillment of my educational pursuit.

My child and I have been assured that my child may refuse to discuss any matters that cause discomfort or that my child might experience as an unwanted invasion of privacy. I am aware that my child may choose not to answer any questions that my child finds embarrassing or offensive.

I understand that my child's participation is voluntary and that my child may refuse to participate or discontinue participation at any time without penalty or loss of benefits to which my child may be otherwise entitled.

This study is unlikely to cause my child distress. However, I understand that if, after participation, my child experiences any undue anxiety or stress or has questions about the research or their rights as a participant that may have been provoked by the experience, Annie George will be available for consultation, and will also be available to provide direction regarding medical assistance in the unlikely event of physical injury incurred during participation in the research.

Confidentiality of research results will be maintained by the researcher. No individual results will be released without the written consent of the parents or guardians of the particular child.

Signature of Parent or Guardian _____ Date _____

Signature of Child/Minor _____ Date _____

There are two copies of this consent form included. Please sign one and return it to the researcher with your responses. The other copy you may keep for your records.

Questions and comments may be addressed to Annie George, Christian Education, Biola University, 13800 Biola Ave, La Mirada, CA. 90639-0001. Phone: (562) 903-6000.

Locally you can contact me: Annie George, Faith Theological Seminary, Manakala, Adoor. Phone: 9349647571

APPENDIX E

Permission Letter to Use the Textbook, God Our Security

Dear Annie,

I was delighted to receive your mail and to learn about your dissertation. I wish you all the very best as you complete your doctoral studies. We are glad that you find *Windows to Encounter* a helpful series for children and youth. Please feel free to use the sections you have mentioned in your e-mail for your dissertation.

I look forward to reading your dissertation.

Warm regards to you and Dr George,

Ajit

APPENDIX F

Tables Displaying Demographic Information about Participating Churches and Demographic Information of Children from Seven Churches with Respect to Age and Gender

Table 20: The Participating Churches

Name of the Church	Number of Years of Existence	Church Attendance	Number of Children (below 18)
Antioch	50	300	65
Colosse	60	150	40
Ephesus	40	75	25
Jerusalem	40	300	60
Philippi	32	300	35
Rome	11	200	45
Thessalonica	14	150	20

Table 21: Distribution of Twenty-Nine Children

Name of the Church	9-year olds		10-year olds		11-year olds		Total
	Boys	Girls	Boys	Girls	Boys	Girls	
Antioch			3	1			4
Colosse		2	1			2	5
Ephesus	2						2
Jerusalem	2	1	2	1	1	1	8
Philippi				1	2		3
Rome		1		3		1	5
Thessalonica			1		1		2
Total	4	4	7	6	4	4	29

APPENDIX G

Children's Expression of Their Awareness of God through Poems, Pictures, and Testimonies

Testimonies of some 9-year-old girls:
1) "When I went to school, a bike came and hit me. God's protection was with me. I had no dangers ever since."
2) Another girl shared two incidents in her life with the title for her writing as "My Experience." "One day I was going to deliver milk to my neighbor's house, a motorcycle almost hit me. This is a great experience that God did." "One day I was going to enter a KSRTC (the government bus), a bus almost hit me."

Testimonies of some 9-year-old boys:
1) "When I was going to school one day, a dog bit me, Then God saved me."
2) "One day while I was walking, an auto rickshaw almost hit me. God was with me then."
3) "One day while I was playing in the water, a piece of glass cut my fingers. God was with me then."

An 11-year-old girl:
"A danger happened when I was almost 5-years-old. God saved me from it when the danger happened. Pappa came home one day while I was taking bath. I began jumping because of the joy that he came. My elder sister jokingly pushed me. I fell and hit my head on the corner of a tile. My head got

a deep cut and began to bleed. There were five stitches. Next day was my father's ordination. God protected me from having any pain on that day."

Testimonies of some 10-year-old girls:
1) "One night I went to a shop to buy some milk. Our scooter was in a workshop. So we went walking. Suddenly a scorpion jumped in front of me. But my father didn't see it. But I saw it. I walked forward, it would have stung me. But my God saved me. Finally a man came and killed it."
2) "One day, I am going to a vegetable shop. I was buying vegetable and fruits; I was coming to our house. When I was coming to our house a bus came straight to me. I did not see the bus. The bus was full of people. I turned back see the bus was near me. I moved away from the bus. God is with us, He saved me from a big accident."

Testimonies of some 10-year-old boys:
1) "When I was riding in the school bus, God helped me."
2) "One day while I was traveling in my bicycle, my leg slipped and I fell into a ditch from the bicycle. Even then God saved me. So I thank him. Another day while I was sitting in my home a wasp bit me. It became swollen then. The next day morning my swelling was gone and God gave me a complete healing."

The following poems show that they can generalize their understanding of God:

> Even if the valley of fear comes
> I won't fear for God is with me
> Even if the valley of death comes
> I won't fear for God is with me
> For that we have to praise and thank him always.
> *(Written by two 10-year-old girls)*

> When I think of the ways in which God cares for me
> I cannot stop praising him
> My God is good to me
> He cares for me in dangers
> *(Written by a 10-year-old girl)*

My God who cares for me
My God who leads me
In my dangers and in my troubles
My Jesus who leads me.
(Written by two 10-year-old boys)

God who saves me from danger
My heavenly father
Jesus who is good
Jesus who is my Savior
My Jesus who saves me from any danger
Saved me from danger
Jesus who gives me joy
(Written by an 11-year-old girl)

Jesus is good to me
In the midst of my trials
He is always good
In how many situations
Always there when I fall
He who is good is my support
Jesus is my right hand
(Written by an 11-year-old boy)

The God who saves me is strong
God who protects me is big
He will not leave me in danger
His strength is great
(Written by an 11-year-old boy)

My God will protect
The God will protect me is great
My God will always save me
God is with me to save me
The hand that supports, the hand that protects is with me
There is a God to embrace me so that I do not go weary
Jesus is a good Lord
(Written by an 11-year-old boy)

Two 10-year-old boys expressed their experiences through pictures. He had given a description of this picture in the activity sheet, "One day while I was going in bicycle doing circus (tricks) when I stopped, the cycle fell into a ditch. Then God saved me."

Figure 1: "God saved me as a car was about to hit me."

Figure 2: "God saved me from falling into a ditch. The moral lesson: God saves us from danger."

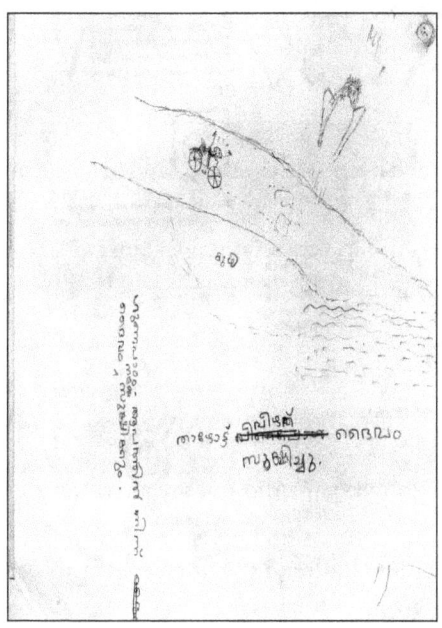

This conversation with a 10-year-old girl happened in the focus group with 10- and 11-year-old girls: This is about the practice of fasting which has surprised the research team. R stands for the researcher and G stands for the 10-year-old girl.

    R: What does God think of you?
    G: (*He expects us*) To fast and pray.
    R: Do you fast?
    G: Yes.
    R: Why do you fast?
    G: For some matters, for healing of my mother.
    R: How long do you fast?
    G: Till night, once a week.
    R: Do you fast every week?
    G: Yes.
    R: Which day?
    G: Every Thursday.

R: Don't you go to school then?
G: Yes, but I do not eat.
R: When did you begin to fast?
G: From 4th grade.
R: Now you are in which grade?
G: 6th.
R: So you have been fasting every Thursday for 2 years?
G: Yes.
R: So parents do not say anything against it?
G: No. Papa and mummy also fast.
R: Who told you to fast?
G: I had a desire to fast.
R: You had a desire to fast?
G: Yes.
R: So mummy and papa did not say anything about it?
G: No.
R: Do any other children in your church fast?
G: I do not know.
R: Have you told anyone about it?
G: No. Three children in my class fast.
R: Why did they begin to fast? Is it because they saw you fasting?
G: No, they also had a desire to fast just like me.
R: Do they fast on Thursdays also?
G: No, sometimes Wednesdays or some other days.

Bibliography

Allen, C. A. "Exploring Children's Spirituality from a Christian Perspective." In *Nurturing Children's Spirituality: Christian Perspectives and Best Practices*, edited by C. A. Allen, 5–20. Eugene, OR: Cascade Books, 2008.

———. "A Qualitative Study Exploring the Similarities and Differences of the Spirituality of Children in Intergenerational and Non-Intergenerational Christian Contexts." Unpublished PhD diss., Biola University, 2002.

Alter, R. *The Art of Biblical Poetry*. New York: Basic Books, 1985.

Anderson, H., and E. Foley. *Mighty Stories, Dangerous Rituals: Weaving together the Human and Divine*. San Francisco, CA: Jossey-Bass, 2001.

Anderson, L. V. *Classroom Assessment: Enhancing the Quality of Teacher Decision Making*. London: Lawrence Erlbaum Associates, 2003.

Barbour, R. *Doing Focus Groups: The Sage Qualitative Research Kit*, vol. 4. London: Sage, 2007.

Barker, J., and S. Weller. "Never Work with Children?: The Geography of Methodological Issues in Research with Children." *Qualitative Research* 3, no. 2 (2003): 207–227.

Barr, J. *The Concept of Biblical Theology: An Old Testament Perspective*. Minneapolis, MN: Fortress Press, 1999.

Bartholomew, C. G., and M. W. Goheen. *The Drama of Scripture: Finding Our Place in the Biblical Story*. Grand Rapids, MI: Baker Academic, 2004.

Bauckham, R. J. *Jude, 2 Peter*. Word Biblical Commentary, vol. 50, edited by D. A. Hubbard and G. W. Barker. Waco, TX: Word, 1983.

Bausch, W. L. *Storytelling: Imagination and Faith*. Mystic, CT: Twenty-Third Publications, 1984.

Beck, J. A. *God as Storyteller: Seeking Meaning in Biblical Narrative*. St Louis, MO: Chalice Press, 2008.

Beckwith, I. *Formational Children's Ministry: Shaping Children Using Story, Ritual, and Relationship*. Grand Rapids, MI: Baker, 2010.

Bellous, J. "The Educational Significances of Spirituality in the Formation of Faith." In *International Handbook of the Religious, Moral, and Spiritual Dimension in Education*, edited by M. De Souza, G. Durka, K. Engebretson,

R. Jackson, and A. G. McGrady, 171–182. Dordrecht, Netherlands: Springer, 2006.

Bishop, K. G. "From Their Perspectives: Children and Young People's Experience of a Pediatric Hospital Environment and Its Relationship to Their Feeling of Well-Being." PhD diss., The University of Sydney, 2008. Accessed 12 August 2010. http://ses.library.usyd.edu.au/bitstream/2123/3962/1/kg-bishop-2008-thesis.pdf

Black, C. C. "The First, Second, and Third Letters of John." In *The New Interpreter's Bible: A Commentary in Twelve Volumes*, vol. 12, 365–469. Nashville, TN: Abingdon, 1998.

Blair, C. E. "Women's Spirituality Empowered by Biblical Story." *Religious Education* 87, no. 4 (1992): 532–544.

Blomberg, C. L. *Matthew*. The New American Commentary, vol. 22. Nashville, TN: Broadman, 1992.

Bhakhry, S. "Children in India and Their Rights." New Delhi: National Human Rights Commission, 2006. Accessed 3 April 2009. http://nhrc.nic.in/Publications/ChildrenRights.pdf

Boadt, L. "The Use of 'Panels' in the Structure of Psalms 73–78." *The Catholic Biblical Quarterly* 66, no. 4 (2004): 533–550.

Booth, W. *The Company We Keep: An Ethics of Fiction*. Berkeley, CA: University of California Press, 1988.

Boyatzis, C. J. "Children's Spiritual Development: Advancing the Field of Definition, Measurement, and Theory." In *Nurturing Children's Spirituality: Christian Perspectives and Best Practices*, edited by C. A. Allen, 43–57. Eugene, OR: Cascade Books, 2008.

Boyatzis, C. J., and B. T. Newman. "How Shall We Study Children's Spirituality?" In *Children's Spirituality: Christian Perspectives, Research, and Applications*, edited by D. Ratcliff, 166–181. Eugene, OR: Cascade Books, 2004.

Boys, M. C. *Tradition and Transformation in Religious Education*. Birmingham, AL: Religious Education Press, 1979.

Branson, R. D. "Musar." In *Theological Dictionary of the Old Testament*, vol. 4, edited by G. J. Botterweck, and H. Ringgren. Translated by D. E. Green, 131–134. Grand Rapids, MI: Eerdmans, 1990.

Brelsford, T. "A Mythical Realist Orientation for Religious Education: Theological and Pedagogical Implications of the Mythical Nature of Religious Study." *Religious Education* 102, no. 3 (2007): 264–278.

Brignall, M. "The Process of Perception." Accessed 23 February 2010. http://www.wisc-online.com/Objects/ViewObject.aspx?ID=OIC3002.

Brooks, J. A. *Mark*. The New American Commentary, vol. 23. Nashville, TN: Broadman, 1991.

Brueggemann, W. *Belonging and Growing in the Christian Community*. Atlanta, GA: General Assembly Mission Board, Presbyterian Church in the United States, 1999.

———. *The Creative Word: Canon as a Model for Biblical Education*. Philadelphia, PA: Fortress Press, 1982.

———. *An Introduction to the Old Testament: The Canon and Christian Imagination*. Louisville, KY: Westminster John Knox, 2003.

———. "Passion and Perspective: Two Dimensions of Education in the Bible." *Theology Today* 42, no. 2 (1985): 172–180.

———. "Vulnerable Children, Divine Passion, and Human Obligation." In *The Child in the Bible*, edited by M. J. Bunge, 329–422. Grand Rapids, MI: Eerdmans, 2008.

Bunge, M. J. "The Dignity and Complexity of Children: Constructing Christian Theologies of Childhood." In *Nurturing Child and Adolescent Spirituality: Perspective from the World's Religious Traditions*, edited by K. M. Yust, A. N. Johnson, S. E. Sasso, and E. C. Rochlkepartian, 53–69. New York: Rowman & Littlefield, 2006.

Burt, P. "'Thus Says the Lord . . .' God's Communication and Children's Understanding." *Journal of Beliefs and Values* 24, no. 3 (2003): 329–338.

Byrne, B. M. "The General/Academic Self-Concept Nomological Network: A Review of Construct Validation Research." *Review of Educational Research* 54, no. 3 (1984): 427–456.

Campbell, A. "Psalm 78: A Contribution to the Theology of Tenth Century Israel." *Catholic Biblical Quarterly* 41, no. 1 (1979): 51–79.

Campbell, D. D. "In Pursuit of the Ideal: Parents' Role in the Spiritual Formation of Young People as Reflected in Wisdom Literature and Ancient Near Eastern Cultural Conventions." 2006. Accessed 22 August 2009. Online.

Cavalletti, S. *The Religious Potential of the Child*, 2nd edition, translated by P. M. Coulter and J. M. Coulter. Chicago, IL: Liturgy Training Publications, 1993.

———. *The Religious Potential of the Child: 6 to 12 Years Old*. Oak Park, IL: Catechism of the Good Shepherd Publications, 2002.

Childs, B. S. *The Book of Exodus: A Critical Theological Commentary*. Philadelphia, PA: Westminster Press, 1974.

Christensen, D. L. *Deuteronomy 1–11*. Word Biblical Commentary, edited by D. A. Hubbard and G. W. Barker, vol. 6A. Dallas, TX: Word Books, 1998.

Clifford, R. J. "In Zion and David a New Beginning: An Interpretation of Psalms 78." In *Traditions and Transformation: Turning Points in Biblical Faith*, edited by B. Halpern, J. D. Levenson, and F. M. Cross. Winona Lake, IN: Eisenbrauns, 1981.

Cole, R. A. *Exodus: An Introduction and Commentary.* Tyndale Old Testament Commentaries, vol. 2. Downers Grove, IL: InterVarsity, 1973.

Coles, R. *The Call for Stories: Teaching and the Moral Imagination.* Boston, MA: Houghton Mifflin, 1989.

———. *The Spiritual Life of Children.* Boston, MA: Houghton Mifflin, 1990.

Copley, T. "The Power of the Storyteller in Religious Education." *Religious Education* 102, no. 3 (2007): 288–297.

Corcoran, H. A. "Biblical Narratives and Life Transformations: An Apology for the Narrative Teaching of Bible Stories." *Christian Education Journal* 4, no. 1 (2007): 34–47.

Craddock, F. B. "The Letter of the Hebrews." In *The New Interpreter's Bible: A Commentary in Twelve Volumes*, vol. 12, 3–173. Nashville, TN: Abingdon, 1998.

Craigie, P. C. *Psalms 1-50.* Word Biblical Commentary, vol. 19, edited by D. A. Hubbard and G. W. Barker. Waco, TX: Word, 1983.

Crain, M. A. "Reconsidering the Power of Story in Religious Education." *Religious Education* 102, no. 3 (2007): 241–248.

Damodaran, K. "Child Labor: An Unresolved Issue." *The Hindu* 14 (8 February 2009).

Darbyshire, P., C. MacDougall, and W. Schiller. "Multiple Methods in Qualitative Research with Children: More Insight or Just More?" *Qualitative Research* 5, no. 4 (2005): 417–436.

Davis, W. D. and D. C. Allison. *The Gospel according to St. Matthew.* The International Critical Commentary, vol 3. Edinburgh: T & T Clark, 1997.

Deconchy, J. P. "The Idea of God: Its Emergence between 7 and 16 Years." In *From Religious Experience to a Religious Attitude*, edited by A. Godin. Chicago, IL: Loyola University Press, 1965.

Dickle, J. "Christian." In *The International Standard Bible Encyclopedia*, vol. 1: A–D, 657. Edited by G. W. Bromiley. Grand Rapids, MI: Eerdmans, 1979.

Downs, P. G. *Teaching for Spiritual Growth: An Introduction to Christian Education.* Grand Rapids, MI: Zondervan, 1994.

Downy, M. *Understanding Christian Spirituality.* Mahwah, NJ: Paulist Press, 1997.

Duff, L. "Spiritual Development and Education: A Contemplative View." *International Journal of Children's Spirituality* 8, no. 3 (2003): 227–237.

Duff, P. A. *Case Study Research in Applied Linguistics.* New York: Taylor & Francis, 2008.

Durka, G. "Through the Looking Glass: Reflections on a Gift to Religious Educators." *Religious Education* 99, no. 4 (2004): 422–426.

Durham, J. I. *Exodus.* Word Biblical Commentary, vol. 3, edited by D. A. Hubbard and G. W. Barker. Dallas, TX: Word Books, 1998.

Dykstra, C. "Faith Development Issues and Religious Nurture." In *Changing Patterns of Religious Education*, edited by M. J. Taylor. Nashville, TN: Abingdon, 1984.

Emmons, R. A. "Emotion and Religion." In *Handbook of the Psychology of Religion and Spirituality*, edited by R. F. Paloutzian and C. L. Park, 235–252. New York: Guilford Press, 2005.

Egan, K. *Imagination in Teaching and Learning: The Middle School Years*. Chicago, IL: University of Chicago Press, 1992.

Evans, C. A. *Mark 8:27–16:20*. Word Biblical Commentary, vol. 34B, edited by D. A. Hubbard and G. W. Barker. Nashville, TN: Thomas Nelson, 2001.

Evans, S. A. "Matters of the Heart: Orality, Story and Cultural Transformation – The Critical Role of Storytelling in Affecting Worldview Change." *Dharma Deepika* 12, no. 1 (2008): 66–77.

Fishbane, M. *Text and Texture*. New York: Schocken, 1979.

Flick, U. *An Introduction to Qualitative Research*. London: Sage, 2006.

Fowl, S. "Some Uses of Story in Moral Discourse: Reflections on Paul's Moral Discourse and Our Own." *Modern Theology* 4, no. 4 (1998): 293–308.

Fowler, J. W. *Becoming Adult, Becoming Christian: Adult Development and Christian Faith*. San Francisco, CA: Harper & Row, 1984.

———. "Faith Development at 30: Naming the Challenges of Faith in a New Millennium." *Religious Education* 99, no. 4 (2004): 405–421.

———. *Stages of Faith: The Psychology of Human Development and the Quest for Meaning*. Victoria, BC: Dove Communications, 1981.

France, R. T. *Mark: A Commentary on the Greek Text*. Grand Rapids, MI: Eerdmans, 2002.

———. *Matthew*. The Tyndale New Testament Commentaries, edited by C. L. Morris. Grand Rapids, MI: Eerdmans, 1985.

Freeman, M., and S. Mathison. *Researching Children's Experiences*. New York: Guilford Press, 2009.

Furnish, D. E. *Experiencing the Bible with Children*. Nashville, TN: Abingdon, 1990.

Gall, M. D., J. P. Gall, and W. R. Borg. *Educational Research: An Introduction*. 7th edition. (n.p.): Pearson, 2003.

Gallagher, M. "Data Collection and Analysis." In *Researching with Children and Young People: Research Design, Methods, and Analysis*, edited by E. K. M. Tisdall, J. M. Davis, and M. Gallagher, 65–153. Los Angeles, CA: Sage, 2009.

———. "Ethics." In *Researching with Children and Young People: Research Design, Methods, and Analysis*, edited by E. K. M. Tisdall, J. M. Davis, and M. Gallagher, 11–64. Los Angeles, CA: Sage, 2009.

Garland, D. "Family Stories: Resources for Nurturing Family Faith in Congregational Life." *Journal of Family Ministry* 18, no. 3 (2004): 26–44.

———. "The Sacred in Family Stories." *Journal of Family Ministry* 19, no. 2 (2005): 41–58.

———. *Sacred Stories of Ordinary Families: Living the Faith of Daily Lives.* San Francisco, CA: Jossey-Bass, 2003.

Garland, D. E. *Mark.* The NIV Application Commentary. Grand Rapids, MI: Zondervan, 1996.

Gerkin, C. V. *Widening the Horizons: Pastoral Responses to a Fragmented Society.* Philadelphia, PA: Westminster Press, 1986.

Gerstenberger, E. S. *Psalms Part 2 and Lamentation.* The Forms of the Old Testament Literature, vol. 15. Grand Rapids, MI: Eerdmans, 2001.

Gibbons, J. L, and D. A. Stiles. *The Thoughts of Youth: An International Perspective on Adolescents' Ideal Persons.* Charlotte, NC: Information Age, 2004.

Gobbel, R. A., and G. G. Gobbel. *The Bible, a Child's Playground.* Philadelphia, PA: Fortress, 1986.

Goheen, M. W. "Reading the Bible as One Story," 2005. Accessed 12 February 2009 from http://biblicaltheology.ca/bluearticles.htm.

Goldingay, J. *Psalms.* Baker Commentary on the Old Testament, vol. 2. Grand Rapids, MI: Baker Academic, 2007.

Goldman, R. *Readiness for Religion: A Basis for Developmental Religious Education.* London: Routledge & Kegan Paul; New York: Seabury Press, 1965.

———. *Religious Thinking from Childhood to Adolescence.* New York: Seabury Press, 1968.

Goodman, R. L. "Nurturing a Relationship to God and Spiritual Growth: Developmental Approaches." In *Teaching about God and Spirituality: A Resource for Jewish Settings,* edited by N. R. Levy, R. L. Goodman, and S. H. Blumbert, 69–96. Denver, CO: A.R.E. Publishing, 2002.

Graue, M. E., and D. J. Walsh. *Studying Children in Context: Theories, Methods, and Ethics.* London: Sage, 1998.

Greeley, A. S. *Religion: A Secular Theory.* New York: Free Press, 1982.

Groome, T. H. *Christian Religious Education.* San Francisco, CA: Harper and Row, 1980.

———. *Sharing Faith: A Comprehensive Approach to Religious Education and Pastoral Ministry.* Eugene, OR: Wipf and Stock, 1998.

Grudem, W. A. *Systematic Theology: An Introduction to Biblical Literature.* Secunderabad, India: OM Books, 1964.

Gundry, R. H. *Mark: A Commentary on His Apology for the Cross.* Grand Rapids, MI: Eerdmans, 1993.

———. *Mark: A Commentary on His Apology for the Cross, Chapters 9–16.* Grand Rapids, MI: Eerdmans, 2000.

Gundry-Volf, J. M. "The Least and the Greatest: Children in the New Testament." In *The Child in the Christian Thought*, edited by M. J. Bunge, 29–60. Grand Rapids, MI: Eerdmans, 2001.

Gupta, N. "An Apocalyptic Reading of Psalm 78 in 2 Thessalonians 3." *Journal for the Study of New Testament* 31, no. 2 (2008): 179–194.

Government of Kerala. Kerala: Education, 2005. Accessed 3 April 2009. http://india.gov.in/knowindia/education_kerala.php

Hagner, D. A. *Matthew 14–28*. Word Biblical Commentary, vol. 33B, edited by D. A. Hubbard and G. W. Barker. Dallas, TX: Word, 1998.

Halkier, B. "Focus Groups as Social Enactments: Integrating Interaction and Content in the Analysis of Focus Group Data." *Qualitative Research* 10, no. 1 (2010): 71–89.

Harney, K., and S. Harney. *Finding a Church You Can Love and Loving the Church You've Found*. Grand Rapids, MI: Zondervan, 2003.

Hauerwas, S. *The Peaceable Kingdom: A Primer in Christian Ethics*. Notre Dame, IN: University of Notre Dame Press, 1983.

Hay, D., and R. Nye. *The Spirit of the Child*. Revised edition. London: Jessica Kingsley Publishers, 2006.

Hays, R. B. "Is Paul's Gospel Narratable?" *Journal for the Study of the New Testament* 27, no. 2 (2004): 217–239.

Hendel, A., W. Messner, and F. Thun, eds. *Rightshore!: Successfully Industrialize SAP Projects Offshore*. Capgemini, Germany: Springerm, 2008.

Hennessy, E., and C. Heary. "Exploring Children's View through Focus Groups." In *Researching Children's Experience*, edited by S. Greene and D. Hogan, 236–252. London: Sage, 2005.

Hesselgrave, D. J. *Scripture and Strategy: The Use of the Bible in the Postmodern Church and Mission*. Pasadena, CA: William Carey Library, 1994.

Hill, M. "Ethical Considerations in Researching Children's Experience." In *Researching Children's Experience*, edited by S. Greene and D. Hogan, 61–86. London: Sage, 2005.

Hoge, Robert D., and Joseph Renzulli. "Exploring the Link between Giftedness and Self-Concept." *Review of Educational Research* 63, no. 4 (1993): 449.

Hood, R. W., P. C. Hill, and B. Spilka. *The Psychology of Religion: An Empirical Approach*, 4th ed. New York: Guilford Press, 2009.

Hultgren, A. J. *The Parable of Jesus: A Commentary*. Grand Rapids, MI: Eerdmans, 2000.

Hyde, B. *Children and Spirituality: Searching for Meaning and Connectedness*. London: Jessica Kingsley Publication, 2008.

Hyde, K. E. "A Critique of Goldman's Research." *Religious Education* 63, no. 6 (1968): 429–435.

India Sunday School Union. *God Our Security: How Do We Get the Security We Need?* Windows to Encounter: Believing Is Living Series, book 4. Konnor, India: Andrew, K. J., G. David, & P. K. Thomas, 1998.

———. *God Our Security: How Do We Get the Security We Need?* Windows to Encounter: Believing Is Living Series, Teacher's Handbook, book 4. Konnor, India: Andrew, K. J., G. David, & P. K. Thomas, 1998.

Issler, K. *Wasting Time with God: A Christian Spirituality of Friendship with God.* Downers Grove, IL: InterVarsity, 2001.

Jackson, J. R. de J., ed. *The Collected Works of Samuel Taylor Coleridge: Logic.* Bolliger Series, vol. 75, 2nd edition. Princeton, NJ: Princeton University, 1981.

Jain, S. *Encyclopedia of Indian Women through the Ages: Modern India,* vol. 4. New Delhi: Gyan Publishing, 2003.

James, R. K. *Crisis Intervention Strategies.* 6th edition. Belmont, CA: Thomson Brook/Cole, 2008.

James, W. *The Principles of Psychology,* vol. 1. New York: H. Holt & Co., 1918.

Jarvelainen, P. "What Are Religious Emotions?" In *Religious Emotions: Some Philosophical Explorations,* edited by W. Leemens and W. Van Herck, 12–26. Newcastle, UK: Cambridge Scholars Publishing, 2008.

John, C. J. "Family Murder Suicides in Kerala," 2000. Accessed 3 April 2009. www.maithrikochi.org/.../Family%20Murder%20Suicides%20in%20Kerala.doc.

John, St. E. D. *Stories and Story-Telling.* New York: Pilgrim Press, 1901.

Jones, T. P. "The Basis of James W. Fowler's Understanding of Faith in the Research of Wilfred Cantwell Smith: An Examination from an Evangelical Perspective." *Religious Education* 99, no. 4 (2004): 345–357.

Jordan, C. F. "Education and Story." *Theological Educator* 33 (1986): 54–63.

Kennedy, A., and J. Duncan. "New Zealand Children's Spirituality in Catholic Schools: Teachers' Perspectives." *International Journal of Children's Spirituality* 11, no. 2 (2006): 281–292.

Kierkegaard, Søren. *Søren Kierkegaard's Journals and Papers,* vol. 1, no. 657. Translated by Howard and Edna Hong. Bloomington, IN: Indiana University Press, 1967–1975.

Klein, R. W. *1 Samuel.* Word Biblical Commentary, vol. 10, edited by D. A. Hubbard and G. W. Barker. Waco, TX: Word, 1983.

Kraus, H. J. *Psalms 60–150. A Commentary.* Translated by H. C. Oswald. Minneapolis, MN: Augsburg, 1989.

———. *Psalms 60–150. A Continental Commentary.* Translated by H. C. Oswald. Minneapolis, MN: Fortress, 1993.

———. *Theology of the Psalms.* Translated by K. Crim. Minneapolis, MN: Fortress, 1992.

Lane, W. L. "Discipline." In *The International Standard Bible Encyclopaedia*, edited by G. W. Bromiley, vol. 1: A–D, 948–950. Grand Rapids, MI: Eerdmans, 1986.

———. *The Gospel according to Mark*. NICNT. Grand Rapids, MI: Eerdmans, 1974.

———. *Hebrews 9–13*. In Word Biblical Commentary, vol. 47B, edited by D. A. Hubbard and G. W. Barker. Waco, TX: Word, 1991.

Lawrie, D. G. "Old Testament Perspectives on Religious Education." *Scriptura* 43 (1992): 1–20.

Leary, C. "Parables and Fairytales." *Religious Education* 81, no. 3 (1986): 485–499.

Lee, J. M. "How to Teach: Foundations, Process, Procedures." In *Handbook of Preschool Religious Education*, edited by D. Ratcliff, 152–223. Birmingham, AL: Religious Education Press, 1988.

Leonard, J. M. "Identifying Inner-Biblical Allusions." *Journal of Biblical Literature* 127, no. 2 (2008): 241–265.

Leupold, H. C. *Exposition of Psalms*. Grand Rapids, MI: Baker, 1969.

Levy, S. M. *Imagination and Faith Journey*. Grand Rapids, MI: Eerdmans, 2008.

Littleton, K., C. Wood, and J. K. Staarman. *International Handbook of Psychology in Education*. Wagon Lane, UK: Emerald Group, 2010.

Lincoln, A. T. *Ephesians*. Word Biblical Commentary, vol. 42, edited by D. A. Hubbard and G. W. Barker. Dallas, TX: Word, 1991.

Lincoln, Y. S., and E. G. Guba. *Naturalistic Inquiry*. Beverly Hills, CA: Sage, 1985.

Longenecker, B. W. "Narrative Interest in the Study of Paul: Retrospective and Prospective." In *Narrative Dynamics in Paul: A Critical Assessment*, edited by B. W. Longenecker, 3–18. Louisville, KY: John Knox Press, 2002.

Longman, T., III. *How to Read the Psalms*. Leicester, UK: IVP, 1998.

Looy, H. "Sensation and Perception." In *Baker Encyclopedia of Psychology and Counseling*, edited by D. G. Benner and P. C. Hill, 1092–1093. Grand Rapids, MI: Baker, 1985.

Macky, P. W. "Biblical Story Theology." *The Theological Educator* 33 (1986): 22–32.

Mandelbaum, D. G. *Society in India: Continuity and Change*, vol. 1–2. Los Angeles, CA: University of California Press, 1970.

Mangel, S. K. *Advanced Educational Psychology*. New Delhi: Prentice-Hall of India, 1999.

May, S., B. Posterski, C. Stonehouse, and L. Cannell. *Children Matter: Celebrating Their Place in the Church, Family and Community*. Grand Rapids, MI: Eerdmans, 2005.

Maya, C. "Suicide Rate Is Down in State." *The Hindu* – the Online Edition, 12 September 2009. http://www.hinduonnet.com/2009/09/12/stories/2009091252840300.htm.
Mays, J. L. *Psalm, Interpretation: A Bible Commentary for Teaching and Preaching*. Louisville, KY: John Knox Press, 1994.
McCann, J. C. Jr. "Psalms." In *The New Interpreter's Bible: A Commentary in Twelve Volumes,* vol. 4, 639–1279. Nashville, TN: Abingdon, 1996.
McGhee, M. "Making Spirits Attentive: Moral-and-Spiritual Development." In *Spirituality, Philosophy and Education*, edited by D. Carr and J. Haldane, 26–39. New York, NY: RoutledgeFalmer, 2003.
McGinnis, C. R. M. "Exodus as a 'Text of Terror' for Children." In *The Child in the Bible*, edited by M. J. Bunge, 24–44. Grand Rapids, MI: Eerdmans, 2008.
McGrath, A. E. *Christian Spirituality: An Introduction*. Malden, MA: Wiley-Blackwell, 1999.
———. *Studies in Doctrine*. Grand Rapids, MI: Zondervan, 1997.
McMillion, P. "Psalm 78: Teaching the Next Generation." *Restoration Quarterly* 43, no. 4 (2001): 219–228.
Meeks, W. A. *The Origins of Christian Morality: The First Two Centuries*. New Haven, CT: Yale University Press, 1993.
Miller-McLemore, B. *In the Midst of Chaos: Caring for Children as Spiritual Practice*. San Francisco, CA: Jossey-Bass, 2007.
———. "Whither the Children? Childhood in Religious Education." *Journal of Religion* 86, no. 4 (2006): 635–657.
Miller, P. D. *Deuteronomy: Interpretation: A Bible Commentary for Teaching and Preaching*. Louisville, KY: John Knox Press, 1990.
———. "That the Children May Know: Children in Deuteronomy." In *The Child in the Bible*, edited by M. J. Bunge, 45–62. Grand Rapids, MI: Eerdmans, 2008.
Mitchell, P. "Why Care about Stories? A Theory of Narrative Art." *Religious Education* 86, no. 1 (1991): 30–43.
Morgan, M., S. Gibbs, K. Maxwell, and N. Britten. "Hearing Children's Voices: Methodological Issues in Conducting Focus Groups with Children Aged 7–11 Years." *Qualitative Research* 2, no. 1 (2002): 5–20.
Montemayor, R., and M. Eisen. "The Development of Self-Conceptions from Childhood to Adolescence." *Developmental Psychology* 13, no. 4 (1977): 314–319.
Murphy, R. E. *Proverbs*. Word Biblical Commentary, vol. 22, edited by D. A. Hubbard and G. W. Barker. Dallas, TX: Word, 1998.
Myers, B. K. *Young Children and Spirituality*. New York: Routledge, 1997.

Nair, V. B. *Social Development and Demographic Changes in South India: Focus on Kerala*. New Delhi: M. D. Publications, 1994.

Neidhart, W. "What the Bible Means to Children and Adolescents." *Religious Education* 53, no. 2 (1968): 112–119.

Nelson, J. M. *Psychology, Religion, and Spirituality*. New York: Springer, 2009.

Newbigin. L. *The Gospel in a Pluralist Society*. London: SPCK, 1992.

———. *A Word in Season*. Grand Rapids, MI: Eerdmans, 1994.

Newby, M. "Towards a Secular Concept of Spiritual Maturity." In *Education, Spirituality, and the Whole Child*, edited by R. Best, 92–107. London: Cassell, 1996.

Nolland, J. *The Gospel of Matthew: A Commentary on the Greek Text*. The New International Greek Testament Commentary. Edited by D. A. Hagner and I. H. Marshall. Grand Rapids, MI: Eerdmans, 2005.

Olam, B. *Psalms: Studies in Hebrew Narrative and Poetry*. Collegeville, MN: Liturgical Press, 2001.

Osborne, G. R. *The Hermeneutical Spiral: A Comprehensive Introduction to Biblical Interpretation*. Downers Grove, IL: InterVarsity, 2006.

Ospino, H. "Unveiling the Human and the Divine: The Revelatory Power of Popular Religiosity Narratives in Christian Education." *Religious Education* 102, no. 3 (2007): 328–339.

Pate, M. C., S. J. Duvall, and D. Hays. *The Story of Israel: A Biblical Theology*. Downers Grove, IL: InterVarsity, 2004.

"Perception." Oxford English Dictionary.com. Accessed 20 February 2010. http://dictionary.oed.com/cgi/findword?query_type=word&queryword=perception&find.x=24&find.y=15.

Perowne, J. J. S. *The Book of Psalms, Vol. 1*. Grand Rapids, MI: Zondervan, 1966.

Peterson, E. *Living into God's Story*. 2006. Accessed 12 June 2009. http://biblicaltheology.ca/bluearticles.htm.

Polit, D. F., and C. T. Beck. *Essentials of Nursing Research: Appraising Evidence for Nursing Practice*. 7th edition. Philadelphia, PA: Lippincott Williams & Wilkins, 2009.

———. *Nursing Research: Generating and Assessing Evidence for Nursing Practice*. Philadelphia, PA: Lippincott Williams & Wilkins, 2008.

Poll, B. J., and T. B. Smith. "The Spiritual Self: Toward a Conceptualization of Spiritual Identity Development." *Journal of Psychology and Theology* 31, no. 2 (2003): 129–142.

Pritchard, G. W. *Offering the Gospel to Children*. Lanham, MD: Cowley, 1992.

Ratcliff, D. "Qualitative Data Analysis and the Transforming Moment." *Transformation: An International Journal of Holistic Mission Studies* 25, no. 2 & 3 (2008): 116–133.

———. "The Spirit of the Past: A Century of Children's Spirituality Research." In *Nurturing Children's Spirituality: Christian Perspectives and Best Practices*, edited by C. A. Allen, 21–42. Eugene, OR: Cascade Books, 2008.

Ratcliff, D., and S. May. "Identifying Children's Spirituality, Walter Wangerin's Perspectives, and an Overview of This Book." In *Children's Spirituality: Christian Perspectives, Research, and Applications*, edited by D. Ratcliff, 7–21. Eugene, OR: Cascade Books, 2004.

Ratcliff, D., and B. Ratcliff. *Childfaith: Experiencing God and Spiritual Growth with Your Children*. Eugene, OR: Cascade Books, 2010.

Reddy, R., and J. L. Gibbons. "School Socioeconomic Context and Adolescent Self-Descriptions in India." *Journal of Youth and Adolescence* 28, no. 5 (1999): 619–631.

Roberts, R. C. "Emotions Research and Religious Experience." In *The Oxford Handbook of Religion and Emotion*, edited by J. Corrigan, 490–506. New York: Oxford University Press, 2008.

Roos, S. A. de. "Young Children's God Concepts: Influences of Attachment and Religious Socialization in a Family and School Context." *Religious Education* 10, no. 1 (2006): 84–103.

Roos, S. A. de., J. Iedema, and S. Miedema. "Influence of Maternal Denomination, God Concepts, and Child-Rearing Practices on Young Children's God Concepts." *Journal for the Scientific Study of Religion* 43, no. 4 (2004): 519–535.

Rosman, S. M. "God Dwells in the Story." In *Teaching about God and Spirituality: A Resource for Jewish Settings*, edited by N. R. Levy, R. L. Goodman, and S. H. Blumbert, 204–211. Denver, CO: A.R.E Publishing, 2002.

Rosenberg, M. "The Self-Concept: Social Product and Social Force." In *Social Psychology: Sociological Perspectives*, revised edition, edited by M. Rosenberg and R. H. Turner, 593–624. Piscataway, NJ: Transaction Publishers, 1990.

Rowatt, W. C., and L. A. Kirkpatrick. "Two Dimensions of Attachment to God and Their Relation to Affect, Religiosity, and Personal Constructs." *Journal for the Scientific Study of Religion* 41, no. 4 (2002): 637–651.

Sampley, J. P. *The First Letter to the Corinthians*. The New Interpreter's Bible: A Commentary in Twelve Volumes, vol. 10, 771–1003. Nashville, TN: Abingdon, 2002.

Sasso, S. E. "The Role of Narratives in the Spiritual Formation of Children." *Journal of Family Ministry* 19, no. 2 (2005): 13–26.

———. "Tell Me a Story about God." In *Teaching about God and Spirituality: A Resource for Jewish Settings*, edited by N. R. Levy, R. L. Goodman, and S. H. Blumbert, 180–188. Denver, CO: A.R.E Publishing, 2002.

———. "When Your Children Ask: A Jewish Theology of Childhood." In *Spiritual Education, Cultural, Religious and Social Differences: New Perspective for the 21st Century*, edited by J. Erricker, C. Otta, and C. Erricker, 22–33. Brighton: Sussex, 2001.

Schwartz, H. "Narrative and Imagination: The Role of Texts and Storytelling in Nurturing Spirituality in Judaism." In *Nurturing Child and Adolescent Spirituality: Perspectives from the World's Religious Traditions*, edited by K. M. Yust and E. C. Roehlkepartian, 191–198. Lanham, MD: Rowman & Littlefield, 2005.

Seymour, J. L. "Editorial." *Religious Education* 102, no. 3 (2007): 237–239.

Shavelson, R. J., J. J. Huber, and G. C. Stanton. "Self-Concept: Validation of Construct Interpretations." *Review of Educational Research* 46, no. 4 (1976): 407–499.

Sherwani, A. *The Girl Child in Crisis*. New Delhi: Indian Social Institute, 1998.

Simmonds, G. "Spiritual Formation." In *The New Westminster Dictionary of Christian Spirituality*, edited by P. Sheldrake, 309–310. Louisville, KY: Westminster John Knox, 2005.

Sinha, D. "Indigenizing Psychology." In *Handbook of Cross-Cultural Psychology: Theory and Method*, vol. 1, 2nd edition, edited by J. W. Berry, Y. H. Poortinga, and J. Pandey, 129–170. Needham Heights, MA: Allyn & Bacon, 1997.

Smalley, S. S. *1, 2, 3 John*. Word Biblical Commentary, vol. 51, edited by D. A. Hubbard and G. W. Barker. Waco, TX: Word, 1984.

Snodgrass, K. R. *Stories with Intent: A Comprehensive Guide to the Parable of Jesus*. Grand Rapids, MI: Eerdmans, 2008.

Steffen, T. *Reconnecting God's Story to Ministry: Crosscultural Storytelling at Home and Abroad*. Waynesboro, GA: Authentic, 2005.

Stewart, S. M. "Children and Worship." *Religious Education* 84, no. 3 (1989): 350–366.

Stonehouse, C. "After a Child's First Dance with God: Accompanying Children on a Protestant Spiritual Journey." In *Nurturing Child and Adolescent Spirituality: Perspectives from the World's Religious Traditions*, edited by K. M. Yust, A. N. Johnson, S. E. Sasso, and E. C. Roehlkepartain, 95–107. New York: Rowman & Littlefield, 2006.

———. *Joining Children on the Spiritual Journey: Nurturing a Life of Faith*. Grand Rapids, MI: Baker, 1998

Stonehouse, C., and P. May. *Listening to Children on the Spiritual Journey: Guidance for Those Who Teach and Nurture*. Grand Rapids, MI: Baker, 2010.

Streib, H. "Faith Development Research at Twenty Years," 15–42. 2003. Accessed 14 January 2010. http://www.uni-bielefeld.de/(de)/theologie/forschung/religionsforschung/forschung/streib/pdf/FDRat20.pdf.

———. "Extending Our Vision of Developmental Growth and Engaging in Empirical Scrutiny: Proposals for the Future of Faith Development Theory." *Religious Education* 99, no. 4 (2004): 427–434.

Suroor, H. "A Controversial Survey on India." *The Hindu*, 19 July 2006. Accessed 8 January 2009. Online edition of India's National Newspaper. http://www.hinduonnet.com/2006/07/19/stories/2006071903331100.htm.

Tamminen, K. "Religious Experiences in Childhood and Adolescence: A Viewpoint of Religious Development between the Ages of 7 and 20." *International Journal of Psychology of Religion* 4, no. 2 (1994): 61–85.

Tate, M. E. *Psalm 51–100*. Word Biblical Commentary, vol. 20, edited by D. A. Hubbard and G. W. Barker. Waco, TX: Word, 1990.

Thompson, J. A. *Deuteronomy*. Tyndale Old Testament Commentaries. Downers Grove, IL: InterVarsity, 1974.

Thukral, E. G., B. Ali, and S. Mathur. "Children: Background & Perspective." 2009. Accessed 16 February 2009. http://infochangeindia.org/200210045933/Children/Backgrounder/Children-Background-Perspective.html.

Tripathy, S. N. *Girl Child in India*. New Delhi: Discovery Publishing, 2003.

Trousdale, A. M., and J. S. Everett. "Me and Bad Harry: Three African-American Children's Response to Fiction." *Children's Literature in Education* 25, no. 1 (1994): 1–15.

Trousdale, A. M., and S. McMillian. "'Cinderella Was a Wuss': A Young Girl's Response to Feminist and Patriarchal Folktales." *Christian Literature in Education* 34, no. 1 (2003): 1–28.

Trousdale, A. M. "Using Children's Literature for Spiritual Development." In *Spirituality and Ethics in Education: Philosophical, Theological and Radical Perspectives*, edited by C. A. Alexander, 30–139. Brighton: Sussex Academic, 2004.

Umman, P. "W(h)ither the Girl Child?" *The Hindu*, 25 April 2010, 14.

United Nations Committee on the Rights of the Child United Nations Children's Fund and Bernard van Leer Foundation. *A Guide to General Comment 7: Implementing Child Rights in Early Childhood*. 2006. Accessed 2 November 2009. http://www.unicef.org/earlychildhood/files/Guide_to_GC7.pdf.

VanGemeren, W. A. *Psalms-Songs of Songs*. The Expositor's Bible Commentary, vol. 5. Grand Rapids, MI: Zondervan, 1991.

Van Manen, Max. *Researching Lived Experience: Human Science for an Action Sensitive Pedagogy*. Albany, NY: State University of New York Press, 1990.

Verma, S., D. Sharma, and R. W. Larson. "School Stress in India: Effects on Time and Daily Emotions." *International Journal of Behavioral Development* 26, no. 6 (2002): 500–508.

Vitz, P. C. "The Use of Stories in Moral Development: New Psychological Reasons for an Old Education Method." *American Psychologist* 45, no. 6 (1990): 709–720.

Von Rad, G. *From Genesis to Chronicles: Explorations in Old Testament Theology.* Minneapolis, MN: Fortress, 2005.

Wallace, C. M. "Storytelling, Doctrine, and Spiritual Formation." *Anglican Theological Review* 81, no. 1 (1999): 39–59.

Walton, J. H., V. H. Matthews, and M. W. Chavalas. *The IVP Bible Background Commentary: Old Testament.* Downers Grove, IL: InterVarsity, 2004.

Wangerin, W. *The Orphan Passages.* Grand Rapids, MI: Zondervan, 1986.

Watson, D. F. "The Second Letter of Peter." *The New Interpreter's Bible: A Commentary in Twelve Volumes*, vol. 12, 321–361. Nashville, TN: Abingdon, 1998.

Webb, R. L. "The Use of 'Story' in the Letter of Jude: Rhetorical Strategies of Jude's Narrative Episodes." *The Journal for the Study of the New Testament* 31, no. 1 (2008): 53–87.

Wenham, G. J. *Genesis 16–50.* Word Biblical Commentary, vol. 2, edited by D. A. Hubbard and G. W. Barker. Waco, TX: Word, 1994.

Wenh-In Ng, G. A. "Beyond Bible Stories: The Role of Culture-Specific Myths/Stories in the Identity Formation of Nondominant Immigrant Children." *Religious Education* 99, no. 2 (2004): 125–136.

Werpehowski, W. "Reading Karl Barth on Children." In *The Child in Christian Thought*, edited by M. J. Bunge, 386–405. Grand Rapids, MI: Eerdmans, 2001.

Westerhoff III, J. H. *Bringing Up Children in the Christian Faith.* Minneapolis, MN: Winston Press, 1980.

———. *Will Our Children Have Faith?* Revised edition. Harrisburg, PA: Morehouse, 2000.

Westermann, C. *Praise and Lament in the Psalms.* Translated by K. R. Crim and R. N. Soulen. Atlanta, GA: John Knox Press, 1981.

Whybray, R. N. *Reading the Psalms as a Book.* Journal for the Study of the Old Testament Supplement Series 222. Sheffield, UK: Sheffield Academic Press, 1996.

Wilson, G. H. *Psalms.* The New NIV Application Commentary, vol. 1. Grand Rapids, MI: Zondervan, 2002.

Williamson, P. R. "Covenant." In *Dictionary of the Old Testament: Pentateuch*, edited by T. D. Alexander and D. W. Baker, 139–155. Downers Grove, IL: InterVarsity, 2003.

Wimberly, A. S. *Soul Stories: African American Christian Education.* Nashville, TN: Abingdon, 1994.

Worsley, H. "How Children Aged 9–10 Understand Bible Stories: A Study of Children at a Church-Aided and a State Primary School in the Midlands." *International Journal of Children's Spirituality* 9, no. 2 (2004): 203–217.

Wright, N. T. *The New Testament and the People of God*. London: SPCK, 1992.

Yoder, G. *The Nurture and Evangelism of Children*. Scottdale, PA: Herald Press, 1959.

Yust, K. M. *Real Kids, Real Faith: Practices for Nurturing Children's Spiritual Lives*. San Francisco, CA: Jossey-Bass, 2004.

Langham Literature and its imprints are a ministry of Langham Partnership.

Langham Partnership is a global fellowship working in pursuit of the vision God entrusted to its founder John Stott –

to facilitate the growth of the church in maturity and Christ-likeness through raising the standards of biblical preaching and teaching.

Our vision is to see churches in the majority world equipped for mission and growing to maturity in Christ through the ministry of pastors and leaders who believe, teach and live by the Word of God.

Our mission is to strengthen the ministry of the Word of God through:
- nurturing national movements for biblical preaching
- fostering the creation and distribution of evangelical literature
- enhancing evangelical theological education

especially in countries where churches are under-resourced.

Our ministry

Langham Preaching partners with national leaders to nurture indigenous biblical preaching movements for pastors and lay preachers all around the world. With the support of a team of trainers from many countries, a multi-level programme of seminars provides practical training, and is followed by a programme for training local facilitators. Local preachers' groups and national and regional networks ensure continuity and ongoing development, seeking to build vigorous movements committed to Bible exposition.

Langham Literature provides majority world preachers, scholars and seminary libraries with evangelical books and electronic resources through publishing and distribution, grants and discounts. The programme also fosters the creation of indigenous evangelical books in many languages, through writer's grants, strengthening local evangelical publishing houses, and investment in major regional literature projects, such as one volume Bible commentaries like *The Africa Bible Commentary* and *The South Asia Bible Commentary*.

Langham Scholars provides financial support for evangelical doctoral students from the majority world so that, when they return home, they may train pastors and other Christian leaders with sound, biblical and theological teaching. This programme equips those who equip others. Langham Scholars also works in partnership with majority world seminaries in strengthening evangelical theological education. A growing number of Langham Scholars study in high quality doctoral programmes in the majority world itself. As well as teaching the next generation of pastors, graduated Langham Scholars exercise significant influence through their writing and leadership.

To learn more about Langham Partnership and the work we do visit **langham.org**

www.ingramcontent.com/pod-product-compliance
Lightning Source LLC
Chambersburg PA
CBHW070235240426
43673CB00044B/1797